THE BATTLE OF LEYTE GULF

THE BATTLE OF LEYTE GULF

by
ADRIAN STEWART

ROBERT HALE · LONDON

© Adrian Stewart 1979
First published in Great Britain 1979

ISBN 0 7091 7544 2

Robert Hale Limited
Clerkenwell House
Clerkenwell Green
London, EC1R 0HT

Photoset by
Specialised Offset Services Limited, Liverpool
and printed in Great Britain by
Lowe & Brydone Limited,
Thetford, Norfolk

Contents

	List of Illustrations	7
1	Plans, Preparations, Preliminaries	9
2	The Submarine Attacks	37
3	The Air Attacks of 24 October	45
4	Admiral Halsey Heads North	67
5	The Action in Surigao Strait	90
6	The Action off Cape Engano	122
7	The Action off Samar Island	144
8	Admiral Kurita Changes Course	178
9	Kamikaze	190
10	Death of a Navy	205
	Bibliography	215
	Index	217

*To Captain Donald Macintyre.
In appreciation of his help and encouragement*

List of Illustrations

between pages 64 and 65

1a Admiral William Halsey
1b Vice-Admiral Thomas Kinkaid
2a Vice-Admiral Jisaburo Ozawa
2b Vice-Admiral Takeo Kurita
3a U.S. carrier *Enterprise*
3b Japanese battleship *Yamato*
4   The Leyte landings: an Avenger provides support
5   Battleship *Yamashiro* under attack
6a Light carrier *Princeton* ablaze
6b The fight to save *Princeton*
7a Bomb-hit on battleship *Yamato*
7b Surigao Strait: destroyer *McDermut*
8a Vice-Admiral Marc Mitscher
8b Rear-Admiral Thomas Sprague
8c Rear-Admiral Jesse Oldendorf
8d Rear-Admiral Clifton Sprague

between pages 128 and 129

9a   Cape Engano: attack on Ozawa's carriers
9b   Carrier *Zuikaku* under attack
10a Light carrier *Zuiho* under attack
10b Battleship *Ise* under attack
11   Samar Island: destroyer *Heermann*
12   Escort carrier *Kitkun Bay* launches Avengers
13a *Gambier Bay* and destroyers lay smoke
13b *Gambier Bay* and destroyers under fire
14a *Gambier Bay* dead in the water
14b *Gambier Bay* left behind to her fate
15   Kamikaze: attack on escort carrier *Sangamon*
16   The end of escort carrier *St Lo*

Credits

Photographs: Imperial War Museum, London; 3a, 3b, 8a; United States Navy Department, the remainder. Maps 1 and 3 are based on the author's researches, maps 2, 4, 5 and 6 are based, with author's amendments, on those in a *History of United States Naval Operations in World War II*, Volume XII "Leyte", by Samuel Eliot Morison published by Little, Brown and Company.

MAPS

1	Strategy and Preliminaries	28
2	The Air Attacks of 24 October	48
3	Surigao Strait: The Torpedo Attacks	104
4	Surigao Strait: The Main Gunfire Phase	109
5	The Action off Cape Engano	127
6	The Action off Samar Island	149

KEY TO MAPS

Japanese Forces — —	Allied Forces ·······
Task Force ....TF	Task Group ....TG
Fleet carrier ....CF	Light carrier CL
Escort carrier ....CE	Battleship ....BB
Heavy cruiser ....HC	Light cruiser LC
Destroyer ....DD	Destroyer escort ....DE
	Submarine ....SS

1

Plans, Preparations, Preliminaries

"This is the Voice of Freedom, General MacArthur speaking. People of the Philippines! I have returned. By the grace of Almighty God our forces stand again on Philippine soil – soil consecrated in the blood of our two peoples ... Rally to me."

This stirring call by General Douglas MacArthur, broadcast through a signal corps microphone on a beach at Leyte Island, marked the successful culmination of the most important amphibious landing in the Pacific war. The origin of this operation may be traced to a conference in Honolulu on 26–27 July 1944 between President Roosevelt, MacArthur, and Admiral Chester Nimitz, Commander-in-Chief Pacific Fleet (CINPAC for short) and Commander-in-Chief Pacific Ocean Areas (CINCPOA) – a position which gave him authority over the entire active Pacific theatre except South-West Pacific Area which was under MacArthur's command. Prior to this date, throughout 1944, there had been considerable dispute as to whether the route for the American advance on Japan should run through the Philippines or Formosa.

General MacArthur was the champion of the Philippines objective. He argued passionately that he had given his and America's word that the islands should be liberated as soon as possible and that, if this word was broken, no Asiatic country would trust the Americans again. He pointed out that thousands of Filipino guerillas were already harassing the Japanese occupation troops, so that in the event of an American assault on the islands the population would wholeheartedly support the invading forces whereas the population of Formosa would be hostile. Quite apart from these political considerations, he emphasized that the Philippines were a more strategically sound target; for, since they could be protected by U.S. sea-power more easily than could Formosa, they would be safer from counter-attack and thus a more suitable base for an assault on Japan. This latter consideration was also urged by the Army's chief logistician, General Brehon

Somervell who claimed that only the Philippines could serve as an adequate spring-board for an advance against Japan because an operation against Formosa could not be supported over 1,800 miles of open sea with the Japanese able to make flanking attacks from Luzon, the most northern of the Philippines, and the Ryukyu Islands.

On the other hand, the Formosa project enjoyed the formidable advocacy of Fleet Admiral Ernest King, Commander-in-Chief United States Fleet and Chief of Naval Operations, whose views, supported by Admiral Nimitz and also by General George Marshall, Chief of Staff of the U.S. Army, were that what he called "battering our way through the Philippines" would be a long, costly process. The capture of Formosa, he believed, would provide a better position for assaulting Japan, bombarding her with long-range air attacks, blocking her supply routes to the south or moving on to Amoy on the China coast as desired. In King's scheme, only Mindanao the most southerly of the Philippines would be occupied for its air bases; the remainder of the archipelago being by-passed and neutralized by air attacks.

There the argument rested until on 26 July, heavy cruiser *Baltimore* carrying the President arrived at Pearl Harbour where Admiral Nimitz boarded her from a tug. When she docked, she was greeted by an imposing delegation of 'top brass' headed by Nimitz's Chief of Staff, Vice-Admiral Charles McMorris. McMorris ordered "Right Face!" but since the admirals had had plenty of time to forget their drill, two of them turned left, much to the delight of the crew of *Baltimore*. The error was quickly corrected, however, and the whole contingent went aboard to be presented to Mr Roosevelt. Meanwhile, as the President was arriving by sea, General MacArthur was arriving by air from Brisbane. Shortly after the admirals had departed, he mounted the gangway, arrayed as usual in khaki trousers, brown leather air-force jacket and Philippine field-marshal's cap.

In discussions aboard the cruiser, and later ashore, MacArthur not only convinced the President that the Central and Northern Philippines – specifically Leyte and Luzon – should be invaded, as well as Mindanao; he won over Admiral Nimitz to this belief also. The latter was already conscious of the weakness of the military forces under his personal command which would be needed for the assault on Formosa and inclined to think that such an assault would need the support of air bases at least in the Central Philippines, so he was able to reach practical agreement with MacArthur on this issue even though no firm decision could be given even now, since this was the responsibility of the Joint Chiefs of Staff. Nimitz's conversion greatly strengthened MacArthur's hand, while over the next month, he further won over General Marshall, who was influenced not only by the question of national honour involved but also by Japanese advances in China. These had demonstrated the deficiencies of the Chinese Nationalist Army and had led to the overrunning of south-east China, including the American air bases there, virtually precluding the possibility of a successful advance through China.

Consequently, although Admiral King continued to argue for the Formosa operation, when the Joint Chiefs of Staff met with the British Chiefs of Staff, the President, Mr Churchill and the Canadian Premier, Mr Mackenzie King, at Quebec on 11 September, a landing on Leyte was agreed with target date scheduled for 20 December. As preliminaries to the Leyte landing, on 15 September, MacArthur's troops were to take the island of Morotai in the Moluccas while Nimitz's Central Pacific forces seized Peliliu in the Palau group. On 5 October, Nimitz would advance to capture Yap in the Carolines and then Ulithi. On 15 October, MacArthur would take Salebaboe in the Talaud Islands, moving on to Sarangani Bay, Mindanao on 15 November. The decision of whether to follow up the invasion of Leyte with that of Formosa or Luzon was still left in abeyance, the verdict being given in favour of the latter on 3 October, by which time the original schedule had been drastically accelerated.

During the early weeks of September, the Southern and Central Philippines had been undergoing heavy carrier-based air strikes from Task Force 38 of the U.S. Third Fleet under the command of Nimitz's subordinate, Admiral William Halsey. At a cost of eight aircraft and ten airmen, Halsey destroyed an estimated 200 planes in the Central Philippines as well as inflicting heavy damage on shipping and land installations. Convinced that Japanese shore-based air strength in this area had been "annihilated", Halsey, on 13 September, radioed to Nimitz that the landings on the Palaus, the Talauds, Yap and Mindanao could be cancelled and the forces allocated for their capture given to MacArthur to support a landing on Leyte as soon as possible. In fact, not only had Halsey over-estimated the damage that his forces had inflicted, which was quickly made good by the enemy flying in reinforcements, but the Japanese air forces had been held back deliberately by Imperial General Headquarters so as to be on hand for the major landings which were already anticipated. However, Nimitz took Halsey's advice apart from insisting on the attack on the Palaus, the by-passing of which he considered too great a risk and the forces designated for which were already embarked. When the suggestion was sent to MacArthur's headquarters, the Chief of Staff, General Richard Sutherland in MacArthur's absence[1] accepted it eagerly, despite having learned from intelligence reports that the enemy strength on Leyte was greater than Halsey thought, because it provided a splendid opportunity to speed up the liberation of the Philippines. He indicated to the Joint Chiefs of Staff in Quebec that if this suggestion were adopted, the landing on Leyte could be advanced to 20 October; whereupon they gave prompt approval to both the cancellation of the intermediate landings and the new target date for the Leyte operation.

This decision was strategically brilliant for, since Leyte is a natural gateway to the Philippines, if it could be captured, this would split the Japanese forces in the islands into two main groups in Luzon and Mindanao, the latter of which would be outflanked and by-passed. Further, unless the Japanese could re-take Leyte, so re-establishing a continuous front, their forces, thus separated, could be overcome in turn. So the capture of Leyte would virtually ensure the successful re-occupation of the Philippines. And once the Philippines were taken, then not only would the Americans have a spring-board for the assault on Japan but the Japanese supply lines to their sources of such essentials as oil and rubber in conquered Malaya and the Dutch East Indies, already threatened by U.S. submarines, would be cut, thus making their defeat a certainty. MacArthur understandably called the Leyte operation "the crucial battle in the war in the Pacific", while in a letter to President Roosevelt from Leyte on 20 October, he wrote that if successful, it would

> strategically as well as tactically cut the enemy forces in two. Strategically it will pierce the centre of his defensive line extending along the coast of Asia from the Japanese homeland to the tip of Singapore and will enable us to envelop to the north or south as we desire. It severs completely the Japanese from their infamous propaganda slogan of the 'Greater East Asia Co-Prosperity Sphere'.[2] Tactically it divides his forces in two and by by-passing the southern half of the Philippines will result in the saving of possibly fifty thousand American casualties. He had expected us and prepared on Mindanao.[3]

On the other hand, the acceleration of the schedule would emphasize

---

[1] On 13 September, MacArthur was *en route* for Morotai on light cruiser *Nashville*.
[2] This was the Japanese name for the areas they had overrun.
[3] Quoted in General Douglas MacArthur's *Reminiscences* p.212.

several risks already inherent in any attack on the Philippines. Leyte was an objective within easy reach of numerous other islands from which the Japanese could throw in reinforcements, whereas the American supply lines were constantly being stretched to greater lengths. Since the nearest allied fighter base would be 500 miles away on newly-captured Morotai, the Americans would have to rely on carrier-based air cover until such time as they could prepare air bases on Leyte itself. This in turn would be far from easy in October since apart from the possibility of a typhoon, the north-east monsoon which commences in that month always brings a great deal of rain, thus inevitably causing delays in airfield construction.

The Japanese, however, had a network of airfields on hand from which to attack the landings or support their ground troops. As Mr Vann Woodward points out:

> The assault upon the Philippines would be unlike any of our landings on the tiny atolls and islands to the eastward, and different from our jungle-locked beachheads in New Guinea. In those operations it had been possible to neutralize enemy airfields. The airfields and emergency strips in the Philippines, some seventy of them operational, would be too numerous to be effectively neutralized and too close to Formosa and the Empire to be cut off from reinforcement.[4]

There was every risk therefore that the defenders could furnish fresh troops and aircraft more quickly than the invaders.

Furthermore, the last-minute change of plans naturally resulted in considerable supply difficulties. The forces detailed for the attack on Yap had types of landing-craft suitable for Yap but less suitable for Leyte where beach conditions were quite different. There was also a critical shortage of certain items, especially motor vehicles and fresh and frozen provisions, and a narrow margin of supplies of all kinds.

As for those preliminary operations that were not cancelled, Morotai was taken without too much difficulty on 15 September. By the time of the major landings, two bomber fields and a fighter strip had been established there; the only Allied base from which fighters and light or medium bombers could reach Leyte. The capture of Peliliu and the near-by island of Angaur proved a different matter, for the enemy commander, Colonel Nakagawa had, as well as the usual beach defences, a formidable system of underground fortifications well

---

[4] *The Battle For Leyte Gulf* by C. Vann Woodward. Woodward was Intelligence Officer in the office of the Chief of Naval Operations.

inland out of range of naval bombardment. The defenders continued their fanatical resistance until the night of 24–25 November when Colonel Nakagawa committed suicide. His garrison had been exterminated but the Americans lost 1,950 men and suffered some 10,000 casualties in all. The capture of the island's airfield on 18 September, however, even though the Americans could not as yet use it themselves, achieved the main object of the operation by removing its threat to the flank of the line of advance to Leyte. Ulithi Atoll with its big, deep lagoon was taken without opposition on 23 September. It provided a perfect fleet base but the weather now proved more deadly than the Japanese for, on 3 October, a typhoon hit the lagoon, sinking or wrecking three LCTs (Landing-Craft, Tank), fourteen LCMs (Landing-Craft, Mechanized), and sixty-five LCVPs (Landing-Craft, Vehicles and Personnel). Also the sea was so heavy for three days thereafter that it proved impossible to provision some of the warships supporting the landing. Accordingly, they had to sail with store-rooms only half full, a factor responsible for the shortage of provisions remarked on previously. The major risks inherent in the attack on Leyte were in fact but slightly reduced by these preliminaries – indeed in the case of Peliliu at least it is arguable that the advantages gained did not wholly justify the cost incurred.

It is not to be supposed that the Japanese were unaware of the Americans' intentions. They had long foreseen such an attack – indeed in contrast to the American disputes, as early as March 1944, Imperial General Headquarters forecast that their enemies would probably make the decisions they ultimately did make. By August top priority had been given to the defence of the Philippines, the attacks on Peliliu and Morotai were accurately foretold and the main assault was estimated for November, which it will be recalled was the original date set. Further, while U.S. Intelligence was not in very good form at this time – even insisting until the very last moment that the Japanese fleet would not take part in defending the islands – the enemy's intelligence service became still better informed with the passing of time. On 7 October, it correctly announced that Third Fleet would shortly launch carrier-plane attacks on Formosa, Okinawa and the Philippines as a prelude to the invasion; predicted that the major landings would take place in the Philippines in the last ten days of October; and even guessed that the target would be Leyte.

The prospect of the Leyte landings filled the Japanese leaders with dismay, for to them even more than to their adversaries, the

Plans, Preparations, Preliminaries

importance of the Philippines was obvious — so obvious that it made their prospective loss dreadful to contemplate. Speaking in Tokyo of the impending action, Admiral Nobumasa Suetsugu, a pre-war commander of the Japanese Combined Fleet, pointed out that this would be

> not a mere battle for the Philippines, but one which will decide whether Japan can maintain or is to be cut off from her communication with the vital resources of the southern regions. For that reason, the outcome of the Philippine operations will be of such a far-reaching nature as to decide the general war situation, and I am certain it will be the greatest and most decisive battle fought.

Similarly, Lieutenant-General Suichi Miyazaki, the Chief of Operations Section of Imperial General Headquarters, considered that: "Viewed from the standpoint of political and operational strategy, holding the Philippines was the one essential for the execution of the war against America and Britain". While after the war, Vice-Admiral Takeo Kurita, who commanded the main enemy force at the Battle of Leyte Gulf, replied to an American enquiry: "The first point is that if you seized the Philippines it would cut off all fuel supply to the Empire [i.e. the Japanese homelands] and that, all supply of fuel being severed, the war in all areas south of the Empire must end. The Philippines were vital to the continuation of the war".

For the purposes of this narrative, however, the most important opinion was that of a stubborn and aggressive gentleman called Admiral Soemu Toyoda, because he was the Commander-in-Chief of the Japanese Combined Fleet, so it would be on his instructions, if at all, that that fleet would attack American forces supporting the Leyte landings. Toyoda was the third C.-in-C. that the fleet had had during the war. The first, the brilliant Admiral Yamamoto, who had been the brain behind the original Japanese conquests, although in fact he had constantly argued against going to war, had been killed over Bougainville on 18 April 1943, when his plane was ambushed by U.S. fighters. His successor, Admiral Koga, met an equally melancholy fate when his aircraft disappeared in a storm over the Philippines on the night of 31 March–1 April 1944; he was replaced by Toyoda who seems to have been a considerably better strategist. With regard to the question of using his fleet should the Philippines be attacked, Toyoda was curt and to the point. He explained after the war,

> Should we lose in the Philippines operations even though the fleet should

be left, the shipping lane to the south would be completely cut off so that the fleet, if it should come back to Japanese waters, could not obtain its fuel supply. If it should remain in southern waters, it could not receive supplies of ammunition and arms. There would be no sense in saving the fleet at the expense of the loss of the Philippines.

Because such loss would thus bring with it the neutralization of the fleet, clearly, should the Philippines be attacked, the Japanese leaders could not hold it back but would be faced with the necessity of committing it and either conquering or dying. As their clever estimate of American intentions gave them plenty of time to decide how best to intervene effectively, during late July and early August 1944, they drew up a plan called *Sho-Go* which means 'Operation Victory'. There were indeed four separate divisions of the plan to cover potential landings on: the Philippines; Formosa, the Ryukyus of which the chief is Okinawa, and Kyushu the most southern of the Japanese home-islands; the main Japanese island of Honshu; and the most northern, Hokkaido. All these were considered essential for the successful prosecution of the war. However, *Sho I* dealing with the defence of the Philippines, by far the most probable target, was naturally the most important.

The *Sho* plan was faced from the outset with two major difficulties, one which it simply had to accept; the other which it was designed to circumvent. The former was that due to an increasing loss of vital tankers to U.S. submarines, the Japanese forces had had to be divided. Towards the end of February, Vice-Admiral Takeo Kurita's 'First Striking Force' which contained the majority of the heavy surface warships including seven battleships, sailed to Lingga Roads near Singapore in order to be near its fuel supplies. Here it was well within range of Superfortresses of the Twentieth Army Air Force based in China, but for some unknown reason, despite strong requests from General MacArthur, this force did not visit Lingga even on reconnaissance until after the Battle of Leyte Gulf was already over. The Japanese carrier forces, known as the 'Main Body' under the command of Vice-Admiral Jisaburo Ozawa, however, had to remain in the Inland Sea of Japan between Honshu and Shikoku to await replacement air crews under training; while a cruiser-destroyer unit, the 'Second Striking Force' under Vice-Admiral Kiyohide Shima was based at Amami-O-Shima in the Ryukyus.

All these separate bodies would have to co-ordinate their movements should they put to sea as parts of a concerted operation but Japanese communications were, by this stage of the war, quite deplorable. Admiral Ozawa stated later that: "Generally speaking naval shore communications were very poor from the standpoint of equipment, technical ability and so on" – which was equally true of those on board ships. Matters were made even worse by the quite unnecessarily complicated Japanese command system. While Admirals Kurita and Ozawa were responsible directly to Toyoda, Shima, and for that matter the Japanese Navy's land-based air fleets, were controlled by Vice-Admiral Gunichi Mikawa, the head of South-West Area Force, whose H.Q. was in Manila and who in turn was responsible to Toyoda. Toyoda thus had the unpleasant task of co-ordinating all naval units, ships and planes alike, long-distance from Tokyo. Army air forces in the Philippines did not come under his command at all, although as will be seen, a certain amount of co-operation was achieved between the services.

The other major disadvantage confronting the Japanese was the fact that their forces were considerably the weaker, particularly in carrier-aircraft. This defect became crucial after the Battle of the Philippine Sea, won for the United States by Admiral Raymond Spruance, and his carrier task force commander, Vice-Admiral Marc Mitscher, on 19–20 June 1944. During this battle, the Japanese lost three carriers; *Taiho* and *Shokaku* to submarines; *Hiyo* to carrier-based air strikes. Far worse was the virtual annihilation of the air groups of three of their carrier divisions by the pilots of the new Hellcat fighters which at last gave the U.S. naval airmen a weapon superior to the famous Zero that the Japanese had possessed since the beginning of the war; and by another Allied creation, an anti-aircraft shell which by means of a miniature radar set in its nose reflecting signals off solid objects such as aircraft, detonated automatically in the close proximity of its target when the intervals between the outward and returning signals became very short. The Japanese started the battle with 430 carrier-aircraft. They ended it with thirty-five. Since a carrier is useless without its planes, the Japanese carrier force could not be effective again until the lost machines and crews could be replaced. Although Admiral Ozawa set to work to train reinforcements with a desperate determination, the handicap of having to start virtually from nothing plus the constant lack of petrol which made it difficult to give the new recruits sufficient flying-hours, proved too great. The carriers could not possibly be ready before November at the earliest which as the *Sho* plan foresaw would probably be too late, allowing them, in consequence, to play only a subsidiary role.

On the other hand, Japan still possessed in Kurita's First Striking Force most formidable gunfire strength — just how formidable will be seen later. The basic intention behind the *Sho* plan was therefore to get this force into the most advantageous position; by which the enemy's high command meant one from which it could attack the landing forces plus their transports, supply ships and close-support units, as soon as possible after the invasion. Avoiding the attack of planes of the American task force, said the *Sho* plan, Kurita's force would "push forward and engage in a decisive battle with the surface force which tries to stop it. After annihilating this force, it will then attack and wipe out the enemy convoy and troops at the landing point". The plan hoped that the big guns of Kurita's battleships would engage the weak amphibious forces within at least two days of the landing.

Accordingly, at Lingga, Kurita's command began intensive training in preparation for their coming task. Experiments were made to discover the best ways of approaching an anchorage and destroying transports at anchor; conferences studied the probable landing-places (three were specified including Leyte Gulf); exercises rehearsed night attacks with the use of flares and radar to assist accurate gunnery and one problem was especially emphasized — anti-aircraft defence.

The *Sho* plan also hoped to remedy the absence of effective carrier support by the use of land-based air attacks. The job of the shore-based naval air forces would be first to strike against the enemy carriers; then, "two days before the arrival of our surface force they will thrust with all their strength on the carriers and transports to open the way for the First Attack Force"; and finally they would join with the naval forces and incidentally the Army air forces in the assault on the transports and the troops on the beach-head. It will be noticed, however, that the mission of both the Navy and Army air forces was purely offensive, no provision being made for cover to be given to Kurita's forces, who were made fully aware that they would have to defend themselves from air attack. Accordingly, increased training in the use of anti-aircraft weapons was initiated, methods were worked out whereby even the battleships' main guns could be turned to fire on attacking planes and evasive tactics were carefully formulated. Each of Kurita's battleships was mounted with an average of one hundred and twenty 25 millimetre machine-guns, each heavy cruiser had ninety such and each destroyer thirty to forty.

While the battleships were given the main role of destruction, the weakened carrier group was recognized as being able only to constitute a subsidiary force to lure away or distract the U.S. carrier forces. "It will facilitate penetration [of the First Striking Force]" stated the *Sho* plan "by diverting the enemy [carrier] task force to the northeast and will join in the attack against the flank of the enemy task force".

Although there were some alterations to this scheme before it was put into practice, it is important to notice that as early as August the Japanese intended to use their carriers as a purely diversionary unit. The main assault would be that by the battleships against the transports and the beach-head. If the carriers could inflict losses on their American rivals so much the better, but such losses would be in the nature of a bonus.

Further, even this early there were definite indications that the carriers were regarded as expendable. They were to be committed even though it was admitted that their covering warships were "not strong enough to screen the carriers". It was considered that the inexperienced pilots would normally fly on to land bases after making their attacks rather than return to their ships, while some carrier-planes might be diverted prior to the battle to operate under the various shore-based air commands. Finally there was the suggestion that carriers with no planes might be used as decoys; those earmarked for this unenviable task being the battleship-carriers (battleships with a flight-deck aft) *Hyuga* and *Ise*, of which more later.

The Japanese weakness in the air was made worse by the final American preliminaries to the invasion. These consisted of a series of assaults by Halsey's Third Fleet on those enemy bases from which Leyte could be reinforced. Accordingly, on 10 October Third Fleet's carrier-planes attacked Okinawa and, arriving on the heels of a convenient typhoon, achieved surprise and enjoyed great success. On 11 October they raided Luzon, and on the twelfth, in excellent flying conditions, they struck at Formosa, 1,378 sorties being flown, plus 974 more the following day. These attacks achieved spectacular results. Although American claims for aircraft destroyed were exaggerated, their final total of about 500 — including those destroyed in Japanese counter-attacks — was good enough. In addition the fliers sank a score of freighters as well as causing very heavy destruction to ammunition dumps, hangars, installations, industrial plants, barracks and the headquarters of Vice-Admiral Shigeru Fukudome, Commander of Japan's Sixth Base (Naval) Air Force which controlled the Second Air Fleet covering Kyushu, Formosa and the Ryukyus. So heavy were the attacks, that Toyoda's Chief of Staff,

Rear-Admiral Kusaka, alerted the Navy's shore-based air forces for *Sho I* (Leyte) and *Sho II* (Formosa) while Toyoda himself, temporarily in Formosa, ordered Fukudome's planes out to attack and destroy Halsey.

These Japanese counter-attacks suffered very heavy losses but achieved nothing at all on the first day. However, on the thirteenth which was of course a Friday, a torpedo-bomber hit and crippled the heavy cruiser U.S.S. *Canberra*, so named in honour of H.M.A.S. *Canberra* that had perished fighting alongside American forces in the Battle of Savo Island on 9th August 1942. Instead of scuttling her, Halsey made the bold decision to salvage her, and she was taken in tow, to be pulled, slowly and painfully, clear of the danger area. To cover this withdrawal, Halsey launched further strikes on Formosa on the fourteenth and also others against the Manila airfields on the fifteenth and sixteenth. Meanwhile the Japanese, eager to whittle down American forces before the big battle started and well aware that the present operations were preliminary to this, hurled in their air forces in a series of attacks which suffered cruel losses with little to show for it. On the fourteenth, light cruiser *Houston* was hit by a torpedo-bomber and disabled but she too was successfully taken in tow. On the fifteenth a 'Judy' dive-bomber hit carrier *Franklin* causing minor damage. These were the only injuries Third Fleet suffered during these raids.

This, however, was not the story reported to Admiral Toyoda. In the heat of fast air-activity, pilots of all nationalities inevitably tend to exaggerate claims, and considering the inexperience of the Japanese pilots, it was perhaps not too surprising that they should indulge in a bout of colossal over-estimation of the damage inflicted. Tokyo Radio put out a claim that eleven carriers, two battleships and three cruisers had been sunk, with eight carriers, two battleships and four cruisers damaged. The Emperor issued a special rescript of commendation while mass celebrations took place throughout Japan. Admiral Toyoda probably did not believe these extreme claims but may well have felt that considerable injuries had been inflicted on the American carriers by the land-based aircraft, as indeed expert opinion, in America as well as Japan, had long predicted would be the case. The fact that Halsey was retiring, while after the thirteenth the weight of American attacks fell sharply away due to the need to give protection to the damaged ships, doubtless appeared to confirm this belief.

Accordingly Toyoda prepared to launch further raids on Third Fleet. He detached some 150 planes under training in his carriers to land bases, principally in Formosa though also in the Philippines. This was carried out despite the strong protests of Admiral Ozawa, who, being by far the most experienced of the enemy commanders in carrier warfare was much more conscious of the probability of over-estimated claims. On the fifteenth and sixteenth, these aircraft with others were thrown into the fray. The results were once more disastrous for the Japanese as their partly-trained airmen were almost completely wiped out in return for a second torpedo hit on *Houston* which was not fatal. These casualties meant that the role of the Japanese carriers, already limited, could now only be that of a decoy.

Meanwhile, Admiral Halsey, hearing of the triumphant Japanese broadcasts, withdrew the majority of his forces from Formosan waters, leaving behind as a bait the crippled cruisers with their escorting screen under Rear-Admiral Laurence DuBose (by now being described by the enemy as "the crippled remnants of the Third Fleet") together with one only of his four carrier task groups. Toyoda at first fell into the trap and on the night of the 14–15 October, he ordered Admiral Shima's Second Striking Force to attack the "remnants". Fortunately for the Japanese, on the sixteenth some experienced pilots not gazing through rose-tinted spectacles had a good look at all Halsey's task groups. Their reports caused Shima to retire hastily before he could be attacked and incidentally dispose of the oft-repeated tale that the Japanese Navy came out to fight at Leyte Gulf because it still believed the fictitious account of Third Fleet's losses;[5] not indeed that it was relevant whether this was believed or not for, as has been seen, the Navy had to fight for the Philippines in any event or perish ingloriously from lack of fuel and/or ammunition. Third Fleet continued its retirement, both the injured cruisers being brought back safely to Ulithi. The American losses in the air were more severe; seventy-six aircraft in combat, thirteen more on operations, and sixty-four aircrew lost.

Most accounts consider the loss of the Japanese carrier-planes to have been a vital one. Thus in the British official history, *The War at Sea*, Captain S.W. Roskill says that these aircraft and crews "might have played a decisive part in the battle for the Philippines now pending"; while Major-General J.F.C. Fuller in *The Decisive Battles of the Western World* says that as Toyoda's decision "meant the loss

[5]The Army section of Imperial General Headquarters certainly did believe that the claims were true and the Philippine invasion would be delayed in consequence, but Toyoda was well aware of the correct position by the evening of the sixteenth, as witness also his prompt reaction to the news of the preliminary American landings.

of Ozawa's half-trained air-crews, more than anything else it wrecked the *Sho* plan". With great respect to these authorities this does not seem to have been so. For many months, it had been planned to use the carriers in a purely diversionary role, their "half-trained air-crews" were probably not capable of operating successfully at sea, and in view of the poor use made by the Japanese commanders of their aircraft and the consequent small results they in fact achieved in the fighting around Formosa, it seems unlikely that they would have had any more success had they been retained for use in the big battle, in which incidentally as will be seen Japanese aerial tactics were again far from good.

Far more serious, therefore, was the loss of land-based aircraft with which the Japanese had intended to make good their carrier deficiencies. Indeed Captain Mitsuo Fuchida, air-operations officer on the staff of the Combined Fleet, considered that this cost Japan the main action. Again, however, this is open to doubt. It is true that the American command of the air was a vital factor in the coming battle – *the* vital factor in the view of both Ozawa and Kurita – but so great was American aerial strength, that this command would still have been effective although not to the same extent, even had the Japanese not suffered their losses at Formosa. Further, the enemy air-commanders deliberately preserved their planes after Halsey's retirement, and so by 24 October had again gathered a useful force under their command.

When the attack on Leyte commenced on 20 October, Fifth Base Air Force controlling the Navy's First Air Fleet in the Philippines under the command of Vice-Admiral Takijiro Onishi, who that day relieved Vice-Admiral Teroaka, had only about 100 aircraft available. However, on the twenty-second, Fukudome flew in everything he had from Formosa bringing the Navy's air strength to between 300 and 400 planes although not all were operational. Some 800 more were ordered from Japan or China of which 180 arrived fairly promptly. Further, since the importance of the Philippines was recognized by everyone, the Army and Navy Air Forces at last co-operated (these were separate organizations and previously the former had refused to help in naval operations) thus enabling Toyoda to count on the help of the Fourth Air Army of Lieutenant General Kyoji Tominaga whose headquarters were at Manila. Tominaga, not having joined in the attacks on Third Fleet since he was apparently not informed of Toyoda's *Sho* alert, had suffered few losses and had some 150-250 aircraft on hand, reinforced by eighty more on the twenty-fourth.

Thus the combined Japanese Air Forces were by no means negligible; also they could easily stage in reinforcements via Formosa and the Ryukyus. The most important point, however, is that the main objective of the Japanese was to get their big guns into effective action. Land-based air attacks were intended to help clear the way for the Japanese battleships but if the way could be cleared by other means as was in fact the case, Japan could still achieve this objective. The battles round Formosa, therefore, while increasing Japanese difficulties, cannot be said to have altered the fundamental positions or strengths of the two adversaries.

Two other incidents in the Formosa battle deserve special mention. On the thirteenth, a Mitsubishi 'Betty' bomber set on fire when attacking carrier *Franklin*, deliberately crashed into the carrier's flight-deck, slid across it, and went over the side into the sea. There had been several such incidents on previous occasions notably in the fighting round Guadalcanal but these were the results of rage or hatred, on the part of individual pilots, usually in planes already on fire or crippled, not part of a preconceived plan.

However, on the fifteenth, came a quite different incident. Rear-Admiral Masafumi Arima took off to attack Third Fleet with the express intention of crashing a carrier. He did not get his chance for he was shot down at a safe distance but this rendered his example no less inspiring. He "lit the fuse of the ardent wishes of his men" by becoming the first of the Kamikaze suicide-pilots. Postponing to a more convenient time a description of this wonderful but terrible organization, it is sufficient here to state that many Japanese commanders, particularly Admiral Onishi, had previously favoured the use of bomb-carrying fighters which would deliberately crash onto the decks of American carriers to make certain of a hit – a desperate measure suggested by the frightful casualties already being experienced in orthodox attacks. Now, since the surface Navy was preparing to risk all in the coming battle, its Air Force decided it must make similar sacrifices and on assuming command of the Navy's First Air Fleet, Onishi took the plunge and began to form a Kamikaze unit. It consisted originally of twenty-six planes (some of which would act as fighter escorts to the suicide attackers) stationed at Mabalacat, Luzon, and was divided into four sections. The following day a second unit of twenty planes was formed on Cebu Island in the Central Philippines. The Americans would learn all about these forces in due course.

At the time that Halsey's Third Fleet was striking at Formosa, Vice-Admiral Thomas Kinkaid's Seventh Fleet of transports, mine-sweepers and supporting warships was sailing from bases at Manus and Hollandia. In all Kinkaid commanded 738 ships, fewer than those taking part in the invasion of Normandy but with a heavier striking power. General MacArthur was aboard light cruiser *Nashville* in his capacity of Supreme Commander of South-West Pacific Area though it was Kinkaid as his naval commander who exercised actual control over the fleet, including the army personnel of Lieutenant-General Walter Krueger's Sixth Army until they disembarked.

The advance-guards of this massive force arrived in Leyte Gulf at about 0630, 17 October. The mine-sweepers under Commander Loud at once set to work to clear the approaches to Leyte while Rear-Admiral Struble's 'Dinagat Attack Group' of transports carrying some 500 men under Lieutenant-Colonel Mucci, supported by Rear-Admiral Hayler with light cruisers *Denver* and *Columbia* and four destroyers, prepared to seize the small islands of Dinagat, Suluan and Homonhon guarding the entrance to the gulf, which having radar stations could notify the enemy of the American approach. At 0800 *Denver* opened fire on Suluan's defences, thereby firing the first shots in the invasion of the Philippines. Twenty minutes later the troops were safely put ashore, routing the small Japanese garrison at the cost of only three casualties. Elsewhere things went even better for although heavy seas delayed attacks on Homonhon and Dinagat until the following day, the former was discovered to be unoccupied, while on the latter the attackers found that Filipino guerilas had already done their work for them.

On 18 and 19 October, Rear-Admiral Jesse Oldendorf, boldly accepting the risks involved, took his gunfire-support ships into Leyte Gulf to reduce the defences and assist underwater demolition teams, despite the fact that the bad weather had prevented the mine-sweepers completing their task. His forces suffered no casualties but on the nineteenth destroyer *Ross* covering the mine-sweepers hit not one mine but two, and although she became the only destroyer in the war to suffer such a dual misfortune and survive, not surprisingly she was put out of the fight.

A final preliminary softening-up came from the supporting escort-carriers of Rear-Admiral Thomas Sprague whose duty was to furnish the troops ashore with direct air cover and assistance. Sprague had eighteen of the small escort-carriers on his strength, but as six of these were mounting guard over the main convoys, only twelve were

Plans, Preparations, Preliminaries

immediately to hand. Since Halsey, then engaged in defending his cripples, was not able to make previously planned strikes on Leyte and Mindanao, Sprague made them for him inflicting further casualties on enemy aircraft on the ground. Still other support was forthcoming from MacArthur's Air Commander General George Kenney whose Far Eastern air forces based in Morotai, Biak and New Guinea made persistent raids on Mindanao and the Dutch East Indies to prevent the enemy from staging in aircraft reinforcements by this route. All was now ready for the main landings on Leyte, due to take place on 20 October which was designated A-Day by MacArthur since the usual name of D-Day was at that time and forever after associated solely with the landings of 6 June in Normandy.

On A-Day, two groups of transports – the northern (Task Force 78) under Rear-Admiral Daniel Barbey carrying X Corps (Major-General Sibert) consisting of 1st Cavalry Division (Major-General Mudge) and 24th Infantry Division (Major-General Irving) and the southern (Task Force 79) under Vice-Admiral Theodore Wilkinson embarking XXIV Corps (Major-General Hodge) made up of the 7th and 96th Infantry Divisions (Major-Generals Arnold and Bradley respectively) – flung their waves of landing-craft onto the beaches, preceded and supported by gunfire from Oldendorf's ships, air attacks from Sprague and Halsey, now operating east of the Philippines, and rockets from landing-craft specially equipped with these. Some 5,500 of these missiles were launched during both the northern and southern attacks in the space of a few minutes. Meanwhile a small force under Admiral Struble seized Panaon Island to the south of Leyte virtually unopposed.

Despite high seas, Japanese mortar fire, the fact that Wilkinson's craft were equipped for landing on coral-fringed Yap not the sandy beaches of Leyte, and the usual difficulties that afflict any large operation, this one went off like clockwork. Admiral Kinkaid who had the responsibility for it was more than reassured. It was, he thought, "the best planned and best executed operation I saw during the whole war".

Japanese forces in the Philippines as from 5 October were under the command of their most distinguished General, Tomoyuki Yamashita, the 'Tiger of Malaya' and conqueror of Singapore. His senior staff officer in that campaign had been Lieutenant-General Sosaku Suzuki who was again serving under him in command of the Central Philippines including Leyte. However, at first the Army's strategy, not as good as that of the Navy, was to fight merely a delaying action on

Leyte, on which was stationed only the 16th Division of Major-General Makino. Also Suzuki, knowing the deadliness of naval bombardment on previous occasions, had determined to place his main defensive line well inland as had been done so effectively on Peliliu. Therefore the Japanese defended the beaches with far less than their usual furious determination. They retreated under pressure, even leaving live ammunition behind in their evacuated bunkers.

In consequence the American beach-head expanded rapidly. On A-Day the southern landing troops captured the town of Dulag and the stronghold Hill 120. The following day the northern forces overran a major obstacle, Mount Guinhandang (Hill 522). Tacloban and Dulag airfields were also taken although both were so badly flooded as to be scarcely fit for use. Tacloban, capital of Leyte with the only docking facilities on the island, fell shortly afterwards. By the twenty-third the versatile 1st Cavalry Division in small boats had secured San Juanico Strait between Leyte and its northern neighbour Samar and made an unopposed landing at La Paz on the latter island while their companions pushed forward into Leyte Valley. By this time 132,400 men together with 200,000 tons of supplies had been landed. On 20 October General MacArthur waded ashore to broadcast the famous announcement of his return, to the people of the Philippines,[6] and on the twenty-fourth, General Krueger set up his Sixth Army command post ashore.

With the landing forces safely established, Admiral Oldendorf's old battleships withdrew to provide cover against enemy interference while Admiral Sprague's escort-carriers furnished fighter protection and laid on strikes to support the troops advancing inland. To the north hovered Halsey's Third Fleet ready to attack any Japanese forces that might threaten Seventh Fleet. The point to notice, however, is that while Seventh Fleet was 'MacArthur's Navy' and Admiral Kinkaid was directly under MacArthur's command, Halsey owed allegiance not to the General but to Admiral Nimitz in Hawaii. Thus the two fleets that were co-operating in support of the same landing had no common superior nearer than the Joint Chiefs of Staff 10,000 miles away in Washington.

This divergence of command caused a sizable increase in the

---

[6]Incidentally, the General almost got more than he bargained for from his broadcast. Fortunately General Yamashita did not believe that MacArthur was really present on Leyte, thinking the photos of his wading ashore were fakes taken in New Guinea. Had he known the truth he would have thrown every available aircraft at MacArthur's headquarters to avenge the death of Admiral Yamamoto.

volume of radio traffic necessary, as well as in the number of circuits to be guarded; hence it led to considerable delay in the passing of messages between the various commanders. Indeed while vastly better than those of the Japanese, American communications were far from good; Admiral Halsey later complaining of "long and intolerable delays in getting urgent messages through". Further, although Nimitz had ordered Halsey that "necessary measures for detailed co-ordination of operations" between the two fleets "will be arranged by their respective commanders", Halsey was later to refer to this directive as being "just so many words and nothing more. They were impossible of accomplishment." The reason was that the rapid changes of plan and acceleration of time-tables noted earlier had made it impossible for Halsey or Kinkaid to take such measures prior to the invasion, while during it each had been too busily occupied to confer with the other. This absence of a supreme commander, a point of which the Japanese were apparently aware, aggravated by the delays in communication, was to lead to a series of misunderstandings, culminating in a near-disaster on the decisive day of battle. Captain Roskill, indeed, considers that:

> It may be that if MacArthur, who was already charged with the chief responsibility for the capture of Leyte, had been given temporary control of all the supporting warships, and if either Kinkaid or Halsey – but preferably the former, because he had been working under MacArthur for a long time – had been placed in sole operational command of the naval side, the troubles of the twenty-fifth of October would have been avoided.

During the first four days of the invasion, Japanese air attacks were few and far between. At the time of the landings a single reconnaissance aircraft appeared – to be promptly shot down. Later the pressure increased and Sprague's sixteen available escort-carriers, the other two having been sent for replacement planes, downed some sixty-six enemy aircraft in protection of Seventh Fleet and the forces ashore. However, in the afternoon of A-Day, a torpedo-bomber hit light-cruiser *Honolulu*, badly damaged her, killed sixty of her crew and trapped a radioman, Leon Garson, below decks for sixteen hours before he was rescued happily unscathed by his ordeal. The following day at dawn, a bomber deliberately crashed into heavy-cruiser H.M.A.S. *Australia* a veteran of Seventh Fleet operations. This, we are assured, was an unpremeditated, individual action not an 'official' Kamikaze attack. But official or unofficial the effect of a bomber charging into a ship is much the same, and the cruiser lost twenty men

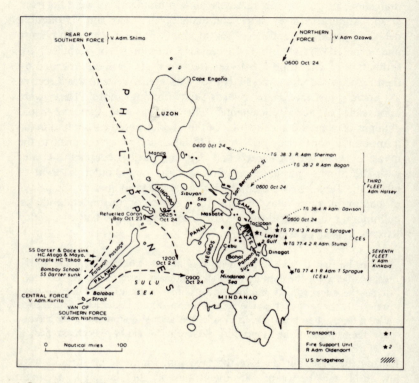

1 Strategy and Preliminaries

The mission of the Central Force under Vice-Admiral Kurita was to attack Leyte Gulf from the north. The Southern Forces under Vice-Admirals Nishimura and Shima were to attack it from the south. The Northern Force under Vice-Admiral Ozawa was to lure the American forces away from the battle area.

The mission of Third Fleet under Admiral William Halsey and Task Force 38 under Vice-Admiral Marc Mitscher was to protect the Leyte landings and "in case opportunity offer or can be created", to destroy the enemy fleet. Seventh Fleet under Vice-Admiral Thomas Kinkaid was to cover and support General MacArthur's landing on Leyte.

including her skipper Captain Deschaineux. Escort-carrier *Sangamon* suffered minor damage from a bomb-hit. Otherwise the naval forces were not harmed.

This comparative freedom from air attack, however, was merely the calm before the storm. The enemy commanders were saving their aerial strength until the time they could, as planned, use it to help clear the way for their fleet. At 0650, 17 October, Japanese look-outs on Suluan sighting the attacking forces broadcast prompt warning to Tokyo. At 0809 Toyoda gave the alert for *Sho I*; the Army leaders, slower to react, following suit the next day. Once again, however, the Japanese shortage of oil bedevilled them. Toyoda dared not commit his fleet immediately in case the operations reported should prove to be a feint to divert attention from a major landing elsewhere, since if they were, his ships thus committed prematurely would have to return due to shortage of fuel just when they would be needed most. Consequently not until 1110, 18 October when he was positive that there was no such deception and that the target really was Leyte, did Toyoda issue instructions for his forces to sail.

The principal Japanese force committed was Admiral Kurita's First Striking Force. This left Lingga Roads at 0100, 18 October for Brunei Bay, North Borneo, where, having refuelled, it split up. On the twenty-second at 0800, Kurita himself left harbour with Battleship Divisions A and B containing in all 5 battleships, 10 heavy cruisers, 2 light cruisers and 15 destroyers. This body was known as the 'Central Force' by the Americans. Kurita's mission was to advance to the west of Palawan, pass south of Mindoro through the Tablas Strait into the Sibuyan Sea and thence, via San Bernardino Strait between Luzon and Samar into the Philippine Sea; finally sailing south off the east coast of Samar to attack Leyte Gulf from the north.

Seven hours after Kurita's departure, Vice-Admiral Shoji Nishimura who had a shorter distance to cover, also left Brunei with Battleship Division C consisting of 2 battleships, 1 heavy cruiser and 4 destroyers. After a wide detour north and west to avoid suspected submarines, Force C turned east, proceeding through Balabac Strait south of Palawan into the Sulu Sea from which its commander intended to progress to the Mindanao Sea and then turn sharply north through Surigao Strait between Leyte and Dinagat to attack the gulf from the south. Meanwhile, Admiral Shima's Second Striking Force of three cruisers, two heavy and one light, plus four destroyers, left Amami-O-Shima in the Ryukyus on the eighteenth and by the twenty-second was west of Luzon heading south for the Sulu Sea with orders to support Nishimura. The forces under Nishimura and Shima were referred to by the Americans as the 'Van' and 'Rear' respectively of the Southern Force.

To assist this gigantic pincer movement, the air forces of Tominaga, Fukudome and Onishi were ordered to commence attacks on the twenty-fourth, the newly formed Kamikazes were alerted, and the Japanese submarine commander Vice-Admiral Miwa ordered eleven submarines into the Philippine Sea to join in the fray.

At this time also, the Japanese Army suddenly awoke to both the strategic disadvantages of the loss of Leyte and the opportunity that the success of the naval operations would yield. It planned to throw in reinforcements so that General Suzuki could drive the Americans into the sea once Kurita, Nishimura and Shima had wiped out their supply and support vessels. As a start, two transport units were detached from Shima's original command to carry troops to Ormoc Bay on the east of Leyte; one commanded by Vice-Admiral Naomasa Sakonju numbering one heavy cruiser, one light cruiser, one destroyer and four transports; the other under Commander Hisashi Ishii containing three destroyers only.

However, the crucial role was to be entrusted to Admiral Ozawa's carrier group. Not only had these vessels long been considered expendable, but the losses of their finest air-crews in the fighting around Formosa meant that they could now expect little success in diversionary attacks on U.S. ships. This, as mentioned earlier, had little real effect on the basic situation, so the ultimate use of the carriers, now hastily decided upon, could perhaps have been foreseen some time previously. It had already been mooted that the battleship-carriers *Hyuga* and *Ise* be used as a purely sacrificial offering to entice American forces north. Now it was decided to make the bait more attractive by adding to them the less important of the carriers with a handful of ill-trained pilots aboard, retaining the more valuable carriers in home waters in the hope that somehow more pilots could be trained to operate from them in the time that the *Sho* operation, if successful, would buy.

In consequence, Ozawa took with him in his Northern Force only the two battleship-carriers, the large fleet carrier *Zuikaku* and three light carriers, *Zuiho, Chitose* and *Chiyoda*, suitably escorted by three light cruisers and ten destroyers (plus a supply unit in case he needed to refuel). Left behind were Japan's three latest large carriers, *Amagi, Unryu* and *Katsuragi*, with two older carriers *Junyo* and *Ryuho*. The mission of the forces that did sail was wholly one of sacrifice. They were to "manoeuvre east of Luzon to lure the enemy northward". The enemy in question was Halsey's vast fleet and both Toyoda and Ozawa held the grim opinion that the Northern Force would be annihilated, but they believed that its sacrifice might clear the way for the heavy Japanese surface forces on which all depended.

On the evening of 20 October, a few hours after Nishimura sailed, Ozawa's ships left Bungo Suido the southern entrance to the Inland Sea. Ozawa expected he would have to fight his way out past U.S. submarines known to be watching the strait, but as it happened the 'wolfpack' which had been on guard had decided on the previous day that their enemy was not seeking battle so, with the concurrence of Vice-Admiral Charles Lockwood, Commander Submarines Pacific Fleet, had retired to hunt targets among merchant shipping. Since the Japanese, apart from not wanting to be reported that early, might well have suffered losses from the submarines, Ozawa's undetected sortie undoubtedly won the first move of the battle albeit by default. His carriers with their almost empty hangars headed south for Cape Engano the north-eastern point of Luzon.

Such was Toyoda's *Sho* plan, described by General Fuller as "Japan's supreme effort of the war" and "one of the most daring naval operations ever undertaken". While most of the senior Japanese officers did not have a great deal of confidence in the plan they all agreed that in the circumstances it was impossible to find a better one. The fact is that the plan all but succeeded and in order to throw into relief the events that follow, it is fascinating to discuss the situation that would have arisen had such success been achieved.

One irony is that the planned destruction of the transports would not have been the greatest of the Japanese successes. Toyoda had originally planned 'X Day', the assault on the transports by Kurita, Nishimura and Shima for 22 October which would of course be within the first two days of the landing as the Japanese considered so important. However, after Kurita had protested that it would be quite impossible for his forces to steam the required distance in time, 'X Day' had had to be postponed to the twenty-fifth.

By this date, however, the bulk of the transports had sailed; the remaining targets consisting of one attack cargo vessel, twenty-three LSTs, two LCMs, and twenty-eight Liberty ships mainly from reinforcement groups. Even these were useful objectives in view of the considerable shortage of supplies. According to Woodward: "Interruption of the flow of supplies, even for a short period would have created an extremely critical situation". There is also the point that an attack on the shipping in the gulf would cost the Americans several valuable officers for Admirals Kinkaid, Barbey and Wilkinson were all present in their amphibious flagships *Wasatch, Blue Ridge* and *Mt Olympus*, together with their staffs and senior commanders like Captain Whitehead, the Commander Air Support Seventh Fleet, who was with Kinkaid in *Wasatch*. Probably, however, the Japanese in any case would just have missed MacArthur since he left *Nashville* to set up his command post ashore about an hour before their forces were due to arrive – but they might have killed him on the beaches, which leads us to the next point for consideration.

After the battle, Admiral Halsey, for reasons that will shortly become clear, insisted that even had Kurita got into the gulf his bombardment of the beaches would have had only a temporary effect on the position ashore, basing his claim on the fact that in the fighting at Guadalcanal the enemy had on several occasions pulled off such a bombardment – though the bombarding units never had half the strength that Kurita had under his command at midday on 25 October – yet had caused only temporary set-backs. However, the position at Guadalcanal was entirely different from that at Leyte in a number of respects. In the first place, though Japanese destroyers had shelled the beaches on previous occasions at night, the first really big bombardment by battleships did not occur until the American troops had been established ashore for over two months with their stores and equipment inland and dispersed. In this connection a most interesting comment comes from Major Frank Hough, who in *The Island War* states that the enemy made their biggest mistake when immediately after the Guadalcanal landings their air attacks "concentrated entirely on the [landing] convoy, ignoring the supplies piled all over the beach in plain sight. Had those supplies been destroyed or even seriously damaged, the expedition would have been doomed at a single stroke, as events were to prove."

The situation on the beaches of Leyte on 25 October was the same as that on Guadalcanal when the Japanese airmen thus "ignored their main chance". The beaches were piled high with food, ammunition and other supplies – equipment for a time even littered the vital airfield at Tacloban. Destruction of these supplies would obviously leave the forces ashore without food or ammunition, while to make matters worse, the temporary headquarters of the Army commanders at Dulag, Palo and San José were practically on the beaches within easy range of even the secondary batteries of ships in the gulf. If they were shelled the troops would be deprived of their leaders as well.

Plans, Preparations, Preliminaries 33

According to General MacArthur whose summary of the situation should be noted:

> Should the enemy [i.e. Kurita] gain entrance to Leyte Gulf, his powerful naval guns could pulverize any of the eggshell transports present in the area and destroy vitally needed supplies on the beachhead. The thousands of U.S. troops ashore would be isolated and pinned down helplessly between enemy fire from ground and sea. Then too, the schedule for supply reinforcement would not only be completely upset but the success of the invasion itself would be placed in jeopardy.

A further difference from the Guadalcanal campaign was that the Japanese forces there could not be supplied or reinforced easily. So much was this so that, although by great efforts accompanied by heavy losses they did at one stage land more troops on the island than their opponents had available, this situation did not arise until the Americans were too firmly established to be dislodged. Indeed for the first two vital months the Americans had odds of two to one at least in their favour.

On Leyte, however, the reverse was the case. The narrow channels between the various Philippine islands, mined, and guarded by land-based aircraft, were not yet accessible to U.S. forces but were so to the Japanese who could thus throw in heavy reinforcements — and did! Even after the Leyte Gulf battle, the enemy despite heavy losses was able to run in some 50,000 fresh troops to assist Suzuki's defenders. These were not sufficient to oust the Americans, but had the latter been deprived of supplies, leaders, transports and supporting air forces, they might well have been — if indeed in those circumstances the Japanese would not have been able to provide much larger reinforcements.

This leads to the final important difference from the Guadalcanal campaign. At Guadalcanal the Americans had the only airfield in the vicinity — Henderson Field on Guadalcanal which they had ready for action within two weeks, both fighters and bombers operating therefrom, while two smaller fighter strips were added later. The Japanese, in contrast, operated long-distance from Rabaul, which meant that their bombers flew unescorted — an easy prey for the American fighters. Even when a landing-strip was built at Bougainville, the Zero fighters had no time to linger over Guadalcanal which they could just reach. Furthermore, even in the first two weeks while the Americans were readying the airfield there were repeated small raids by six or seven bombers but no really heavy attacks were launched.

On Leyte, however, again the opposite was true. Apart from the newly captured airfields on Leyte the Americans had none within 500 miles, while as a result of continuous torrential rain and unsuitable subsoil, it proved impossible until the end of October to use any aircraft on Leyte except a handful of Lockheed Lightning fighters. Not very many were present thereafter for quite a time. The enemy, however, with scores of airfields available was able to mount attacks which were far from light. "Ammunition dumps and oil-tanks were razed almost nightly", reported General MacArthur who considered that not for two and a half years "had the Japanese blanketed an Allied position with such powerful sustained and effective air action".

In these conditions the escort carriers of Seventh Fleet were of immense importance. Ironically enough the Japanese did not know of their existence, but they lay right in the path of their advancing forces. If these ships had been annihilated on the twenty-fifth, and as it was two-thirds had to withdraw on the evening of that day and the remainder at the end of the month, at which date fortunately eighty fresh fighters arrived at Tacloban to provide some relief, then the troops would have been deprived of air support as well as supplies for the crucial period when they were striving to maintain their establishment ashore against enemy counter-attacks.

In his official *History of United States Naval Operations in World War II*[7] Professor S.E. Morison remarks:

> The great unanswered question is: Supposing *Sho I* worked, and the pincer on our amphibious forces pinched, what would the Japanese Navy do about Halsey's Third Fleet when it swallowed the Ozawa bait and turned south again? There were no land-based air forces capable of handling Halsey. Apparently the Japanese planners never thought of that; or if they did, estimated that the damage they would inflict in Leyte Gulf would ruin the invasion and cause Nimitz to send Third Fleet home.

In fact it appears that the Japanese had no intention of waiting for Third Fleet to return. According to Kurita's Chief of Staff, Rear-Admiral Tomiji Koyanagi, after getting through to Leyte Gulf and shooting up the transports and beach-head, the Central Force planned to retire through Surigao Strait which, it will be remembered, the Southern Force was supposed to have penetrated. In other words the Japanese were not to meet Halsey but to depart on a route which would carry them clear of him.

[7] Volume XII *Leyte*.

Plans, Preparations, Preliminaries 35

Therefore it would seem that the Japanese planners did estimate that the damage they would inflict in Leyte Gulf would be sufficient in itself. It also seems that Morison admits that such estimate was correct for he later remarks: "One need only think what would have happened had Operation *Sho-Go* worked. General MacArthur's Army would have been cut off like that of Athens at Syracuse in 413 B.C. Third Fleet alone could not have maintained its communications." This view is amply supported by a signal from Halsey to MacArthur on 26 October, asking when land-based aircraft could take over on Leyte, in which he said: "After 17 days of battle my fast carriers are unable to provide extended support for Leyte but 2 Groups are available 27 October. The pilots are exhausted and the carriers are low in provisions, bombs and torpedoes."

Thus the Japanese plan gave them the opportunity of inflicting spectacularly heavy casualties on their opponents including several top military and naval commanders. If this were taken it would in turn result in very heavy losses if not complete catastrophe to Sixth Army. What effect this catastrophe would have had on the war is debatable but it might well have been considerable. It would have provoked furious controversy among those who considered the Philippine campaign a mistake in any event. It would have presented a heavy blow to the Filipino people for whose sake the landing had been arranged. Coming as it would have done after a run of American victories, it would have had a correspondingly dampening effect on American morale by threatening an unbearable prolongation of the war. It would have given the Japanese vital time to train new airmen to equip those new big carriers remaining in the Inland Sea. And it would have been followed by the further heavy losses and terrifying strain that were indeed to be inflicted by the 'Kamikazes'.

In this connection, it is worthwhile to reflect that the intention of the Japanese in the war was never to occupy the American homeland which they knew to be militarily and logistically impossible but, having seized as much territory as possible, to fight to hold this until their enemies, exhausted by the prodigious efforts needed to recapture it, were prepared to allow them to keep at least part of their conquests in return for a cessation of hostilities. This scheme had not worked for a number of reasons, chief of which was that the Americans had adopted 'island-leapfrogging' under which they seized only the most vital enemy bases, by-passing and isolating the rest – as Mindanao was by-passed by the Leyte invasion for example – but it could work yet. As Morison remarks: "the Japanese war-lords were playing for time. America might yet tire of the War". If they could show the Americans that the reconquest of the Philippines which had been under American protection would be impossible or at least dreadfully costly, might they not be able to retain some of their conquests in the south in the "colonial territories" of which the U.S. disapproved, or at least special privileges therein, in return for a voluntary surrender of the Philippines?

Yet whatever be the opinion as to the possible long-term results of the *Sho* plan's success, there can be no doubt of its short-term effect which Woodward thus summarizes: "Should Kurita succeed in carrying out his mission, and come through with even half his ships, he could isolate our troops on Leyte, and, at his leisure, destroy the shipping, aircraft and supplies that were vital to the operation. The effect would have been a disaster of incalculable proportions."

These then were the enormous prizes at stake when almost every ship in the Japanese Navy left its harbour to steam east or south for the Leyte Gulf — and the largest naval battle in history.

2

The Submarine Attacks

The most interesting aspect of the Battle of Leyte Gulf is not its sheer size, although certainly it was gigantic in scale. Fought across an area of almost 500,000 square miles, lasting over several days, the action saw joining battle slightly more ships with a fifth greater tonnage than those present at Jutland. Such a comparison ignores the presence of the transports in the gulf, which were scarcely of value in a naval action but which were one of the main targets of Japanese attacks; it also ignores the presence of submarines which did no damage at Jutland but inflicted considerable damage at Leyte Gulf; most of all it ignores air power, represented at Jutland by some five seaplanes but at Leyte Gulf by hundreds of aircraft on each side.

Yet it is in its variety of naval warfare that the chief interest of Leyte Gulf lies. Previously there had been two main types of battle fought in the Pacific. There had been short-range actions where ships had attacked each other with gunfire or torpedoes, almost invariably under cover of darkness. There had been long-range actions between forces built around carriers which had struck at each other over hundreds of miles of sea. Yet hitherto never had the two types been actively employed in the same battle. At Leyte Gulf they were; they even overlapped, for one vital round of the conflict saw carrier-planes furiously assaulting surface vessels which at the time were themselves shelling the carriers whence the attacking planes came. Apart from the mine, which as previously mentioned had some slight effect in the preliminary period, every naval weapon previously known was employed, while two new ones made their first appearance: 18-inch naval guns were seen in action and the new tactic of suicide-crashing was introduced on an organized basis by a formation of several planes. And the battle began with "one of the most successful co-ordinated attacks on record" launched by submarines.

In the early hours of 23 October, strong patrols of these deadly underwater craft lay west and north of the Philippines to give advance warning of the approach of the enemy. Two such were *Darter* under Commander David McClintock and *Dace* whose skipper was Commander Bladen Claggett. Their patrol area was at the southern entrance of Palawan Passage lying west of the long island of that name, between it and the 'Dangerous Ground' a series of unpleasant reefs and shoals in the South China Sea, many of which bore the names of unfortunate ships that had met with disaster thereon in the past. At midnight, the submarines were surfaced a few yards apart exchanging information. At 0116, *Darter*'s radar located a contact at 30,000 yards range. Commander McClintock, the senior officer of the team, called through his megaphone: "We have radar contact! Let's go!" Both submarines closed the enemy. They estimated his strength at eleven heavy ships plus six destroyers, promptly reporting this by radio. Admiral Halsey received the message – first sighting report of any of the approaching Japanese forces – at 0630. Although an assault under cover of darkness would have been safer, McClintock considered it essential to track the enemy ships until early dawn before striking so as to be able to give as exact an account as possible of their composition. Two more contact reports were sent off by the submarines in the night-hours variously estimating the size of the hostile fleet. In fact this was throughout considerably under-stated. *Darter* and *Dace* had located the strongest enemy of all – Admiral Kurita's Central Force.

Prior to the subs' attack, though not afterwards, this force was composed as follows:

> 5 battleships: *Yamato, Musashi, Nagato, Kongo, Haruna.*
> 10 heavy cruisers: *Atago* (Kurita's flagship), *Maya, Takao, Chokai, Myoko, Haguro, Kumano, Suzuya, Tone, Chikuma.*
> 2 light cruisers: *Noshiro, Yahagi.*
> 15 destroyers: *Kishinami, Okinami, Hayashimo, Akishimo, Hamanami, Fujinami, Shimakaze, Nowake, Urakaze, Isokaze, Yukikaze, Asashimo, Kiyoshimo, Hamakaze, Naganami.*

The fleet was based upon the super-battleships *Yamato* and *Musashi*, the largest battleships ever built and the biggest warships to take part in World War II. To gain some idea of their size, it is worth recalling that the German giants *Bismarck* and *Tirpitz* displaced 42,500 tons with an armament of eight 15-inch and twelve 5.9-inch guns. *Yamato* and *Musashi*, 863 feet long, had a standard displacement of 64,170 tons, being nearly 72,000 tons when fully laden. They packed a considerably more powerful punch having nine

The Submarine Attacks 39

18.1-inch guns with twelve 6.1-inch weapons forming an ample secondary battery. The 18.1-inch main batteries, set in three triple turrets, two forward and one aft, were the largest naval guns in existence. The barrel of any one of these was 75 feet long, alone weighing 162 tons. They fired shells weighing 3,200 pounds a distance of $22\frac{1}{2}$ miles, far outranging the 16-inch shells which were the biggest any American battleship possessed. Yet in spite of their bulk, they were fast ships; four turbine engines developing 150,000 horsepower, giving them a speed of 27.5 knots, only $2\frac{1}{2}$ knots slower than the big German ships that were two-thirds their size.

This considerable rapidity for their tonnage was due to Japanese skill in shipbuilding, demonstrated since the war in their vast tankers. The *Yamatos* were extremely beautiful ships with graceful, soaring bows and backward-slanting, streamlined funnel and mast. They represented the very latest stage in battleship construction but alas for them they had to face the swarms of aircraft that had now become the new rulers of the sea, relegating battleships of whatever strength to a vulnerable secondary importance.

Compared with these monsters the 16-inch gunned *Nagato* and the 14-inch gunned *Kongo* and *Haruna* were definitely less dangerous. In their own way, however, the heavy cruisers were just as remarkable. They were bigger than their American counterparts which did not exceed 10,000 tons, ranging from 11,200 to 13,300 tons. While the American 'heavies' had nine 8-inch guns, all the Japanese ones had ten such, except *Tone* and *Chikuma*, both of which had been in the Pearl Harbour attack force, which had eight.

On the twenty-third when the submarines located it, this immensely powerful force was steaming in two distinct groups, each of which consisted of two columns. The port column of the first group was led by Kurita in his flagship, heavy cruiser *Atago*, followed by *Takao*, *Chokai*, and battleship *Nagato*. To starboard *Myoko*, *Haguro* and *Maya* led *Yamato* and *Musashi*. Some six kilometres astern came the second section; on the port side the battleship *Haruna* preceded by *Kumano* and *Suzuya*; to starboard *Kongo* preceded by *Tone* and *Chikuma*. The two light cruisers and the destroyers hovered on each flank of, or in between, the columns. Yet none were stationed in advance of them, a fact that was of considerable assistance to *Darter* and *Dace*.

Admiral Takeo Kurita, Commander of the Central Force, was an officer of thirty-eight years service. He was a 'big-ship' man who did not value carriers highly before the war. In consequence he had hitherto usually operated in a secondary or escorting role, guarding transports in the invasion of the Dutch East Indies and commanding a bombardment group at Midway. A past experience which gave encouragement in view of his present role was that he had pulled off the big bombardment of Guadalcanal by battleships on 14 October 1942 with great success. Yet in many respects Kurita seems to have lacked the exceptional resolution that was the great strength of most Japanese admirals. He had retired from his Guadalcanal bombardment as the result of an attack by four motor-torpedo-boats. At the Philippine Sea, he had not shown marked enthusiasm for the combat having been the first to counsel retreat. He had a very healthy respect for American air attacks as a result of raids by carriers *Saratoga* and *Princeton* on Rabaul on 5 November 1943 which had crippled a strong cruiser force under his command. He seems also to have been singularly heedless of the risks of submarine attacks. On the twenty-second, his look-outs more than once identified bamboo poles as periscopes, causing nervous gunners to open fire on them. Also his radio room had warned him that a submarine had been heard transmitting close at hand. Yet Kurita took no precautions. The absence of picket destroyers has already been noted; in addition, Kurita, with a closely-restricted schedule to meet, was steaming at a mere 16 knots. He remained blissfully unaware that throughout the night *Darter* to port and *Dace* to starboard were hanging onto his flanks sending out their reports, preparing to submerge at dawn for a combined attack on his fleet.

Shortly after 0600, in the half-light, *Darter* closed the nearest column. At 0632 she began launching the six torpedoes in her bow tubes at Kurita's flagship, heavy cruiser *Atago*. "After firing two into him and one straight ahead," remarked McClintock "target was roaring by so close that we couldn't miss so spread the remainder inside his length." McClintock then swung hard to port to bring the stern tubes to bear on the cruiser next in line. A minute later, four more torpedoes leapt towards heavy cruiser *Takao*.

On board the Japanese ships look-outs sighted the wakes of the torpedoes but so close had *Darter* approached that hurried orders to wheel and engine-room were far too late. Four torpedoes hit *Atago*, shattering her along her entire length. Hearing the shock of explosions McClintock whipped his periscope back to see "the sight of a lifetime". So close that all of her could not be seen at once with the periscope in high power, *Atago* was "a mass of billowing black smoke from Number One turret to the stern. No superstructure could be

The Submarine Attacks

seen. Bright orange flames shot from the side from the bow to the after turret. Cruiser was already down by the bow which was dipping under. Number One turret was at water level. She was definitely finished." Eighteen minutes later the cruiser disappeared leaving a black sheet of oil on the surface – the first fatal casualty of the battle.

When his flagship went down Admiral Kurita was forced to swim for safety with his staff, being somewhat ignominiously fished out of the water by destroyer *Kishinami*. Some 360 officers and men were lost including half Kurita's key communications personnel. Since poor communications and poor control were to prove the curse of the whole operation, McClintock probably achieved an even more important success than he realized. He also made his contribution towards shaking Kurita's nerve, a factor which was to prove of importance later.

Behind the stricken flagship, *Takao* with a minute's longer warning had swung forty-five degrees to port. This saved her from *Atago*'s fate but two torpedoes found their mark, blowing off her rudder and two propellers and flooding three boiler-rooms. Since she could not possibly continue in this state, she was sent back to Brunei for repairs accompanied by destroyers *Naganami* and *Asashimo*. *Darter* had thus single-handed ensured that Kurita would have four ships less with which to attack Leyte Gulf. Depth charges aimed at the submarine fell well wide. Some twenty-five minutes after her own attack, *Darter* heard "four distinct torpedo explosions in rapid succession". *Dace* was in action also.

To escape from *Darter*'s attentions, the Japanese squadron had made a sudden alteration of course to starboard but it then resumed its original course putting Commander Claggett in a perfect position for attacking the starboard column. He had a "beautiful view" of the first two ships (*Myoko* and *Haguro*) correctly identifying them as *Nachi*-class cruisers. Since he was an enthusiastically optimistic character, Claggett decided that these targets were not good enough. The third ship in line seemed much more promising. "He looks larger than the two cruisers that have just passed ahead", remarked the Commander. "He has two stacks, and superstructure appears much heavier. Sound also reports target screws as heavier and slower than those of cruisers." Accordingly, assessing this vessel as a *Kongo*-class battleship which was worthy of his attention, Claggett prepared to attack her. In reality, she was heavy cruiser *Maya* which was of slightly less tonnage than the two preceding ships although she was still a better target since she belonged to a class later than the *Nachis* and was designed as an improvement on them. She had indeed more armour than the *Nachi*s, her reduced tonnage being due to the use of lighter alloys. The massive bridge that drew Claggett's attention contained the latest equipment associated with fire-control and communications; also the cruiser was one of the most powerfully armed vessels in the fleet. Even so it was perhaps a pity that Claggett was not still more greedy and did not wait for the fourth ship to pass – *Yamato* would surely have been big enough for anyone.

As it was, at 0654, *Dace* fired six torpedoes at *Maya*. Four of them hit. The wretched *Maya* burst into a sheet of flame from stem to stern, being shaken violently by terrific magazine explosions that were so loud that Claggett was alarmed lest *Dace* might have sustained damage also. Only four minutes after being struck the cruiser sank amid clouds of smoke and spray, with a very heavy loss of life. Four destroyers promptly counter-attacked with depth-charges which exploded all around *Dace*. She was violently rocked by these but a quick check showed that she had suffered no damage.

With Kurita now on *Kishinami*, command was taken over by Rear-Admiral Matome Ugaki in *Yamato*. He promptly ordered the surviving ships to increase speed to 24 knots so as to clear this unhealthy area. The Japanese fled north in a state of considerable alarm. Understandably look-outs now saw submarines everywhere, several depth-charge attacks being launched against further bamboo poles reported as periscopes, while evasive action followed evasive action. It was late afternoon before Kurita, accompanied by his staff, was able to be transferred to *Yamato*, there to resume tactical control of Central Force.

The adventures of *Darter* and *Dace* were not over, however. Like his partner, Commander McClintock was determined to inflict the maximum possible damage on the enemy. He had no intention of allowing the crippled *Takao* to escape. *Darter* returned to periscope depth at 0920 but found the injured cruiser too well guarded by her destroyers, while three aircraft were on patrol overhead. For five hours McClintock tried to get at his potential victim but in vain. Finally he decided that he would track *Takao*, now slowly retiring southward, in preparation for a combined attack with *Dace* to finish her off after dark.

Luck however had now deserted *Darter* albeit apparently not her crew. The two submarines had by this time been navigating the dangerous waters of Palawan Passage for twenty-four hours on dead reckoning alone, since their enforced submergence had prevented their officers learning their position from sightings of Palawan, while clouds

The Submarine Attacks

obscured the stars. At midnight both were racing on the surface for a position ahead of the cruiser from which they could spring their attack. In approximately an hour such a position could be reached. On *Darter*'s bridge McClintock with his officer of the watch, Lieutenant Skorupski, peered into the pitch black night. Then without warning, "we hit something and we were riding over it as a whale noses up out of the water", recorded McClintock. "We took a large up-angle and the stern went under as far as the engine-hatch. Then all of a sudden the stern rode up and we came to rest high and dry."

A mere quarter-knot error in estimating a current had caused *Darter* to crash into Bombay Shoal, a coral reef forming a particularly unpleasant part of the well-named 'Dangerous Ground'. The impact registered on the sound gear of one of the Japanese destroyers which promptly charged onto the scene, closing to a range of 4,000 yards. "That," commented McClintock "may not sound so close on shore, but it sounded close then to us sitting on that reef." Luckily, the enemy did not appreciate what had happened, so soon drew away.

At high water, *Darter*'s crew made every possible attempt to get her off her undesired resting-place in vain. There was nothing for it but to abandon ship before daylight inevitably brought attacks from hostile forces. "Down below all equipment was destroyed. Sledgehammers were used on the radar and radio. Confidential gear was burned, choking everybody with smoke." Then shortly after 0400, the men began transferring to *Dace* which had closed up to the reef to render assistance. Fifty-pound demolition charges were placed on *Darter* to complete her destruction and at 0555 with the whole crew safely aboard *Dace* one or two of these went up though not enough to wreck the sub. Four torpedoes fired by *Dace* hit the reef causing only minor damage, but twenty-one 4-inch shell-hits along *Darter*'s water-line ensured her uselessness to the enemy, though it was another six days before further shells from 'friendly' submarines finally finished her off. As *Dace* pulled away, an enemy bomber appeared, but happily this attacked wrecked *Darter* while her companion dived to safety.

Despite the loss of *Darter* with the consequent escape of *Takao*, there is no doubt that the Americans had won this round of the battle. To complete the story happily, *Dace* with the full crews of both submarines on board reached Fremantle, Western Australia, safely eleven days later. Since she now carried over twice as many men as her normal complement, conditions were far from ideal, with men sleeping on empty torpedo skids and living (poor devils!) on mushroom soup and peanut-butter sandwiches. Fortunately, the elation of their common victory prevented any tension among the sailors, and, said Commander Claggett "made a pleasant cruise out of what could have been an intolerable situation".

The attacks just described were the most important contributions made by U.S. submarines to the battle but they were by no means the only ones. If *Darter* and *Dace* had the honour of first locating enemy forces, submarine *Bream* enjoyed the distinction of firing the first shots. Early on the twenty-third while *Darter* and *Dace* were tracking Kurita, *Bream*, patrolling off Manila Bay, sighted Admiral Sakonju's transport unit. This consisted of heavy cruiser *Aoba*, light cruiser *Kinu* and destroyer *Uranami*, which were calling in the bay to collect their transports. *Bream* closed to attack this force. 'Closed' is the right word – she could even see men running to their battle stations. Nevertheless of six torpedoes launched at *Aoba*, only one hit. This produced a tremendous flash and so damaged that heavy cruiser that she took no further part in the proceedings, having to be towed into Manila harbour by the *Kinu*, which afterwards rejoined the transport group.

Nor was Kurita to escape the attention of other submarines. *Angler* picked up his fleet to the north of Palawan shortly after dark, tracking it as it headed for the Mindoro Strait. Early on the twenty-fourth *Guitarro* also made contact, correctly estimating that Central Force was proceeding towards the Sibuyan Sea. Although neither was able to attain an attacking position and although their preoccupation with Kurita enabled both Nishimura and Shima to break into the Sulu Sea without being engaged or even located, their sighting reports were of the greatest value. Admiral Halsey's Third Fleet had plenty of warning of the approach of Kurita's vessels. A strong reception was duly prepared for them. Central Force had already undergone submarine attacks on the twenty-third; on the twenty-fourth it would be faced with attacks in a different but even deadlier form – attacks from the air.

3

The Air Attacks of 24 October

On 24 October, three task groups of Third Fleet were stationed to the east of the Philippines about 125 miles apart. Third Fleet, the strongest in the world, was normally divided into three task forces containing fast carriers, amphibious vessels and supply ships respectively. However Admiral Wilkinson's amphibious craft had been allocated to Kinkaid's Seventh Fleet for this mission, while although Captain Acuff's Task Force of oilers, fleet tugs, ammunition ships etc., was vital if the carriers were to continue to operate — it refuelled all three available task groups on the twenty-third for example — it was obviously not intended to participate in battle.

This, however, was the function of Third Fleet's carrier division, Task Force 38, whose commander Vice-Admiral Marc Mitscher had had charge of the fast carriers at the Philippine Sea, remaining in command at his own request after Halsey relieved Spruance as the Fleet Commander. Since the detachment of Wilkinson had resulted in Third Fleet and Task Force 38 becoming identical, however, Halsey exercised direct control on the twenty-fourth, constantly sending orders to his task group leaders without reference to Mitscher. This, as will be seen, had unfortunate consequences.

Task Force 38 contained four task groups but not all were present at this stage. On the evening of the twenty-second Vice-Admiral John McCain's Task Group 38:1, consisting of fleet carriers *Wasp* (his flagship), *Hornet* and *Hancock* with light carriers *Monterey* and *Cowpens*, escorted by heavy cruisers *Chester, Pensacola, Salt Lake City* and *Boston*, light cruisers *San Diego* and *Oakland* and fourteen destroyers, had been sent to Ulithi for rest and reprovisioning. In view of the fact that the task force had just completed ten months of activity the last two of which had, in the opinion of Admiral Mitscher, seen more intensive action than any other in the war, while "no other force in the world has been subjected to such a period of constant operation without rest or rehabilitation", it was logical for Halsey to take such a step, but it was unfortunate that the task group he chose to rest was the one with the most carriers and most planes of the four. An odder decision came when Halsey received news of the submarines' sightings on the twenty-third. Although he cancelled the proposed departure of another group, he did not recall McCain who had orders to strike at Yap on his way to Ulithi, apparently wanting confirmation of the reports from his pilots first. The result was that the strongest of his task groups could not take part in the actions of the twenty-fourth.

Even with McCain's departure, Halsey still had available the tremendous strength of Task Groups 38:2, 38:3 and 38:4 led respectively by Rear-Admirals Gerald Bogan, Frederick Sherman and Ralph Davison. Although there was a considerable transferring of individual ships, particularly destroyers, from one group to another, these units early on the twenty-fourth were composed as follows:

Farthest north was Group 3 stationed east of central Luzon some 60 miles off Polillo Island. This Group numbered:

Fleet carriers: *Essex* (Sherman's flagship), *Lexington* (Mitscher's flagship).

Light carriers: *Princeton, Langley*.

Battleships: *Massachusetts, South Dakota*.

Light cruisers: *Sante Fe, Birmingham, Mobile, Reno*.

Destroyers: *Clarence K. Bronson, Cotten, Dortch, Gatling, Healey, Porterfield, Callaghan, Cassin Young, Irwin, Preston, Morrison, Cogswell, Caperton, Ingersoll, Knapp*.

In the central position was Group 2, some 50 miles east of San Bernardino Strait. This was the smallest Group containing:

Fleet carrier: *Intrepid* (Bogan's flagship).

Light carriers: *Cabot* and *Independence*, which latter controlled pilots specially trained for night operations.

Battleships: *Iowa, New Jersey* (Halsey's flagship).

Light cruisers: *Biloxi, Vincennes, Miami*.

Destroyers: *Owen, Miller, The Sullivans, Tingey, Hickox, Hunt, Lewis Hancock, Marshall, Halsey Powell, Cushing, Colahan, Uhlmann, Stockham, Weiderburn, Twining, Yarnall*.

Finally about 60 miles east of southern Samar sailed Group 4:

Fleet carriers: *Franklin* (Davison's flagship) and the veteran *Enterprise* that had fought at the Battles of Midway, Eastern Solomons, Santa Cruz and Philippine Sea with conspicuous success.

Light carriers: *San Jacinto, Belleau Wood*.

The Air Attacks of 24 October

Battleships: *Washington* (flagship of Vice-Admiral Willis Lee, Commander Battleships, Pacific Fleet) and *Alabama*.
Heavy cruisers: *Wichita, New Orleans*.
Destroyers: *Maurey, Gridley, Helm, McCall, Mugford, Bagley, Patterson, Ralph Talbot, Wilkes, Nicholson, Swanson, Laws, Longshaw*.

It will be noted that Third Fleet was lavishly equipped with both battleships and carriers. Of the former, *Iowa* and *New Jersey* of 45,000 tons with nine 16-inch guns were, apart from *Yamato* and *Musashi*, the largest battleships in the world. The other four were of smaller tonnage (35,000 tons) but also carried nine 16-inchers. All were capable of 28 knots or more — over 30 in the case of *Iowa* and *New Jersey* — together forming a force able, single-handed, to take on even Kurita with a very good chance of success. The carriers also mounted sufficient aerial strength to be able to deal with anything the enemy could bring against them. Although the numbers of planes varied on each ship, the five fleet carriers on hand on the twenty-fourth carried an average of forty-two Hellcat fighters, superior to anything the Japanese possessed, thirty Helldiver bombers and eighteen of the splendidly adaptable Avengers which could be used for reconnaissance or as torpedo-bombers or glide-bombers as desired; while each of the six light carriers was equipped with an average of twenty-two fighters and nine Avengers. It can readily be appreciated therefore that Task Force 38 alone had the resources to cope with all the Japanese forces without assistance from Seventh Fleet.

At dawn, Halsey ordered all three task groups to launch search planes to hunt for the enemy over a wide area stretching from central Luzon to northern Mindanao, covering the Sibuyan and Sulu Seas; the areas of search for the groups being made over-lapping for additional security. The planes were divided into search teams, each consisting of one Helldiver accompanied by two Hellcats. Each team was ordered to cover ten degrees of the arc of search assigned to its particular group. However, Halsey made another strange decision at this point in that he failed to order any searches to the north or north-east, an omission which was to cause trouble later. Shortly after 0600 all teams had flown off. Additional fighters were stationed at intervals from their parent ship to relay radio reports. Flying weather was very good with visibility clear. The airmen roared out over the vivid blue seas from which the magnificent volcanic peaks of the islands reared abruptly heavenwards.

At 0746 Lieutenant (Junior Grade) Max Adams, pilot of a

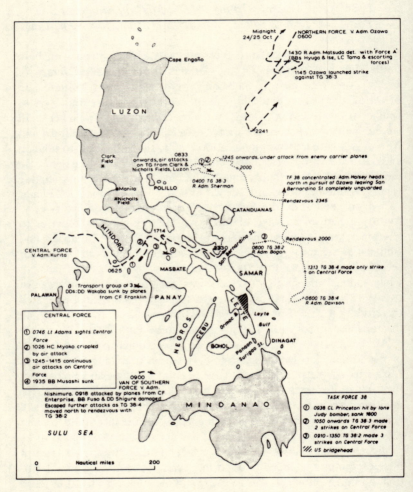

2 The Air Attacks of 24 October

The Air Attacks of 24 October

Helldiver from *Intrepid*, detected a radar contact. Followed by his escorting fighters he investigated, shortly thereafter sighting a large number of ships, their white wakes clearly visible cutting across the blue sea. Kurita's Central Force, still in two sections, was then rounding the southern cape of Mindoro to enter the Tablas Strait. The Japanese were steaming in two circular dispositions with their battleships and heavy cruisers forming an inner ring while the light cruisers and destroyers made an outer one around them, a formation designed for protection against air attack. Kurita still commanded five battleships and seven heavy cruisers, with the mighty *Yamato* and *Musashi*, now sighed by American airmen for the first time, looming formidably in their midst.

The search planes at once reported the position and composition of Central Force to their relaying fighters from whom Admiral Halsey received the news at about 0820. To proceed through San Bernardino Strait to attack Kurita was impossible for the waters of the strait were presumably mined, with the location of the minefields known only to the Japanese. Also Admiral Nimitz had specifically ordered that no ships were to pass through the strait without his express permission.

However, with the air-strength Halsey had to hand, the problem of dealing with Kurita was easily solved. Five minutes after hearing this information, Halsey (by-passing Mitscher as usual) ordered Sherman and Davison to concentrate on Bogan's Group 2 off the strait and prepare to launch air strikes. He also at last ordered McCain's Group 1 to reverse course to proceed for a rendezvous with Captain Acuff's tankers preparatory to re-entering the action as soon as possible. However, since McCain was now some 600 miles east of Samar, there would be no chance of his adding to the American might before the following day.

Meanwhile, other sightings were being recorded – indeed 24 October provided a quite unprecedented number of these. Both Japanese transport units were quickly located. At almost the same time that Adams sighted Kurita, another search team from *Intrepid* spotted Sakonju's group. They attacked, hitting the biggest target, light cruiser *Kinu*, on the bow with a 1,000-pound bomb. However, damage was only slight, while two separate strafing attacks on the cruiser by fighters from *Essex* did no damage at all.

At 0800, search planes from carrier *Franklin* of Davison's Group 4 spotted the other transport force, consisting of destroyers *Wakaba*, *Hatsushimo*, and *Hatsuharu*, west of Panay. Two teams combined to attack them with bombs and rockets, scoring at least two hits, possibly more, on the division's flagship, *Wakaba*. This luckless destroyer sank five minutes later taking with her the unit leader Commander Hisashi Ishii. Davison now launched a special strike of eleven bombers escorted by eleven fighters from *Franklin* against the remaining destroyers. This raid caused only minor damage but convinced the enemy of the folly of proceeding. Accordingly, *Wakaba*'s ex-companions, having rescued her survivors, promptly returned to Manila. Japanese numbers were being steadily whittled down.

About an hour later bigger game was sighted in the form of the Van of the Japanese Southern Force. This arm of the great pincer movement, it will be recalled, was composed of two separate fleets. The more powerful of these was Admiral Nishimura's command which early on the twenty-fourth was well across the Sulu Sea, some 50 miles south-west of Negros and north-east of Mindanao. It was composed of battleships *Yamashiro* (flagship) and *Fuso*, both 34,700 tons, mounting twelve 14-inch guns with a speed of 24 knots; heavy cruiser *Mogami* a 12,400 tonner with ten 8-inch guns which had earned a fine reputation in the early part of the war, together with heavy damage at Midway where only her great durability enabled her to survive, and at Rabaul; and four destroyers, *Yamagumo, Asagumo, Michishio* and *Shigure*.

Sixty miles behind Nishimura steamed Admiral Shima's Second Striking Force made up of heavy cruisers *Nachi* (flagship) and *Ashigara*, each carrying ten 8-inchers, escorted by light cruiser *Abukuma* which had been one of the Pearl Harbour strike-force, and four destroyers: *Shiranuhi, Kasumi, Ushio* and *Akebono*. On the evening of the twenty-third, Shima had arrived at Coron Bay in the Calamian Islands where he hoped to find a tanker waiting for him. Since the tanker in question had left to re-fuel Kurita's ships, Shima was forced to supply his destroyers with fuel from the cruisers. He then sailed south-east into the Sulu Sea at 0200 on the twenty-fourth.

Although the combined strength of the Southern Force was thus considerable, its part in the operation was bedevilled from the start by faulty, over-hasty planning. Nishimura's battleships had never fought or even apparently trained with *Mogami* and the destroyers before. The Admiral only met his ships' captains at a conference at Brunei Bay when their task was explained to them. This it seems in no way perturbed Nishimura. A gruff, eccentric sailor who had commanded fleets during the conquest of the Dutch East Indies, though without any great distinction, he preferred an independent command, reacting

The Air Attacks of 24 October

to advice or suggestions from his officers, many of whom had ideas very different from his own, by merely remarking: "Bah! We'll do our best!"

Admiral Shima was even more badly served by the Japanese High Command. He originally sailed simply under orders to attack Leyte Gulf from the south. He knew nothing of Nishimura's part in the plan at this time, learning of it only by an intercepted radio message. He was never informed of the route of Nishimura's approach. Since, as previously mentioned, Nishimura and Shima owed allegiance to two different commands with their nearest common superior, Admiral Toyoda, in Tokyo, Shima did not attempt to join forces with his colleague. Had he done so, furthermore, he as senior officer would automatically have taken command. As he presumed that Nishimura had a better knowledge of the situation, he preferred to attack in support of Nishimura but separately. Both fleets observed radio silence so could make no arrangements for co-ordination by this means. The first contact between them was to be in an unpleasantly literal manner when two of their cruisers collided in Surigao Strait.

Nishimura's fleet being nearest to the gulf was the first to be sighted – by Lieutenant Raymond Moore from the veteran *Enterprise* of Davison's Group at about 0900. *Enterprise* was a ship which had a splendid fighting reputation to live up to, so on sighting the enemy, who were steaming in a tight formation which placed the heavy ships in the middle with the destroyers on both flanks, Moore not only reported his find but called up the carrier's remaining scouting aircraft, twenty-six in all, for an assault which was launched at about 0918.

Hurtling out of the sun, with fighters strafing and firing rockets to clear the way for the bombers following close on their tails, *Enterprise*'s airmen pushed home their attack through heavy, accurate anti-aircraft fire. The battleships opened up with their main batteries at a range of 10 miles – the first instance of a tactic the Americans were to encounter throughout the day's fighting. Even so, only one Hellcat was brought down. Its pilot, Commander Fred Bukatis, leader of the fighter squadron, crash-landed in the sea not far from the enemy ships. His comrades did everything possible to help. Despite continued fire from the Japanese, one of the bombers dropped a life-raft, while fighters circled overhead to keep off any enemy aircraft that might attempt to intervene. After Bukatis had reached his raft safely, his friends, estimating his rate of drift, broadcast this information to every fleet headquarters, to the Army Air Force at Tacloban and to all submarine H.Q.s. Six days later Bukatis was rescued by submarine *Hardhead*, "none the worse for his ride".

In return, the attacking pilots claimed numerous hits but, as usual, the damage done was considerably over-estimated – only two bombs really found their mark. Battleship *Fuso* was hit on her stern. Her two seaplanes caught fire on their catapults starting a blaze that lasted for an hour, leaving her deck sadly blackened. Destroyer *Shigure* was struck in Number 1 turret, which was put out of action together with its crew. Neither ship had her speed or navigation affected, however. The formation maintained its speed. Yet Nishimura who had a long way to go, with the consequent prospect of several further attacks, was understandably concerned. He sent a signal to Kurita, who never received it, that his part of the operation was not going successfully.

To the astonishment of the Japanese, no further attacks followed this first one. Shima's ships, unknown to him, were sighted by a V Army Air Force bomber shortly before midday, but he was not attacked at all. The Americans appreciated that the two Southern Forces were bound for Surigao Strait, and, believing them to be closer together than they were, estimated that they formed the two sections of one single force – as indeed they should have done. Nonetheless Admiral Halsey continued with his planned concentration off San Bernardino Strait. Admiral Davison reported that this was taking him out of range of the Southern Forces but Halsey persisted in his decision to throw his entire strength against the larger Central Force, with pleasant results for Nishimura and Shima who were thus able to cross the Sulu Sea into the Mindanao Sea without further damage.

Halsey may well have been justified in leaving the Southern Forces to Seventh Fleet which was very capable of dealing with them. It is interesting to observe, however, that at no time did he specifically inform Kinkaid that he was doing so. This failure to keep his fellow commander fully notified of his intentions showed a dangerous lack of co-ordination on Halsey's part. He was to repeat this error not long afterwards – this time with nearly fatal results.

Before Halsey could deliver his planned blows at Kurita, Japanese land-based aircraft were already striking at his own ships. There were three separate enemies facing the Americans; Fukudome's naval air forces, Tominaga's Army air forces and Onishi's Special Attack Force – the Kamikazes.

The last-named had sent out sorties on four successive days from 21 to 24 October but with complete lack of results. Not only were the

The Air Attacks of 24 October

American task groups not damaged, they were not even located. The Japanese lacked sufficient reconnaissance aircraft with the consequence that the would-be raiders were constantly following false trails. Also the weather in the Philippines was poor. The towering cumulo-nimbus thunder-clouds prevalent at the time of year frequently caused sudden changes of weather bringing with them rain, wind and poor visibility which rarely proved a handicap to the American pilots but to the inexperienced Japanese presented overwhelming obstacles. The rain squalls also provided excellent hiding-places for the American ships of which their commanders were adept at taking full advantage, while the lack of radar in Japanese planes made it virtually impossible for them to discover targets that had taken refuge therein.

In consequence the Kamikaze pilots were forced to return from every sortie either by rain or by lack of fuel after a fruitless search. On the afternoon of the 21 October, three bomb-laden Zeros took off from Cebu on such a mission only to encounter bad weather. Two of the aircraft turned back but the leader Lieutenant (jg) Kuno, refusing to give up, headed instead to Leyte Gulf in the hope of discovering a target there. He never returned and his ultimate fate remains unknown.

While the Kamikazes were unable to find American carriers on the twenty-fourth as on previous days, Tominaga's Fourth Air Army was not even looking for them. The Japanese air commanders had apparently arranged that Army Air would concentrate on the vessels in the gulf together with any targets on the beaches. This Tominaga did, striking frequently at the landing area throughout the day. So persistent were these attacks that Sprague's escort carrier pilots had to confine themselves to the work of interception to the detriment of missions in support of the soldiers ashore. Their defence was well worthwhile, however, for Tominaga lost nearly seventy planes to their fighters or anti-aircraft gunners, while the only real misfortune suffered by Seventh Fleet on the twenty-fourth was the torpedoing in the evening of oiler *Ashtabula* without great harm being done, although very minor damage was also caused by near-misses on *Leutze*, one of Oldendorf's destroyers. Attacks on land installations were equally unsuccessful. The only serious incident was the raid on Tacloban airfield on the night of the twenty-fourth to the twenty-fifth which set fire to a fuel dump.

Thus any assaults on Third Fleet would have to come from Japanese land-based naval planes. Such attacks were required by the

Sho plan so Admiral Fukudome, who transferred his headquarters to Manila on the twenty-second, accordingly prepared to deliver them. Bad weather prevented his fliers from locating Third Fleet until the evening of the twenty-third when Sherman's Group 3 was spotted. Throughout the night, this group was grimly tracked by 'snoopers' who resolutely refused to be shaken off. Night fighters launched to drive them away were able to shoot down one, but dawn found five more, widely separated to avoid attack, still in contact. Since the rest of Halsey's fleet remained undetected, it was inevitably against Sherman's force, built around carriers *Essex* and *Lexington*, and light carriers *Princeton* and *Langley*, that Fukudome flung his airmen.

Shortly before 0800, while Sherman was steaming south to rendezvous with Bogan, simultaneously preparing for an attack on the Central Force, his radar operators discovered a group of about forty enemy aircraft approaching from the direction of Luzon. Immediately afterwards a second raid of similar size was detected close behind the first. A few minutes later, yet another, some sixty strong, was also reported.

Sherman was not well placed to meet these attacks. In addition to the planes engaged in searching for enemy shipping, he had launched a twenty-plane strike to hit enemy aircraft in the area of the Manila airfields, whence ironically his present opponents had come. The Americans claimed some thirty-five planes destroyed in this vicinity, yet in retrospect it seems surprising that they were not retained for defence considering that the Group Commander knew that he was being watched by the enemy with an air attack therefore a strong probability. When this attack materialized, only twelve Hellcats were aloft on combat air patrol. Hastily postponing the planned raid against Kurita, Sherman ordered up twelve more fighters from *Langley*, twelve from *Princeton*, eleven from *Lexington* and seven from *Essex*. Fortunately the warning given by radar was sufficient to enable these to gain the height needed to intercept while the task group sought shelter under the usual convenient rain squalls.

The resulting air-battle which lasted about an hour and a half effectively shattered Japan's shore-based air fleets, graphically demonstrating the deterioration in her pilots' standards. Each of the three raids was broken up by the fighters; flaming or smoking aircraft plunging into the sea all around the exultant American ships. The Hellcats from *Princeton* alone claimed thirty-four enemy planes destroyed. *Lexington*'s fighters downed thirteen, seven of which were dive-bombers. Yet the most spectacular achievement of all came from

The Air Attacks of 24 October

the seven Hellcats of *Essex*'s Air Group 15, rightly nicknamed in the Service 'The Fabled Fifteen', whose leader was a certain Commander David McCampbell.

McCampbell at the time of this action was already a veteran having personally shot down seven enemy aircraft during the Battle of the Philippine Sea. He was to end the war with a total of thirty-five, the highest by a U.S. naval pilot. At 0833 his group intercepted the third and largest enemy raid, which consisted of some thirty fighters with about the same number of dive-bombers or torpedo-bombers at a lower level, when they were still 30 miles away from their targets. When the Hellcats attacked, the bombers dived through the overcast pursued by five of the Americans, but McCampbell and his 'Number Two', Lieutenant (jg) Rushing, pressed home their assault on the escorting Zeros which did not follow their charges down. Indeed having quickly lost seven of their number, the Japanese fighters concentrated entirely on protecting themselves by orbiting in a tight circle which it was impossible to attack.

Accordingly McCampbell and Rushing calmly maintained an altitude of 23,000 feet, knowing that their adversaries would have to start for home when their fuel ran low. On the break-up of the circle, they relentlessly chased the formation shooting down stragglers or those attempting to climb to their own height. There was nothing to it – so at least said the laconic McCampbell; "It was simply a question of watching for an opening, knocking them down, converting into altitude the speed we had obtained in the dive and then waiting for a couple more to lay themselves open." They were "very careful not to expose ourselves and to conserve ammunition by withholding our fire until within very close range".

When, after an hour, shortage of fuel finally enabled the remnant of Air Group 15's victims to escape, McCampbell and Rushing re-joined their companions, none of whom had even been damaged apart from being struck by flying debris from their targets. Unable to reach *Essex* because of their diminishing fuel supply, the entire flight landed safely on *Langley*.

McCampbell's pilots had seen ninety-five minutes of combat. Those who had attacked the enemy bombers had destroyed eleven between them. Lieutenant Rushing had personally destroyed six fighters. Commander McCampbell who had exactly two rounds of ammunition remaining in his guns, had shot down no less than nine enemy aircraft, the greatest success recorded by any Allied pilot in World War II. This figure does not include half-a-dozen other planes that the Commander had sent down spinning or smoking but which were not seen to crash; a comparison of the numbers of the enemy at the beginning and at the end of the action shows that most of these were almost certainly also destroyed. Although he apologetically explained that his foes just would keep flying into his sights, McCampbell was promptly awarded America's V.C., the Congressional Medal of Honour.

Yet despite their successes, the Americans were also to suffer cruelly at the very moment that their triumph seemed assured. At 0938 all carriers were untouched while all organized raids had been broken. Suddenly, without the slightest warning, out of a low cloud shot winged death in the form of a solitary Judy dive-bomber. This plane's unknown pilot, who must have been as skilful and experienced as he was valiant, had escaped detection by brilliant use of cloud-cover. Now, timing his opportunity beautifully, as the carriers emerged from the rain squalls turning into the wind to recover their fighters which were short of fuel and ammunition and while their radar screens thus cluttered up by these were unable to distinguish friend from foe, he launched his single-handed attack. Ignoring a formidable amount of anti-aircraft fire, he made a perfect approach run on light carrier *Princeton*, dropped his 550-pound bomb with uncanny accuracy, passed astern still apparently untouched by the anti-aircraft gunners – and was shot into the sea by a fighter from *Langley*.

Too late! The bomb striking *Princeton*'s flight-deck, plunged through three decks, finally exploding in the ship's bake-shop where the luckless bakers were instantly killed. The blast entered a hangar. Here six torpedo-carrying Avengers had been hastily stowed when the air attack had first materialized. There had been no time to remove or disarm their weapons. Also the aircraft had full auxiliary wing-tanks as well as their normal fuel load in preparation for the strike on Kurita. Aviation fuel, the death-warrant of so many carriers, was soon in roaring flames while the torpedoes began exploding one after the other.

Conditions rapidly worsened as the fires spread. Choking smoke drove men from the hangar and, worse, from the damage-control and fire-fighting stations, though the ship's engineers continued at their posts in gas-masks for twenty minutes until ordered aloft for safety. Electric power started to fail in several parts of the vessel. Anti-aircraft ammunition began to go off. Fire on the flight-deck drove several men overboard and five fighters had to be pushed into the sea. Finally, shortly after 1000, a number of terrific detonations from the

The Air Attacks of 24 October

exploding torpedoes brought *Princeton* virtually to a stop heading into the wind. The explosions split open her deck, blew the forward elevator — 25-foot square — high into the air, after which it fell back into the pit, and hurled the after elevator onto the flight-deck upside-down. A great pillar of smoke a thousand feet high towered above the stricken carrier. Twenty minutes after the first major detonation, Captain Buracker ordered all crewmen except fire-fighting parties of some 240 men to abandon ship.

When *Princeton*, was struck, Admiral Sherman cancelled his move southward to join Bogan. Instead he took the remainder of his group clear of the cripple but manoeuvred within range to give air cover. Destroyers *Gatling, Irwin* and *Cassin Young*, joined after the first big explosion by light cruisers *Birmingham* and *Reno* and destroyer *Morrison*, remained by the wounded *Princeton* to render assistance or to rescue her crew.

As these little ships clustered about their charge, a small enemy air raid attempted to attack her. Fighters from *Langley* shot down four Jill torpedo bombers in the nick of time before they could launch their deadly weapons. Two Judy bombers then tried to destroy *Langley* herself but were brought down by anti-aircraft fire. *Reno*'s gunners shot down two more torpedo planes. The attack caused no damage.

With this nuisance disposed of, the supporting warships under the direction of Captain Thomas Inglis of *Birmingham* turned to their rescue work. While *Reno* stood by to provide anti-aircraft protection if needed, the remainder prepared to take off survivors. This was not easy for the sea was making up, pounding *Princeton* and her would-be helpers together. Wounded men were transferred to *Irwin*, a hazardous business as the vessels were rising and falling at different rates, causing a constantly changing gap. Hundreds of others slid down lines from the flight-deck into the water, to swim to nets put down over the destroyers' sides. The rough seas claimed some victims but the majority were picked up safely; 600 by *Irwin*, 400 by *Morrison*. Yet others drifted astern, where, to make matters still more unpleasant, sharks appeared. Machine-gunners on the destroyers drove these off, allowing most of the unfortunate sailors to be rescued by ships' boats.

Once *Princeton*'s crew, apart from her fire-fighters, had been evacuated, all attention was concentrated on quenching the carrier's fires. A party of thirty-eight volunteers from *Birmingham* under Lieutenant Reed was put aboard her, while all ships, including *Reno*, began hosing water onto the flames from every side in spite of smothering clouds of thick black smoke pouring all over them.

For two and a half hours Captain Inglis and his devoted team battled to save their comrade, most of them being damaged in one way or another in the process. *Irwin* was bashed into the carrier on several occasions, sustaining injuries topside which included some to her torpedo director. *Birmingham* suffered even greater harm, two of her 5-inch guns being put out of action. Commander Price of *Morrison*, trying to furnish aid from the starboard, found his ship jammed against *Princeton*'s overhanging side. She proved of great assistance to the fire-fighters, but at heavy cost. Her foremast, funnels and forward fire director were crushed, her searchlight platform smashed and her bridge badly battered. Heavy debris including, of all things, a Jeep and an electric aeroplane tractor slid off *Princeton* to crash onto the destroyer's bridge, whence they bounced onto the main deck. Attempts by *Irwin* to drag her loose resulted in the tow-lines breaking but did manage to shift *Morrison* sufficiently for that unlucky destroyer to wrench free under her own power.

While *Princeton* and *Morrison* were still locked together, a submarine contact was reported. *Birmingham* and *Reno* reluctantly cast off only to discover the alarm was a false one. Meanwhile, however, yet another air raid had been signalled. This report was correct – forty fighters, twenty-eight dive-bombers or fighter-bombers and eight torpedo-planes from Admiral Ozawa's Northern Force were on their way to aim a further blow at Sherman's ships.

This attack could have had unfortunate consequences for the *Princeton* group, but luckily Ozawa's pilots quite rightly ignored them in order to concentrate on the undamaged carriers. Some indeed had no chance of selecting targets at all. The raid was launched in two divisions. The first, composed of Zero fighters and fighter-bombers, was dispersed harmlessly 45 miles north-east of Sherman's main group. The second larger wave was intercepted only some 20 miles from the carriers. Vicious dog-fights took place with the Hellcats as usual having the better of it, seven fighters from *Lexington* alone downing nine enemy planes in a matter of minutes.

Yet however much the skill of the Japanese naval airmen had declined since Pearl Harbour, one characteristic remained at the highest level. Seven Judys burst through the fighter screen to plummet down in the face of heavy gunfire with such ferocious determination that some Americans were later to believe, erroneously, that they were suicide planes. Three of them were shot down. The others also failed to receive the due reward for their gallantry, for although they scored

The Air Attacks of 24 October

two near-misses on *Langley* and one each on *Essex* and *Lexington* none of these did more than minor damage.

This attack from the Northern Force ended before 1400 – for good since there were now too few Japanese carrier-planes available for the strike to be repeated. However, Fukudome continued to send off minor raids from shore throughout the afternoon. Most of these were driven off by combat air patrol without sighting their targets. About 1515, five Judys dodged the Hellcats to attack *Essex*. All bombs missed and two of the enemy were brought down. A few minutes later, a lone Judy near-missed *Lexington* in a determined individual attempt, escaping unhurt afterwards.

This symbolic action marked the end of Japan's orthodox landbased air attacks. Fukudome had shot his bolt. He was unable to make any further contribution to the battle. Sherman's pilots had destroyed 120 planes while defending their ships. Only ten American aircraft were lost during these combats.

Furthermore, it seemed that no fatal consequences had befallen any of Sherman's vessels. By this time unceasing efforts had quenched all except one of *Princeton*'s fires. This remaining fire was still very dangerous, however, for it was approaching the torpedo storage aft of the hangar in which a number of excess bombs had been placed. Yet considering that there had been no major explosions for five hours despite the flames that had raged in this area during that time, it was thought that any possible explosion would already have taken place. Prospects of saving the ship were believed to be very high.

Captain Buracker now requested that *Princeton* be taken in tow. Since *Reno* had no towing gear, Captain Inglis decided to bring his own *Birmingham* alongside the burning carrier to fight the fires and give this required assistance. At 1523, *Birmingham* had closed to within 50 feet, with a line out forward between the two ships. The cruiser's decks were thick with personnel – fire-fighting and rescue squads, men handling the tow-lines, medical officers and orderlies, anti-aircraft gunners, officers of the watch, and no doubt anyone who could be spared from other jobs eager to see what was happening.

At this moment the bombs exploded devastatingly, tearing off *Princeton*'s stern and flight-deck, hurling forth a hail of what are usually called 'splinters' – a hopelessly inadequate word for large savage steel missiles which included on this occasion broken gunbarrels, steel helmets, tool chests, beams from the deck and even huge metal plates. *Birmingham* was deluged by this lethal storm. Literally in a flash, she became, said Captain Inglis "a veritable charnel house of dead, dying and wounded". Two hundred and twenty-nine of her crew were killed. Four hundred and twenty more including the captain were wounded, many of them very badly. "Blood ran freely down the waterways and continued to run for some time." The ship's superstructure was "perforated to an almost unbelievable extent".

Yet despite the numbing suddenness of the catastrophe, the crew's discipline prevented any sign of panic. Indeed the disaster brought out the best in most of them, giving rise to numerous actions of extraordinary unselfishness. Hideously wounded men, insisting that they were all right, asked that their friends be seen to first. Those less badly hurt tried to assist the more serious casualties. Those with clean cuts, when told that the men bleeding more profusely must first be treated "agreed cheerfully in every case". Even the most gravely injured, some of whom were suffering from shock, or were in considerable pain until morphine took effect, "remained quiet and fully co-operative with those attempting to render first aid".

The blast of the explosion also decimated the fire-fighters on *Princeton*. Scarcely a single man remained uninjured. One of those struck down was Captain John Hoskins who, scheduled to take command of the carrier in the near future, had come aboard to get into the feel of things. His right foot was so mangled that a medical officer had to amputate it with a sheath-knife. Despite the handicap of an artificial foot, however, he later commanded a carrier task force in the Korean War, with the rank of Rear-Admiral. In the after part of the carrier there were no survivors at all. Rescue parties found only mangled corpses.

Although even now *Princeton* still appeared seaworthy, no other ship was available to take her in tow. Also the fires which had sprung up furiously again as a result of the explosion were threatening the fuel tanks and main magazines, which, because of the lack of water-pressure had not been properly flooded. Further attempts to save her could only invite another tragedy to a rescue vessel. Accordingly at 1600, the damage control parties were ordered to abandon ship. They were picked up safely by *Gatling*, the evacuation being completed by 1638. Shortly afterwards Admiral Sherman ordered that the blazing carrier be finished off by torpedoes.

This task was first entrusted to destroyer *Irwin* but because of damage sustained in crashing into the carrier during earlier rescue work, her torpedo director was useless. Extraordinary things happened to her torpedoes. The first swung left, hitting *Princeton*'s bow too far forward for serious damage. The second swung right,

The Air Attacks of 24 October

missing altogether. The third, turning round in its tracks, came straight back at the destroyer which dodged it just in time. Torpedoes four and five missed. Torpedo six incredibly repeated the performance of number three, missing *Irwin* by a narrower margin. Perhaps fortunately, the destroyer was then relieved from her assignment.

Light cruiser *Reno* now took her turn with better success, launching two torpedoes which found *Princeton*'s forward fuel tanks. With one final colossal upheaval she totally disintegrated. Such was the American command of the air that *Princeton* was the first major U.S. warship to be sunk by air attack since January 1943. She took to the bottom with her all her thirty-four planes except three which, having been airborne when she was hit, were able to land on other carriers. Thanks to the work of her companions she lost only 108 dead or missing with 190 wounded — less than half the casualties of poor *Birmingham*. Nor were the efforts of the fire-fighters entirely wasted. They had provided valuable practical information which was to play an important part in saving at least three fleet carriers which would otherwise have perished from their injuries later in the war.

Sherman now prepared to proceed south to his rendezvous with the rest of Third Fleet, but those ships that had been damaged in the fight to save *Princeton* were detached to Ulithi for repairs. As *Birmingham, Gatling, Irwin* and *Morrison* steamed away, Captain Inglis, still full of fight, called to Admiral Sherman on the voice-radio: "Goodbye! Good luck! And hit them hard for us!"

Even while *Princeton* was battling with the flames, her fellow carriers of Task Force 38 were already "hitting them hard", as Kurita's Central Force could testify. Kurita had expected air attacks but nothing like the scale of those that developed. At 0810 he sighted three aircraft (Adams with his escort) to the north tracking his force. Tension had reached an almost unbearable peak when at about 1020, luminous specks on the radar screen closed rapidly as the first attack came in.

This raid, consisting of twenty-one Hellcats, twelve Helldiver bombers and twelve Avenger torpedo-planes, from Bogan's Group 2, found Central Force in Tablas Strait heading into the Sibuyan Sea. At once Kurita's gunners opened fire with everything they had, the battleships even firing with their main batteries. The shells burst spectacularly in pinks, purples and whites, ejecting phosphorus or silver balls. Under this barrage, two crippled Avengers lurched away to crash-land in the sea. A Hellcat went straight down in flames. Yet the other pilots pushed on, attacking from every side at once.

When the planes turned again for home the super-battleship *Musashi*, struck by one bomb and one torpedo, was leaving a trail of oil from a ruptured tank. Heavy cruiser *Myoko*, hit by a torpedo astern had two shafts damaged reducing her speed to 15 knots. Kurita ordered her to return to Brunei, which she did safely. Four heavy cruisers had now been lost to Central Force. It would take much more, seriously to affect the monstrous *Musashi*, however, and she steamed on with the rest into the Sibuyan Sea.

Kurita was now faced by a series of successive raids. There was very little he could do about this since although he called repeatedly for fighters to cover him, he received virtually no response. It will be remembered that the *Sho* plan called on the Japanese Navy's land-based airmen not to defend their ships so much as to clear the way for them by attacking the carriers from which American planes could come. This Fukudome tried to do but he only located one of the American task groups, his only victim was *Princeton*, and he broke his air fleet in the course of the attempt. "There could be no clearer demonstration," says Morison, "of the futility of air counter-attack as opposed to interception."

In consequence only a handful of naval fighters were able to provide Kurita with even a token protection. American fighters shot down four of these. Another group of fourteen was driven off by heavy anti-aircraft fire from the ships they were trying to protect; in the circumstances Kurita's gunners understandably treated all planes as hostile. It is indicative of the lack of co-operation between the Services that Kurita neither asked or expected that Army fighters should give him cover. The scarcity of air-opposition was the main reason for the Americans' astonishingly minor casualties. In the whole day the attackers lost only eighteen aircraft.

The second of these strikes, again from Group 2, arrived at 1245 when Kurita had advanced 30 miles to enter the Sibuyan Sea. The fourteen Hellcats, twelve Helldivers and nine Avengers concentrated on *Musashi*, hitting her with four torpedoes and two bombs. As the aircraft gathered for their return flight, they noticed a large explosion on the giant amidships. Her speed was reduced to 22 knots and her manoeuvrability was also affected. Slowly she began to fall out of the formation while her bow dropped lower in the water.

Next on the scene came the dive-bombers and torpedo-bombers from *Essex* and *Lexington* of Group 3, which attacked at 1330. The troubles that this group had suffered before it could launch its strike

The Air Attacks of 24 October

reduced the value of the blows it could deliver. All the Avengers and most of the Helldivers from *Lexington* were armed only with 500-pound general purpose bombs which would not be effective against anything bigger than a destroyer. The reason was that these aircraft had been armed originally for a proposed attack on targets in Luzon, and after Fukudome's attacks, with the possibility of more to come, no one dared to open the magazines to re-equip them with torpedoes in view of the potential danger this would involve. Further, bad weather caused five torpedo-planes and five dive-bombers from *Lexington* to lose their way. They had to return to their carrier. Thick clouds also handicapped *Lexington*'s planes in their attack — it was apparently not their lucky day. Japanese anti-aircraft fire was also more accurate than usual, downing three torpedo-planes and so damaging two dive-bombers that they could not land on their parent ship but had to 'ditch' close by.

None the less, for all these manifold misfortunes, the planes, particularly those from *Essex*, gave a fine account of themselves. The Japanese were later understandably confused about the times when various injuries were suffered, while the American reports are conflicting. To add to the confusion three other attacks were made by Third Fleet during the afternoon and they tended to overlap with each other and with the one just described. Consequently, different accounts give contradictory pictures of the action as well as crediting different strikes with the hits in fact scored. However by examining the reports made by the various raids, remembering that the damage claimed in each case was almost certainly greater than that really achieved, it is possible to arrive at the most likely answers to the problems of who did what.

Acting on this principle, it seems that this strike by Group 3, which claimed numerous bomb or torpedo hits on battleships, did in fact score two bomb hits forward on *Yamato* and four torpedo and four bomb hits on *Musashi* which was already partly unmanoeuvrable after her previous damage. The former's thick hide saved her from serious harm. One of the bombs, indeed, was seen by Admiral Koyanagi to explode instantaneously on striking her foredeck without penetrating at all. *Musashi*, however, was now severely hurt. The bombs made a shambles of her topside, flattening some of her anti-aircraft guns, but it was the torpedoes striking at her vulnerable sides that really did the damage. Her forecastle sank so low in the water that the higher seas came right over it to break against her huge fore-turrets. That it was this raid that caused this damage appears confirmed by the pilots' report that a *Yamato*-class battleship was "dead in the water and down at the bow" after their attack. *Musashi* was down at the bow all right, while if she was not dead in the water her speed was drastically cut, since her commander Rear-Admiral Toshihei Inoguchi dared not steam at more than 12 knots for fear of plunging by the bow. Accompanied only by heavy cruiser *Tone*, *Musashi* fell astern of her companions.

Thrice more during this terrible afternoon, air attacks (one from each task group) savaged the wretched Central Force. That from *Lexington* and *Essex*, their second, claimed several bomb hits but not one torpedo hit was recorded. As will be seen, it could not therefore have been this attack which finally doomed *Musashi*. During the later attacks, *Yamato* was hit twice more forward. A fire was started but quickly controlled. The effect of the bombs together with those that had found her earlier did reduce her speed, although only to 26 knots. *Nagato* was also hit twice, her communication system being damaged. *Haruna* suffered minor injury from five near-misses. Probably this raid was responsible for much of the bomb damage just quoted.

The other hits or near-misses were scored by twenty-one Helldivers and eighteen Avengers, escorted by twenty-six fighters, from Davison's Group 4. This group had not been able to attack previously since first the aircraft that had hit the Southern or Transport Forces had had to be recovered. However, as Mr Vann Woodward remarks: "It is evident from the determination with which the squadrons from *Enterprise* and *Franklin* pressed home their attack that the pilots were bent on making the most of their single opportunity."

This raid indeed achieved the most spectacular results of the day. The airmen reported numerous hits on the main Japanese group, some of which may have been actual hits on *Yamato* or *Nagato*. It is clear, however, that they threw most of their weight at *Musashi*. Cruiser *Tone* was able to dodge all attacks aimed at her but crippled *Musashi* had no chance. The pilots claimed no less than eight torpedo and eleven bomb hits on a *Yamato*-class battleship, which they thought was "probably sunk". They were not far wrong. Japanese accounts give differing estimates of just what hit *Musashi* in the final attack on her which could only have been this one, but the most conservative version was six bombs and four torpedoes, while reliable senior officers estimated as many as ten of each. If so *Musashi* took a total of nineteen torpedoes and seventeen bombs during the course of her ordeal.

In any event her damage was now too much even for a titan such as

Admiral William Halsey

Vice-Admiral Thomas Kinkaid

Vice-Admiral Jisaburo Ozawa

Vice-Admiral Takeo Kurita

Air-power: U.S. carrier *Enterprise*

Gun-power: Japanese battleship *Yamato*

The Leyte landings: an Avenger provides support

The early actions: battleship *Yamashiro* under attack

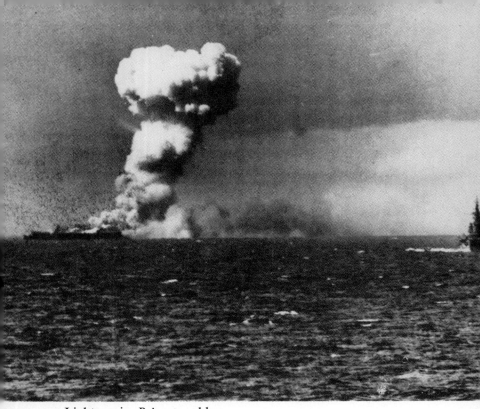

Light carrier *Princeton* ablaze

The fight to save *Princeton*: light cruiser *Birmingham* closes to assist

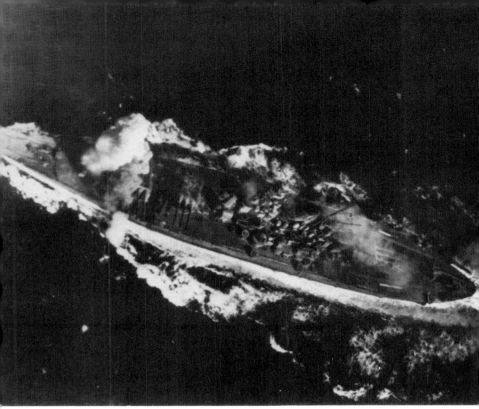

Sibuyan Sea: bomb-hit on battleship *Yamato*

Surigao Strait: destroyer *McDermut*

Vice-Admiral Marc Mitscher

Rear-Admiral Thomas Sprague

Rear-Admiral Jesse Oldendorf

Rear-Admiral Clifton Sprague

The Air Attacks of 24 October

her. She had become unmanageable, listing to port with her flooding uncontrolled. Admiral Ugaki her divisional commander ordered Inoguchi to beach her on Sibuyan Island but even this was now quite impossible. For four hours her death agonies continued. Destroyers *Kiyoshimo* and *Hamakaze* relieved *Tone* in standing by her at about 1830. Her list increased relentlessly. At 1935, the largest battleship ever built rolled slowly over to port and sank. She took down with her Admiral Inoguchi, thirty-eight other officers and 984 men. The destroyers rescued the remainder of the crew and, withdrawing from the battle, took the survivors to Manila. In the course of her career, the giant *Musashi* had never fired her 18.1-inch guns at anything but aircraft.

"If we are attacked by planes as often as this," stated Admiral Ugaki "we will have expended ourselves before reaching the battle area." Kurita was of the same opinion. The fate of *Musashi* which he had believed to be unsinkable was a shocking blow to his morale. Ahead lay narrow straits where, with restricted room in which to manoeuvre, he would find it even more difficult to fight off air attacks. And, while he hesitated, yet another of these fell upon his ships.

This, the sixth and last of the day, consisted of sixteen fighters, twelve dive-bombers and three torpedo-bombers from *Intrepid* and *Cabot*. In view of the small numbers, it could not possibly have been this strike which finished off *Musashi* although some individual planes may have attacked her. Further, as this was the third mission of aircraft from these carriers, the pilots were undoubtedly so fatigued that it was not likely they would achieve much. They made only very modest claims for their attack which probably did no damage, but they did reinforce Kurita's decision to retire. By the time that the last planes from this raid left at about 1600, Central Force was some 14 miles west of its previously reported position, retiring on a westerly course.

For the time being at least, the Japanese had had enough. About now Kurita signalled to Toyoda that he had been under attack from more than 250 planes – which was true – and that "it is therefore considered advisable to retire temporarily from the zone of enemy air attacks and to resume the advance when the battle results of friendly units permit". Hoping that Ozawa's decoys from whom he had had no news might do their work of enticement or that the air fleets of Onishi and Fukudome would be able to neutralize the enemy carriers, Kurita also sent similar messages to all these commanders.

At 1714, about an hour before sunset, Kurita had received no reply from his Commander-in-Chief — a delay typical of Japanese communication difficulties. On the other hand, he had suffered no more attacks since reversing course. Perhaps Ozawa, or the land-based air forces, or both, were now succeeding in their tasks. Kurita again turned about. His battered but still very powerful force with four battleships, including *Yamato*, six heavy cruisers, two light cruisers and eleven destroyers, seven hours behind schedule now, headed back towards San Bernardino Strait at 20 knots.

At 1925, Toyoda's reply was at last received: "All forces will dash to the attack trusting in Divine guidance". Toyoda was later to explain this cryptic message as conveying that "damage could not be limited or reduced by turning back so advance even though the fleet should be completely lost". In view of the death-or-glory nature of the whole project there is no doubt that he was telling the truth. Shortly afterwards, in any case, he expressly ordered Kurita: "A change in the programme of the First Striking Force would cause the failure of our offensive. Let this force go on according to plan."

Kurita replied that he would press forward to reach Leyte Gulf at 1100, 25 October. At 2224 he signalled to his warriors that he would proceed along the east coast of Samar to the American anchorage. "It is strongly desired," he ordered "that the whole force throw its entire power into the fray so as to attain its aim."

At the time of this pep-talk, Kurita was fast approaching San Bernardino Strait, gateway to the Philippine Sea. By this time also, although he could not know it, there was nothing whatever there to stop him.

4

Admiral Halsey Heads North

In the opinion of Admiral Halsey, "there was one piece missing in the puzzle" — the Japanese carriers. He was rightly confident that they were "sure to be employed in some manner in any operation as great as that revealed on the morning of the twenty-fourth".

Since American Intelligence had located the carriers in their home waters, a logical place to find them would be to the north or north-east of the Philippines coming straight from their base to Leyte Gulf. Therefore at 1155, Halsey attempted to retrieve his earlier omission by ordering Sherman to launch search teams in these directions. Unfortunately, the unwelcome attentions of Fukudome and Ozawa prevented Group 3's commander from doing so until 1405 when Helldivers from *Lexington* were sent off. Even then there were no fighter escorts available since these were now re-fuelling and re-arming after beating off the air raids or were on combat air patrol to guard against further attacks. The bombers flew off through a sky dotted with clouds, handicapped by numerous rain-squalls, while back on their carrier, the staff officers waited eagerly for word of any sightings.

At 1540, the first such report came in from Lieutenant (jg) Walters, announcing that he had spotted a strong enemy fleet, which due to cloud and anti-aircraft fire, he incorrectly evaluated as four battleships, one of which he described as having a flight-deck aft, five or six cruisers and six destroyers. A few minutes later another pilot sighted, well to the north, two big 2,700-ton *Terutsuki*-class destroyers. Still Halsey received no news of the missing carriers.

Finally at 1640 came the last sighting of this crowded day when Lieutenant (jg) Crapser located a force which he inaccurately described as containing two fleet carriers, one light carrier, three light cruisers, possibly one heavy cruiser and at least three destroyers. Crapser was not content merely to report his find. After ensuring that his message had reached other planes so was certain to get through, he climbed to 7,500 feet, then plunged through a cloud-bank to bomb the enemy. His bombs failed to release and he pulled out of his dive just in time. At this moment five Zeros appeared from nowhere but Crapser's gunner shot one down as the pilot escaped into the convenient clouds.

Halsey now knew the approximate positions of all the Japanese ships. He was duly gratified to learn that the Northern Force of carriers had finally been detected. He would have been less pleased had he known that the enemy commander was even more delighted by this than he was.

Vice-Admiral Jisaburo Ozawa who led the Northern Force was an officer of exceptional gallantry and competence. A powerful, heavily-built man, unusually tall for a Japanese, he was a notable figure, but his record of service was even more impressive. Possessed of qualities that called forth both admiration and affection from his subordinates, together with the reputation of having the ablest strategic brain in the Japanese high command, he was appointed a professor in the Naval Academy in 1935 and Chief of Staff to the Combined Fleet in 1937-8. His most important contribution to his country's naval thinking was that he became, very early on, a fervent advocate of the value of aircraft-carriers and the use of mass-attacks by carrier-planes.

On the outbreak of war, Ozawa was entrusted with the task of escorting the Malayan-invasion convoys. During the planning of this operation he showed immense moral courage by opposing suggestions by the naval staff that lengthy bombardments be carried out before landing; instead insisting on accepting the Army's claims that surprise and meteorological considerations required the abandonment of such preliminaries "even at the risk of annihilation" of his ships by air attacks as the naval staff feared. This risk proved to be much exaggerated but the action shows clearly Ozawa's determination to achieve co-operation with the Army; a determination which was emphasized further after the fall of Singapore by his suggesting the formation of a society to promote friendship between the military and naval units engaged in this operation – an example which Japan's other leading officers would have done well to follow. After distinguishing himself during the remainder of the Malayan campaign he displayed further talents in the course of the capture of Sumatra and Java.

In November 1943, Ozawa took over command of all carrier forces, also becoming C.-in-C. of First Mobile Fleet comprising over 90 per cent of Japan's surface navy. That he was rightly so appointed can be seen from Morison's description of him as "an officer with a scientific brain as well as a seaman's innate sense of what can be accomplished with ships; a worthy antagonist to Mitscher and

Spruance". Unfortunately for Ozawa, by the time he achieved this post he was faced not only by these talented opponents but by greatly superior numbers, pilots of considerably higher training, and superior equipment in the form of the Hellcat fighter and the proximity-influence shells. It was therefore not exactly surprising that at the Battle of the Philippine Sea the Japanese forces were heavily defeated, though small blame can be attributed to their admiral whose tactics were good and whose personal courage in desperate circumstances was quite sublime.[1] After the war, Ozawa, who "bore himself with dignity and composure" probably made in the opinion of Woodward, "the most favourable impression" on the American naval interrogation mission of all the high-ranking Japanese officers.

On 24 October, Ozawa's forces were really far weaker than reported. They consisted only of:

Fleet carrier: *Zuikaku*.

This carrier was a veteran of the attack on Pearl Harbour, and the Battles of Coral Sea, Eastern Solomons, Santa Cruz and the Philippine Sea.

Light carriers: *Chitose, Chiyoda* and *Zuiho*.

The last-named was another veteran which had provided air-cover for the planned occupation force at Midway, and had fought at Santa Cruz and the Philippine Sea.

Battleships: *Hyuga* and *Ise*.

These were originally equipped with twelve 14-inch guns, but as a result of Japan's carrier losses, they had been converted to hybrid battleship-carriers by the end of 1943. The four heavy guns aft were removed, leaving them eight apiece; in their stead the deck was raised two levels and covered with a flight-deck with a lift in the centre. They were intended to house twenty-two seaplanes, which would be launched by catapults situated to port and starboard just forward of the flight-deck – it was hoped that twenty minutes would suffice to launch these. After their attack, the planes would land not on the short deck but in the sea, to be hoisted aboard by cranes. However, so great were Japan's losses in aircraft and pilots that none of the special planes needed ever became available, with the result that the ships remained merely battleships with a much-reduced armament.

Light cruisers: *Oyodo, Tama, Isuzu*.

---

[1] Ozawa tendered his resignation after the battle but Toyoda refused to accept it, presumably realizing that he had no one of equal ability with whom to replace Ozawa and no one else would have done better or perhaps even as well in the particular circumstances in any case.

Destroyers: *Shimotsuki, Hatsutsuki, Wakatsuki, Akitsuki, Fuyutsuki, Suzutsuki, Kuwa, Maki, Sugi, Kiri,* the first six named being of the big 2,700-ton *Terutsuki*-class.

In addition, kept well out of the battle to the north, Ozawa had a supply unit containing destroyer *Akikaze*, six escort vessels, and two oilers.

Clearly these vessels would not pose a very great threat to the massive strength of Third Fleet even if the carriers had their full complement of planes aboard — but this was not the case. When he sortied from the Inland Sea, Ozawa's four carriers held a grand total of fifty-two Zero fighters, twenty-eight Zero fighter-bombers, twenty-five Jill torpedo-bombers, the seven Judy dive-bombers that made such a brave attack on Sherman, and four Kate high-level bombers.[2] The carrier-battleships had no planes at all. Light cruiser *Oyodo* had two reconnaissance aircraft.

Also the standard of the pilots was appallingly low; so much so that it was assumed that after making their strikes most if not all would have to fly to bases in the Philippines since they would be unable to land on their parent ships. Ozawa apparently flew several off to shore-bases without even using them for attacks. He had ample reason to doubt the abilities of his airmen; on 21 October and the following days he sent out nine reconnaissance planes daily, of which an average of three a day failed to return.

However, as we know, the Northern Force was there not to attack the American ships but to lure them away from the battle zone so that Central Force would have a clear run to the gulf. Their weakness was irrelevant. As Sir Winston Churchill grimly remarks in *The Second World War*: "They were only bait and bait is made to be eaten". Nor were the Japanese leaders unaware of their prospective fate. "I expected complete destruction of my fleet," said Ozawa after the war, "but if Kurita's mission was carried out, that was all I wished." His Chief of Staff, Captain Toshikazu Ohmae, agreed that because Northern force deliberately approached close to Third Fleet "on purpose to lure your ships to the north" they stood no chance of escape; "surely we would be sunk; that was our mission". With

---

[2] The Americans avoided difficulties caused by the complicated Japanese system of aircraft classification, plus the problem of pronunciation, by giving each enemy type an arbitrary code-name; the bombers having ladies' names such as Judy or Jill; the fighters men's names — Oscar or George for instance. The exception was Mitsubishi's famous fighter Type 0, which although officially code-named 'Zeke', in practice always remained known as the Zero.

splendid unselfishness Ozawa and his command coolly prepared to do everything possible to carry out this difficult, appallingly dangerous and probably fatal task.

By the twenty-fourth, Ozawa, who had steered a course which took him outside the range of American search-planes from Saipan (so as to avoid being spotted too early), was manoeuvring off Cape Engano, the north-eastern tip of Luzon. He naturally did not wish to steam too far south since the farther north he could persuade Halsey to chase him the better. One of his reconnaissance pilots sighted Sherman at 0820. Thereafter Ozawa tried continuously to get someone to attack him. He deliberately broke radio silence on various frequencies but an undetected fault in his transmitter which later prevented him from communicating effectively with his fellow-commanders resulted in these temptations being unnoticed by the Americans.

Then at 1115 another search-plane also located Sherman's vessels and half-an-hour later Ozawa hurled his airmen at this target. Three of the pilots, losing touch with their fellows, soon returned to their carriers. The others pressed on but, as we have seen, they did not enjoy the success they may have deserved. Most of the planes were shot down although some fifteen to twenty fled to bases ashore, while only a handful returned to Ozawa. By midnight his entire aerial forces numbered only twenty-nine – nineteen Zero fighters, five fighter-bombers, four Jills and one Judy.

These losses did not bother the Japanese Admiral too much but by now he was thoroughly disheartened by his inability to persuade his opponents to notice him. It was "imperative", he considered, to help Kurita by attracting the Americans onto his own forces. Fearing that they were ignoring him deliberately having detected the ruse, he determined to compel their attention by bringing them to battle with a surface fleet. Accordingly, at 1430 he ordered Rear-Admiral Chiaki Matsuda to head south with an advance group containing Matsuda's flagship *Hyuga*, *Ise*, light cruiser *Tama*, and destroyers *Shimotsuki*, *Hatsutsuki*, *Wakatsuki* and *Akitsuki*, in order to "divert the enemy effectively".

Then in quick succession, the Americans sighted Matsuda's group; destroyers *Fuyutsuki* and *Suzutsuki*, detached as pickets; and lastly Ozawa's own carrier force. The Japanese commander whose communication staff picked up the reconnaissance plane's message together with the acknowledgement, was delighted for it now seemed that his mission could succeed after all. At 2000, however, he heard that Kurita had reversed course to retire. Since he believed that this meant that the *Sho* plan, in which he had not had much faith although admitting it was the only possible hope in the circumstances, had collapsed, he turned back also but by 2110, he had received further information including an order from Toyoda to attack as planned. He therefore recalled Matsuda, sent his two picket-destroyers home and steamed southward to the sacrifice, determined to "carry out diversionary operations at all costs". He correctly guessed what Halsey would do on learning his position, so for the rest of the night he manoeuvred first north then south in order to be sufficiently close to the American Admiral to be both a threat and a tempting target, yet sufficiently far away "to lure your forces further north". His clever enticement was about to succeed beyond his wildest expectations.

At this moment the character of Admiral William Halsey was of quite crucial importance. No one in the American Navy had a greater reputation. At the start of the war, he had been in charge of a carrier group built around *Enterprise*. During the first six months of hostilities, he commanded so many carrier-strikes against enemy bases, including the famous raid by Lieutenant-Colonel Doolittle's Mitchell bombers on Tokyo, that his name became virtually synonymous with this new form of warfare. A skin disease put Halsey on the sick-list just before Midway but on 15 October 1942, Nimitz, thinking that an aggressive leader was needed, appointed him Commander South Pacific, entrusted with the task of taking the hideous but vital island of Guadalcanal. Halsey conducted the hard Solomons campaign from an office desk in Noumea until mid-1944. This was a tedious assignment for him, so when he took over Third Fleet on 24 August, it was scarcely surprising that he was "spoiling for a fight".

Halsey was undoubtedly a very fine strategist as his insistence on speeding-up the Leyte campaign emphasized. Yet his greatest contributions lay in the field of morale. His confident personality was inspiring. His popularity among thousands of sailors who had never even seen him was astonishing. Called 'Bill' by his friends, he quickly became 'The Bull' to the newspapers. Although nobody who knew him ever referred to him by this nickname, it somehow symbolized the figure he presented to the world of the aggressive, impulsive, determined fighter. The value of his influence in this respect was incalculable.

Yet Halsey had one great defect which weakened all his virtues, "He hated the enemy," says Morison, "with an unholy wrath." When Halsey heard of the attack on Pearl Harbour he is reported to have said that after the war the Japanese language would be spoken only in

Admiral Halsey Heads North

hell. When Admiral Yamamoto died in an air-ambush, Halsey is supposed to have expressed regret because he would have preferred to see Yamamoto — then labelled an arch-aggressor, now ironically known to have consistently warned against the conflict with America — dragged through Washington in chains. Even if these stories grew in the telling, they were definitely representative of the Admiral's attitude.

Because he loathed his enemy he came to despise him; because he despised him he constantly under-rated him — in war the most dangerous mistake that can be made. He prophesied victory as early as 1943. Afterwards he was to comment: "I knew my statement could not possibly be true. I wanted to exaggerate as the Japanese exaggerate, to break down their morale." Yet his opinion can also be explained, partly at least, by the fact that his scorn for his foes had made him over-estimate the prospects of success against them.

Since he did not think his opponents worthy of his steel, Halsey frequently threw all prudence to the winds, remarking: "I believe in violating the rules. We violate them every day." Hardly had he taken command of the South Pacific zone when, scorning defensive fighting, he ordered his country's last two serviceable carriers to attack a superior enemy force. He could quite easily have lost them both with disastrous results. As it was, in the Battle of Santa Cruz on 26 October 1942, one, *Hornet* was sunk, while *Enterprise* was damaged, having her forward elevator put out of action. That Halsey later came to appreciate he had taken an unjustified risk is shown by his observation that he would never again let the enemy 'suck' his carriers to the north.

Yet on the whole the Admiral's rash confidence was not affected by mishaps to forces in his area of command — not even by the Battle of Tassafaronga on the 30 November 1942 when a Japanese destroyer squadron inflicted an incredible defeat on an American heavy cruiser force that enjoyed the advantage of surprise. Of course any subordinate commander who allowed himself to be defeated by the under-rated Japanese could expect no sympathy from Halsey. His endorsements on such action reports showed "extreme displeasure" or were "scathing indictments" — in contrast with the milder reactions of Nimitz — while at least one captain who was deprived of his command was later admitted by Halsey to have acted for the best.[3]

---

[3] Plentiful illustrations of Halsey's reactions to his subordinates' misfortunes are to be found in S.E. Morison's *The History of United States Naval Operations in World War II* — Volume V *The Struggle for Guadalcanal; August 1942-February 1943*.

In view of the above it comes as no surprise that Halsey was one of those who censured Spruance for over-caution at the Battle of the Philippine Sea. Spruance who had been covering the American landings on Saipan, on hearing of the approach of an enemy fleet at first set out to meet it; but not making contact he refused to continue a brave but blind advance, instead turning back "so as to reduce the possibility of the enemy passing us in darkness". Standing strictly on the defensive he awaited the Japanese attack. By doing this he was able to keep all his fighters in hand for interception, so, as mentioned earlier, he virtually annihilated the Japanese air strength. In contrast, had he attacked, his planes would have been faced with 200 Zeros plus the strong anti-aircraft strength of a Van Group, deliberately pushed out as a tempting bait by that dangerous officer Ozawa; while had the Japanese eluded Spruance altogether to attack the landing-forces with their aircraft, anything could have happened. Also it may be observed that when Spruance did strike against the enemy ships, even although by then there were few fighters to oppose his airmen, successes were more limited than had been hoped. It is true that most of the Japanese carriers escaped but for the future they were useless except as decoys since they never replaced their lost airmen. However there was considerable resentment by the airmen in Spruance's fleet, at being held back and not going after the enemy carriers. Mitscher supported this view and Halsey, never an admirer of the defensive under any circumstances, and tending to identify himself with the airmen as a result of his previous exploits, was determined he would act more aggressively should he encounter a similar situation.

In addition to Halsey's own inclinations, it seemed to him that he had in his operational orders encouragement not to follow Spruance's prudent example. His instructions were to "cover and support forces of the South-west Pacific [i.e. Seventh Fleet] in order to assist in the seizure and occupation of objectives in the Central Philippines" and to "destroy enemy naval and air forces in or threatening the Philippine area". Unfortunately, because of the criticisms made of Spruance's tactics, another clause was added reading: "In case opportunity for destruction of major portion of the enemy fleet is offered or can be created, such destruction becomes the primary task."

Thus Halsey was in effect given two different objectives and while this would not matter so long as he could both protect Seventh Fleet and the beach-head, and destroy any enemy forces that appeared, there was a possibility that circumstances would arise where these two duties would conflict. The question then would be which would have

Admiral Halsey Heads North

preference. Was Halsey to treat this order to achieve the destruction of an enemy fleet as implying it was justifiable to risk leaving the beach-head unprotected in order to do so? It does seem clear that this was not the intention of the chief American commanders and that Halsey had little excuse for not appreciating that if in doubt the safety of the amphibious operations must have priority. A few days before the battle, he informed Nimitz that, since the necessity to give such cover was hampering his actions, he was contemplating operations in the China Sea. Nimitz replied that his orders were unchanged; any restrictions imposed by protecting Seventh Fleet were unavoidable. Further General MacArthur had "emphatically made clear" to Halsey during discussions in early October that he deemed Halsey's main task to be the provision of air-support. He informed the Admiral:

> The basic plan for this operation in which for the first time I have moved beyond my own land-based air-cover was predicated upon full support by the Third Fleet; such land-based cover is being expedited by every possible measure, but until accomplished, our mass of shipping is subject to enemy air and surface raiding during this critical period. Consider your mission to cover this operation is essential and paramount.

Despite these clear promptings, however, Halsey obstinately persisted in regarding the protection of MacArthur's forces as subsidiary to the aggressive role of attacking enemy shipping; doubtless because this accorded with his own fighting instincts. It is a wry comment on the Admiral's opinion of his enemies that these correctly anticipated that by putting forward their attractive bait they could rely on diverting Halsey whereas in the Mariana landings they had realized that such a ruse would not succeed with the prudent Spruance.

Bearing these points in mind, let us detail the problem facing Halsey. He knew that Japanese forces were approaching from three different directions but he had already decided to leave the Southern Forces to Kinkaid; also he had intercepted messages from Seventh Fleet's commander showing that steps were being taken to deal with these; accordingly he rightly excluded them from his considerations. There remained the Central and Northern Forces. Unfortunately Halsey's information on these was derived from the reports of his airmen which tended to be far from accurate.

Small blame for this is attributable to the pilots. As Woodward, himself an Intelligence officer, understandingly remarks:

While the pilot is trained in identification and drilled in careful observation, his closest look at a target is often at the end of a dive where flak is thickest and danger greatest, and where he has many things to think about in addition to the bridge structure and the precise number of gun turrets of the ship under attack. Rain, gun smoke and clouds often interfere with vision and photographs do not always settle disputes. Errors in identification and position of targets were notoriously frequent.

Such errors, indeed, abounded on the twenty-fourth. For instance the first report by Adams, otherwise a model of accuracy, mistook a battleship for a heavy cruiser. The last three strikes on Central Force apparently did not see one of the *Yamato*-class ships, but since both were attacked during these raids one must have been mis-identified; yet surely they were distinctive enough. Crapser's report on Ozawa's ships correctly evaluated *Zuikaku* but of the three light carriers, one was assessed accurately but another was believed to be a large fleet carrier while the third was not sighted at all. Walters reported four battleships with Matsuda's advance group yet only two were present. Both of these had the noticeable flight-decks aft but only one such was remarked on. During the following day, pilots constantly believed that the big *Terutsuki*-class destroyers were light cruisers while the real light cruisers were thought to be heavy cruisers.

Peculiar errors in positioning also occurred. For example the first raid from Sherman's Group reported that *Musashi* was some 20 miles astern of formation and that they did not attack her. Morison, accepting this, believes that this strike did not hit *Musashi* which presumably therefore in his opinion had taken a total of nine torpedoes plus several bomb hits in the former raids. However, there were only two of these and although Japanese accounts vary the times when *Musashi* was damaged, all agree that she received her early torpedo hits in three separate attacks. Also if it be accepted that all this damage was done in the first two strikes, it must have been the second that did by far the most. All accounts (including Morison's) credit the first raid with only one torpedo hit. This must be correct for when the next raid arrived three hours later, *Musashi* was still in formation, seemingly undamaged. This would mean that the second attack scored eight torpedo hits. There were only nine torpedo-planes in this strike one of which was forced by anti-aircraft fire to do a 'water-landing'. That all the others hit a target still free to manoeuvre would be incredible even if anything like this percentage had been claimed, which it was not. Finally by the time *Musashi* had had this amount of damage, she was not alone as reported by Sherman's pilots; she had *Tone* with her. It is difficult to see how 11,000 tons worth of heavy cruiser could have passed quite unnoticed.

Therefore the only possible explanation is that this raid did attack *Musashi* after all. This is confirmed by the Japanese statement that she was somewhat astern of the main group after the second strike but *Tone* did not join her until after the third – this one – which caused further injuries; while as mentioned earlier the stories by the pilots in this attack of the damage they inflicted accord with the Japanese accounts of *Musashi*'s third instalment of troubles. The real error would appear to have been that the battleship was not anything like the distance reported astern of her fellows. It will be remembered that this raid was handicapped by bad weather which no doubt caused the pilots' confusion.

Another strange sighting was made by the airmen of the last attack of the day, whose perceptions were probably becoming dulled by fatigue. They reported that two *Kongo*-class battleships were circling, apparently uncontrolled, some distance from the other ships, one being on fire and listing. Yet neither *Kongo* nor *Haruna* left the formation, nor was either damaged. Again the answer must be that they were far closer to the rest of the force then reported – the vessels were milling about in some confusion at the time. As for the fire or other injuries described, these were cases of "wishful thinking".

Calculation of damage inflicted was always the least reliable part of aircraft reports. To the difficulties detailed previously must be added the effect of human nature. The flash of a warship's guns would be reported as a bomb hit. A pillar of water from a near-miss would become a torpedo hit. A ship sending out a smoke-screen would be reported as on fire. And with the sheer speed of air-combat, it was inevitable that several pilots, all in perfect good faith, would claim the responsibility for a real success.

These errors consistently occurred in the day's activities. The attackers of Nishimura claimed three bomb hits on each of his battleships; in reality one hit was scored on a battleship and one on a destroyer. During the attacks on Kurita, pilots reckoned that six torpedo hits and six bomb hits on various heavy cruisers was a conservative estimate; the torpedo that crippled *Myoko* was the only genuine achievement. The strike on Kurita by Group 4 believed a destroyer was "probably sunk". No destroyer suffered more than minor damage. The same raid reported that a light cruiser had been seen to roll over. No Japanese cruiser, heavy or light, was lost during the day.[4]

However, the strange thing is that although such mistakes were "notoriously frequent", Halsey apparently accepted the reports at face-value. Once again there seems little excuse for him, since the same error was avoided by his most experienced subordinate.

Vice-Admiral Marc Mitscher, a slight, wiry man with a leathery face described by Morison as "a simple unassuming gentleman with a soft voice and quiet manners" knew more about carrier warfare than any other American officer. He had learned to fly as long ago as 1915 when serving on the battleship *North Carolina* which carried just one aircraft. Thereafter his career was concerned exclusively with naval aviation, either afloat or ashore. He captained carrier *Hornet* during the Doolittle raid and the Battle of Midway Island. Later he commanded various shore-based air forces before taking carriers to attack the Marshall Islands and Truk; subsequently assuming the leadership of Fast Carrier Forces Pacific Fleet in March 1944, in which role he was Officer in Tactical Command at the Philippine Sea. He enjoyed an immense reputation not only for technical ability but also for the extreme concern he displayed for his pilots. Rescue operations were to him, at least as important as more active tasks. At the Philippine Sea his anxiety for his airmen struggling back after dark, led him to risk his career by lighting up every ship to assist in their recovery; luckily no enemy submarine made its appearance.

An officer of Mitscher's ability could be expected to allow for human error when assessing combat reports. His flagship, carrier *Lexington*, was with Sherman's group and it is most instructive to see how he and his staff toned-down the dramatic stories of that group's airmen before releasing them to Halsey. For instance pilots from the group's second raid stated among other things that they had scored seven 1,000-pound and two 500-pound bomb-hits on a *Yamato*-class ship which they "observed to stop dead in the water". In fact, they probably made only two hits on *Yamato* whose speed was not affected. Mitscher reported to Halsey only that an unidentified battleship had been damaged. Even more significant was his comment that because of clouds the estimate of damage was considered poor.

It does seem then that if only Halsey had made use of Mitscher's special talents he would have received a far more accurate impression

---

[4]Full details of the pilots' claims will be found in Vann Woodward's *The Battle for Leyte Gulf*.

Admiral Halsey Heads North

of the harm inflicted. Unfortunately the Fleet Commander's eagerness for action after years of service ashore had resulted in Mitscher being by-passed for days to such an extent that, says Morison, he "had become little more than a passenger in his beloved Fast Carrier Forces Pacific Fleet". Admirals Bogan and Davison, whose forces rendezvoused outside San Bernardino Strait at 2000, accordingly did not send their reports via Mitscher, away to the north, but direct to Halsey's flagship, battleship *New Jersey* in Group 2. Halsey, confident as ever, did not adopt the cautious attitude of his carrier-commander to the estimates thus received.

After the war, Halsey was to protest that "we had rather good evaluation of pilots' reports at this time". He further excused himself by saying "I did think Kurita had been rather badly mauled by our pilots particularly in their [*sic*] upper works and that their fire control would be poor". He considered that the poor shooting of Kurita's ships off Samar later in the battle bore him out in this. With all respect, this is just not so. Kurita's shooting off Samar was, as will be seen, exceptionally accurate for a short period until his targets escaped into rain-squalls or smoke-screens or both. Then it fell away badly because the Japanese radar was hopelessly ineffective. Further, the leading Japanese officers expressly contradicted Halsey by confirming that all surviving ships were in good fighting condition. The damage to *Yamato*, said Koyanagi, was "not so great as to interfere with fighting or navigation," while Kurita reported "nothing important on other ships".

However, the real retort is that whatever Halsey may have said after the war, he said something different during it. In his action report, after quoting numerous false bomb or torpedo hits as actual damage, he stated that "reports indicated beyond doubt" that Kurita's force "had been badly mauled with all its battleships and most of its heavy cruisers tremendously reduced in fighting power and life"; while in a dispatch to MacArthur and Nimitz on the twenty-fifth he reported that he believed the Central Force "had been so heavily damaged in the Sibuyan Sea that it could no longer be considered a serious menace to Seventh Fleet". He also stated that the "battle efficiency" of the enemy had been "greatly impaired by torpedo hits, bomb hits, topside damage, fires, and casualties". All this gave a very different emphasis from his post-war utterances.

The fact is that Halsey ironically made exactly the same mistake that his foes had made during the Formosa operation – one which he had then loudly derided. On hearing Radio Tokyo's false claims he had broadcast that having "salvaged" all his sunken ships he was "retiring at high speed toward the Japanese fleet". This caused great amusement at the time but Seventh Fleet were to be less joyful when they discovered that ships with battle efficiency "greatly impaired" or "tremendously reduced in fighting power and life" according to Halsey, were in reality virtually untouched; that a unit considered "no serious menace" numbered four battleships, six heavy and two light cruisers and eleven destroyers; that vessels "dead in the water", "on fire and listing", "down at the bow", or "circling uncontrolled" were capable of making 26 knots; and that a "capsized" cruiser had somehow succeeded in righting herself.

Since he was thus not over-concerned with the danger from Central Force, which in any case the latest news indicated to be retiring, Halsey now turned his full attention to the Northern Force — just as the Japanese had planned. Once more he accepted his pilots' description of this as gospel, consequently believing there were heavy gunnery units therein. Yet, again, there seems no real justification for his mistake.

All American commanders should have known from intelligence reports that there were only nine Japanese battleships in existence. Since seven of these had been located in the Central or Southern Forces there could be only two in the north, these being, by process of elimination, *Ise* and *Hyuga* unsighted elsewhere. The report of a battleship with a flight-deck aft afforded confirmation, for this could only have been one of these two. The account of four battleships to the north must therefore be incorrect while the only capital ships that could be with Ozawa possessed only eight of their 14-inch guns apiece. This was the conclusion reached by Admiral Kinkaid from the information received after "we had counted noses carefully"; as it was also by Vice-Admiral Lee, Halsey's battleship commander, and by Mitscher who reported to Halsey that Matsuda's group contained four battleships *or* heavy cruisers.

Indeed the best estimate of the strength of the Northern Force was that made by Mitscher. He believed that a small surface force built around two battleships would be quite capable of dealing with Ozawa in a night action — as of course was true. Since he thought that the four battleships with Bogan or Davison had been detailed by Halsey to guard San Bernardino Strait[5] he would have available only the two

---

[5] These four battleships had been provisionally allotted to a surface force called 'Task Force 34' — of which much more later.

in Sherman's group, *Massachusetts* and *South Dakota*, but deeming these sufficient, at 1712 he ordered Sherman to detach them plus two light cruisers and a squadron of destroyers to steam north after dark to engage the Northern Force with gunfire. This good idea, however, was soon to be overruled by Halsey.

The question also arises whether Halsey could have realized that Ozawa's carriers, being denuded of planes, were merely an attractive bait. Although at first glance this might seem impossible, in practice there was information available which might at least have raised a doubt in Halsey's mind — as it did in the mind of Admiral Lee for one.

As was mentioned earlier, the Japanese had for some time considered the use of empty carriers as decoys. The Americans had got on the track of this and in the summer of 1944 Cincpac-Cincpoa Intelligence circulated a translation of a Japanese manual *Striking Force Tactics* referring to just such a device. This scheme was confirmed by a talkative officer prisoner of war[6] whose interrogation was published in "Seventh Fleet Bulletin" on 13 October 1944. Now the enemy manual expressly named the ships to be used as the heart of the decoy force as being *Hyuga* and *Ise*. One of these had definitely been reported to the north, while the logic of circumstances suggested the other one would be there also. However, the red light thus shown roused no response in Halsey who presumably was either unaware of or disbelieved this information. Had he been disposed to think along these lines, he might have found the weak reaction to Crapser's attack somewhat significant. As it was, estimating that Ozawa had been responsible for sinking *Princeton*, he ranked the Japanese carrier force as "a fresh and powerful threat" — the main danger and target for attack.

Halsey believed that he had three alternative courses now open to him. There was incidentally also a fourth alternative which he may well have considered — as he certainly should have. At 1512 — i.e. half an hour before contact was made with any of the Northern Force — Halsey had issued a battle plan stating that a group to be called 'Task Force 34' "will be formed" to deal with Kurita if he sortied from San Bernardino. This was to consist of battleships *Iowa, New Jersey, Washington*, and *Alabama*, escorted by three heavy cruisers, three light cruisers and two squadrons of destroyers, with Halsey as O.T.C. and Lee commanding the battle line. Bogan and Davison were to keep

---

[6]This officer was a survivor of light cruiser *Natori* sunk off the Philippines on 18 April 1944 by submarine *Hardhead*.

their carriers clear of the fighting. One of the Fleet Commander's alternatives was: "Divide the forces, leaving Task Force 34 to block San Bernardino Straits while the carriers with light screens attacked the Northern Force."

This alternative Halsey rejected. Over-estimating the strength of the Northern Force's surface units, he wanted to bring all his own heavy guns into action – in contrast to Mitscher, who as seen, believed two battleships would be quite enough. He was also concerned lest the Japanese shuttle-bomb the ships left outside the strait by flying planes backwards and forwards between carriers and airfields, as had been attempted in the Philippine Sea action. He felt that a surface force like Task Force 34 would be particularly vulnerable to such attacks.

However, while this may have been true earlier in the war, it was not so by late October 1944, when Japan's air-power and the skill of her airmen alike had been so terribly reduced. The fighting off Formosa and the day's raids on Sherman had afforded recent confirmation of this. Indeed had not the enemy weakness in the air been one of the factors that persuaded Halsey personally to advise acceleration of the Leyte time-table?

Again it seems that many another officer was better informed of the situation. Mitscher at first believed that his chief was leaving Task Force 34 to watch San Bernardino alone, but saw no danger in that. Admirals Nimitz and Kinkaid, as will be seen, continued to believe that the battleships had been left on guard until the following day, yet the former raised no objection to this, while the latter considered it "a perfect battle plan". Their view was to be abundantly justified by the fact that during the remainder of the fighting there was to be no serious air raid, apart from the new weapon of the Kamikazes which attacked only Seventh Fleet and which in any event would have inflicted far less serious damage on the armoured battleships than they did on the unarmoured escort carriers.

However, the most important outlook was surely that of Lee who would have commanded the detached battle line. He said after the battle that he would have been only too glad to have been ordered to cover the strait without any air cover. It would seem that this finally disposes of the validity of Halsey's argument.

Of course if Third Fleet's commander insisted that Task Force 34 must have air-protection, there was another alternative that he did not mention in his action report. This was to leave one of his carrier groups to stay with Lee while the remaining two went north after Ozawa. Halsey presumably either did not think of this or more probably determined against it since he wanted to keep his entire aerial strength intact for hitting Ozawa. Yet he had under his control 401 fighters, 214 dive-bombers and 171 torpedo-bombers (not counting the survivors from *Princeton*). These were surely far more than were needed to take care of the Japanese carriers even had these been fully equipped as he thought. The detachment of, say, Admiral Bogan's group, the smallest, could not possibly have weakened Third Fleet's striking power too much. Yet the Admiral insisted on keeping his force intact. The "time-honoured principle of concentration" ruled supreme. It was to continue to do so for 14 hours, 33 minutes precisely.

Another possibility that Halsey did expressly consider was to "maintain integrity of our own entire striking strength, concentrated off San Bernardino Straits". This would have the advantage of his ships remaining together, while still able to watch both Kurita and Ozawa. The trouble, according to Halsey, was that this would permit Ozawa "to function as planned unmolested"; but in his dispatch immediately after the battle he gave the real reason: "It seemed childish to me to guard statically San Bernardino Straits". He was not the man to wait passively for his enemy to emerge – particularly since at this time there was a possibility that Kurita would not emerge at all.

Yet would such a decision have involved a static defence? It depends of course what is meant by "statically". By "statically" remaining on guard of the Saipan landings, letting his enemy attack him, Spruance had shattered Japan's naval air force. Even as Halsey was pondering his alternatives Kinkaid's forces in Surigao Strait were "statically" waiting to ambush and annihilate the enemy approaching from the south. As Morison puts it: "Battle line might have been detached to guard San Bernardino Strait not statically but actively. But Halsey wished to deal the Northern Force a really crushing blow."

In the event, Halsey determined on adopting yet another course of action, namely to "strike the Northern Force with all of our own striking strength concentrated and leave San Bernardino Strait unguarded". Whatever may have been the explanations given both at the time and later, it seems that the two main factors behind the decision were these: one (to quote Morison), "Japanese carriers gave Halsey blood in the eye and he was taking no chances of letting one guilty flattop escape"; two, (to quote Fuller), "It would appear that he was so carried away by the idea of destroying the Northern Force that the security of Kinkaid's northern flank was entirely overlooked. Well may it be asked," adds Fuller "would so immense an oversight have been possible, had there been present a supreme commander who could have viewed the battle as a whole? The lack of such a commander would seem to have been the crucial American error."

Halsey, however, assessed the matter differently. "It was recognized," he claimed, that the Central Force "might sortie and inflict some damage", but he believed that the injuries it had suffered would prevent it from doing very much. He considered that Kinkaid was strong enough to deal with such a threat; but he knew that Kinkaid's vessels were preparing to tackle the Southern Forces, so should have appreciated that they could only be guarding Surigao Strait, in no position to proceed to the north; also that if they repelled the southern attack, they could still not leave Leyte Gulf unprotected to take station off San Bernardino, even had there been time to do so or their old battleships been suitable for the purpose. In any case Halsey "calculated that the Third Fleet could return in time to reverse any advantage" Kurita might gain – though how they would do this remained obscure then and afterwards.

At 2022, Halsey ordered Groups 2 and 4 to steam north at 25 knots for a rendezvous with Sherman about midnight. At that point, Mitscher would take charge of all groups for the attack on the enemy carriers. The first of the battle's fateful decisions had been made. Everything the Americans possessed went racing to the north. Not even one destroyer remained on picket duty at San Bernardino to signal warning of any approach by Central Force.

To make the position still more dangerous, a misunderstanding between the chief American commanders resulted in Kinkaid believing that the strait was still guarded by his colleague. When Halsey issued his battle plan stating that Task Force 34 "will be formed" he intended it to be a mere preparatory indication of future intentions. This message was addressed to all Task Force and Task Group Commanders of Third Fleet, and to Admirals King and Nimitz for information. It was also intercepted by Admiral Kinkaid who read it with considerable satisfaction. Not picking-up some modifying instructions, he and his communications officer, Commander Shaefer, thought that it was not a mere plan for future battle but a direct order – a command that the force "will be formed" – now! This was not only a perfectly reasonable interpretation of the wording used but furthermore one that was also made by Mitscher, by Nimitz and by Rear-Admiral Cooke, Deputy Chief of Naval Operations in

Washington — which would seem to give Kinkaid's view sufficient justification.

The really fatal confusion, however, came at 2022, when Halsey sent this signal to Kinkaid: "Am proceeding north with three groups to attack enemy carrier force at dawn". Doubtless Halsey did not make the more clear signal that he was proceeding north with all his forces because he was thinking of McCain's Group 1 which in fact was also ordered to proceed north at this time, refuel from Captain Acuff's tankers, launch search-planes to locate Ozawa next morning, and in due course join Mitscher; but which was not going north *with* the Admiral. None the less, this wording was exceptionally unfortunate, for looking at it, it must be conceded that it does give a definite impression that only three groups were going with Halsey, leaving behind another which was not.

Having heard the earlier dispatch about Task Force 34, Kinkaid promptly thought that this must be Halsey's fourth group; that while that officer was taking his carriers with him, he would leave four battleships with escorting vessels to guard against Kurita. Mentally congratulating his fellow commander on his "perfect battle plan", Kinkaid concentrated his attentions on Nishimura. Again it is only fair to Kinkaid to emphasize that Mitscher who, as noticed earlier had given instructions for the use of the two battleships he believed would be the only ones available to him, also thought at first that Task Force 34 was going to be left on guard; while Nimitz believed until the following day that the battleships were watching the strait; he was as horrified as anyone when he found they were not.

There was indeed an additional reason why Kinkaid should assume that San Bernardino Strait was secured. In his operation plan he had stated: "Any major enemy naval force approaching from the north will be intercepted and attacked by Third Fleet covering force", which, remarks Morison, "was a natural interpretation of Halsey's orders from Nimitz to engage the enemy fleet if and when an opportunity occurred". Morison believes that Kinkaid "was entitled to assume that the northern sector was being taken care of. Task Force 38 was in a position to do it and one could fairly assume from the operation plan that Halsey would do it".

In these circumstances, it seems unarguable that Halsey was most unwise in assuming that he could just leave Kurita to Kinkaid as he had already left Nishimura, without any definite notice that he had done this. Surely he was bound to make it crystal clear to Seventh

Fleet that he was no longer protecting them. Certainly Seventh Fleet thought so. Kinkaid was to state that: "In the absence of information to the contrary from Halsey, anything else was unthinkable"; while Rear-Admiral Clifton Sprague whose escort carrier group was in the unfortunate position of being nearest to San Bernardino, was of the opinion that: "In the absence of any information that this exit was no longer blocked, it was logical to assume that our northern flank could not be exposed without warning".

Thus the situation had arisen that not only had Halsey's impulsiveness given Kurita a clear run to Seventh Fleet but his unlucky signals had caused Seventh Fleet to be quite unaware of this. Not until 0412 on 25 October did Kinkaid, on the prompting of his Operations Officer, Captain Cruzen, make a formal enquiry of Halsey as to whether Task Force 34 was guarding the strait. This message provided an example of the American communications trouble mentioned previously for it did not reach Halsey until 0648, when it took a further fifteen minutes for him to send off the discouraging news that his battleships were still with him. "Six minutes earlier," writes Morison drily, "the escort carriers had received a much more emphatic answer in the same sense from the muzzles of Kurita's guns."

Even after the orders to head north, there was always a chance that the decision would yet be countermanded. The night-fliers from light carrier *Independence* were still keeping track of Kurita. At 2030 one of them sighted him off the middle of Burias Island heading for San Bernardino. When this contact was plotted, it became apparent that the Japanese were travelling at over 20 knots. Halsey would not believe this. Since details of the ships spotted had not been given, he concluded that they were only a few undamaged vessels. A signal was sent to Kinkaid that part of the enemy force had been sighted in the position indicated — although such an account was based on Halsey's own belief rather than on any evidence.

Next, at 2120, another *Independence* snooper sighted Kurita's ships, then proceeding in single column at 20 knots, rounding Aguja Point, Burias Island, still heading for the strait. This news did not reach Halsey until two hours later and for some unknown reason he never passed it on to Kinkaid. Although Seventh Fleet Commander, confident that Task Force 34 was protecting his northern flank, would doubtless have taken no action in any case, this must be cited as a further illustration of Halsey's failure to co-ordinate his actions with

Admiral Halsey Heads North

those of his colleague or to keep him properly informed of developments. Further amplifying details of the sightings continued to come in after midnight, by which time with the rendezvous with Sherman successfully completed, all three groups, proceeding at 16 knots so as not to risk missing the Japanese carriers in the dark, were some 165 miles north-east of the strait. These revealed that the force under Kurita contained several battleships one of which was estimated as being of the *Yamato*-class. This surely should have warned Halsey that more than a few undamaged units were involved. He stated later that he "recognized the possibility" that the Japanese "might plod through San Bernardino Strait and go on to attack Leyte forces" – yet how could the speed of Kurita's ships, reported as between 20 and 24 knots, possibly be called "plodding"?

However, the Admiral obstinately insisted that it would be better to press on than turn back. Despite the threat of a *Yamato*-class battleship among other capital ships, he was somehow still able to conclude that Kinkaid could look after these as well as the Southern Forces. He contented himself with the reflection that: "From long experience with the Japs, their blind adherence to plan and their inability to readjust disturbed plans, the Commander Third Fleet had long ago adopted a policy of attacking first". Unfortunately, this was a day when Halsey was to make all the mistakes he accused his foes of making. As Woodward puts it: "The Commander of the Third Fleet did not readjust his own disturbed plans – did not even admit they were disturbed. He adhered to his strategy of attacking the Northern Force with everything he had, leaving San Bernardino Strait unguarded in spite of the reported progress of the Central Force."

It should not be supposed that every officer in the task force agreed with Halsey's actions. The Admiral was later to grumble that "now it is the Monday after the Saturday game" everyone claimed to have appreciated the situation better than he did. It is of course terribly easy to be wise afterwards but on this occasion Halsey had no ground for complaint. Neither Mitscher nor Kinkaid had second sight yet each was wiser than Halsey before not after the event. And while Halsey's ships were steaming north, at least three of his chief subordinates were trying to prevent him from taking this potentially disastrous step.

Rear-Admiral Gerald Bogan, the commander of Task Group 38:2 which contained Halsey's *New Jersey*, having seen the night-planes' reports, discussed the matter over the radio telephone – known as TBS (Talk Between Ships) – with Captain Ewen, skipper of *Independence*. The latter notified him of another factor; that the navigation lights in San Bernardino Stait, long blacked-out, had now been sighted burning brightly. This to Bogan was the final confirmation that Kurita was coming through the strait. Considering it essential that Lee's battle line with his own Group 2 in support be detached to take care of Kurita, he prepared a message to Halsey which included the report about the navigation lights; then called him personally over the TBS. When he had read out this information, his only reward was the retort of a staff officer who in "a rather impatient voice" snapped back: "Yes, yes, we have that information". Admiral Bogan fell silent.

Previously to this, an even more distinguished gentleman had also protested. Vice-Admiral Willis Lee commander of Halsey's battleships had a considerable reputation as a strategist. An alert man whose studious manner was emphasized by spectacles; a pre-war director of training who had suggested many improvements in combat equipment; an expert on radar; the victor of the night Battle of Guadalcanal on 14-15 November 1942 where he displayed imperturbability and quick thinking in equal proportions; and the commander of battle line at the Philippine Sea; he was an officer whose advice, frequently sought, was always worth taking. Unfortunately it was not accepted on this occasion.

After considering the early sightings as they came in, Lee had reasoned that the Northern Force was a decoy with little if any striking power while the reversal of course by the Central Force must prove temporary. Before sunset he sent a signal to Halsey stating his views. A brief acknowledgement was the only result. After the night-planes' reports arrived, Lee sent Halsey a further message by TBS saying that he was certain Kurita was coming out. This had no effect either.

Finally Admiral Mitscher's Chief of Staff, Commodore Arleigh Burke, the victor of the Battle of Cape St George on 25 November 1943, was convinced by the night-fliers' signals that Central Force was "still very much afloat and moving toward San Bernardino". Burke considered it vital to detach Lee's battle line to stop it. Together with Commander Flatley, the Operations Officer whose opinion was identical, he hastily awoke Mitscher who had retired to sleep, begging him to "tell Halsey" to take this action. However, Mitscher was in a most difficult position. Having been ignored for so long he thought

Admiral Halsey Heads North

that his superior must have further information that he did not possess. Finally he asked if Halsey had received the reports. When told that this was so, he replied: "If he wants my advice, he'll ask for it"; and went back to sleep. The northward advance was not checked.

After 2320, the night-planes lost track of Central Force. Thereafter, as *Independence* went north with the rest of the fleet, she had to recall them. From then on, Morison notes, "every pair of eyes, every search radar, every search plane, every thinking mind and fighting heart in Task Force 38 was turned northward toward Ozawa – exactly as the Japanese intended".

Behind the backs of the retiring Americans, Kurita's ships were speeding through the dangerous shoals and narrow channels of San Bernardino Strait at 20 knots. This was, incidentally, an exceedingly fine feat of navigation, especially after dark. At 0035, in single column in the constricted passage, they emerged into the Philippine Sea. As they appeared they presented an unpleasantly easy target. Had the battleships of Task Force 34 been waiting for them, with the help of their radar they could have deluged each enemy ship in turn as she moved out of the strait. They could have steamed at right-angles to the entrance so as to bring their full broadsides to bear on ships whose forward guns only could return their fire. In short, under these favourable circumstances there is little doubt that they could have routed Central Force. But Task Force 34 was no longer on guard.

The Japanese, of course, unaware of this, were expecting to have to fight their way out. All their crewmen were at action stations; lookouts peering anxiously into the night. To their astonishment, nothing happened. Pleasantly surprised, Kurita headed south towards Leyte Gulf.

5

The Action in Surigao Strait

Fortunately for the Americans, while Third Fleet was actively racing in the wrong direction, Seventh Fleet was quietly guarding the southern entrance to Leyte Gulf. Its leader even took satisfaction from the fact that apart from occasional air raids he could stay in port to "prepare without serious interruptions for a night action", thereby allowing his tactical dispositions and plans to be "checked and counterchecked by all concerned". This of course would have been anathema to Halsey, but his fellow fleet commander was of a very different temperament.

Vice-Admiral Thomas Kinkaid had spent his early career in battleships or cruisers. He commanded a cruiser division at the Battles of Coral Sea on 7–8 May 1942 and Midway on 4 June 1942, showing considerable ability. He was an admirable 'big gun' officer, as demonstrated by his formulation of tactics to counterbalance the greater experience of the Japanese in night-fighting during the Guadalcanal campaign. The fact that his successor disregarded his ideas, in consequence of which he suffered the disastrous defeat of Tassafaronga, merely emphasized the wisdom of Kinkaid's tactics, which were subsequently put into effect with great success. If he had been in command at Tassafaronga, the result could have been very different.

Yet despite his 'big-ship' background, Kinkaid, like Ozawa, was a firm believer in the effectiveness of air power. He commanded a carrier group built around *Enterprise* in the Battle of the Eastern Solomons on 24 August 1942. He was the unlucky tactical commander whom Halsey rashly ordered to attack a far superior force with America's two remaining carriers at the Battle of Santa Cruz. Although having the worst of this encounter, he inflicted serious losses on his foes despite being outnumbered, while his calm resolution largely compensated for his lack of experience in such operations. Finally at the Battle of Guadalcanal, the Admiral kept damaged *Enterprise* out of danger but was able to attack enemy ships with her aircraft with great effect; while also detaching Lee's battleships from his screen for the decisive blow at the right moment.

The Action in Surigao Strait

Next Kinkaid turned to amphibious operations, being transferred in November 1942 to command the North Pacific Force charged with the recapture of Attu and Kiska in the Aleutian Islands. Learning that he could not be given sufficient forces to take Kiska, the nearer of these, he decided on temporarily by-passing it so as to capture Attu with a smaller force, thereby cutting off Kiska and making its later conquest much more easy. In this he succeeded only too well, for, after Attu had fallen, the Japanese took advantage of its fog-girt conditions to evacuate Kiska before the Americans could attack it. Yet evacuations, even as brilliant as this one, cannot win wars, while this illustration that it was possible to by-pass enemy-held islands with impunity was vital, for it proved the start of the 'island-leapfrogging' by which the United States countered Japan's strategy of selling space for time. Within a few weeks of the Attu landing, Nimitz was proposing other outflanking movements of a similar nature.

It was fitting that Kinkaid should play an important role in this new strategy. In November 1943, he took command of Seventh Fleet. This he led in a series of amphibious assaults, leaping along the coast of New Guinea, capturing some enemy bases while isolating others, which could be neither supported nor relieved because the dense jungles made land travel impossible. Finally in July 1944 after an advance of 1,300 miles which had cut off some 135,000 enemy troops, MacArthur's forces completed the reconquest of New Guinea and the General was ready to fulfil his dream of returning to the Philippines. Kinkaid handled the seaborne aspects of this advance with his usual quiet skill despite a shortage of forces, which included a lack of air support. Seventh Fleet had four squadrons of amphibious Catalinas, each with its tender, but apart from these depended on General Kenney's South-west Pacific Air Force. However, for landings on 22 April 1944 at Aitape, Seventh Fleet borrowed eight escort carriers from Fifth Fleet. These Kinkaid put to good use – a preview of his employment of these vessels at Leyte. The Admiral was of course under MacArthur's command during all these operations. He had, says Morison, "a difficult role to play as head of 'MacArthur's Navy', since that great general, for all his genius, at first imperfectly understood the limitation and capabilities of sea power. But he learned from Kinkaid." Also, although relations between the American Army and Navy were wonderful when compared with the disputes among the Japanese, there was a healthy rivalry between them and one can think of certain admirals who would not have taken kindly to coming under the orders of their sister service. However, no difficulties arose with Kinkaid, who, again like Ozawa, was a champion of inter-service co-operation, no one being more appreciative of his loyalty than was MacArthur.

Seventh Fleet's Commander had need of his coolness on the evening of 24 October. He was, as has been seen, confident that Third Fleet was guarding his northern flank but he was aware of the threat to the south posed by Nishimura and Shima. There had been considerable difficulty in tracking these groups and estimating their strength. Nishimura, as mentioned, was attacked by Davison's Group 4 but was not halted. Later his ships were sighted by a Navy Liberator from Morotai, while Shima was spotted by a V Army Air Force bomber. During the afternoon, no attacks were made on either force, nor were they even sighted for Davison was called north by Halsey to join in the attacks on the Central Force while the escort carriers had their hands full with their various duties of support or protection in the gulf. After dark, Sprague could not make any flights since he had no night fighters and even if he had had any would not have been able to use them since none of his air-crews was trained to make deck-landings at night. Kinkaid had only four radar-equipped Catalinas ('Black Cats' as they were called) for night searches. Two of these were sent off after dark to reconnoitre the Mindanao Sea but they could not locate their enemies and one was accidentally shot down by American motor-torpedo-boats — although fortunately these made some amends by rescuing all the crew. However, Kinkaid correctly estimated that the Japanese would attempt to force Surigao Strait that night. Long before nightfall, he had made all necessary preparations to prevent this.

Since A-Day, Surigao Strait had been guarded by Squadron 54, a patrol of seven destroyers, *Remey, McGowan, Melvin, Mertz, McDermut, Monssen* and *McNair* — under the command of Captain Jesse Coward on board the first-named. On the afternoon of the twenty-fourth, these ships, all new 2,100 tonners, were still on watch between Leyte and tiny Hibuson Island. Before evening, however, they formed merely the first line of a terrific concentration of fire-power.

At 1215 Kinkaid warned every naval and merchant vessel under his command to prepare for a night attack by enemy surface forces. He was rightly satisfied that he could deal with the ships commanded by Nishimura and Shima, which he believed to be two sections of the same force, even though reports received had somewhat overestimated their numbers, crediting them with two battleships, eight cruisers and ten destroyers. However, he had determined by early afternoon that

The Action in Surigao Strait

he would achieve the destruction, not merely the repulse of the enemy, so, believing that Halsey was guarding his northern flank, he decided to allocate almost his entire gunnery and torpedo strength to the defence of the strait.

Accordingly, at 1443, Kinkaid ordered Rear-Admiral Oldendorf as Commander of the Bombardment and Support Group to station his forces across the narrow 12-mile-wide stretch of water between Leyte and Hibuson, where Surigao Strait enters Leyte Gulf, in preparation for a night action. He added the cruisers and destroyers of Rear-Admiral Russell Berkey's Close Covering Group to Oldendorf's command as further reinforcement. A screen of destroyer-escorts and patrol craft was left guarding the remaining transports, the three amphibious flagships and cruiser *Nashville*, for although General MacArthur was eager to have his flagship take part in the battle, Kinkaid rightly refused to risk the life of his distinguished passenger. Sprague's escort carriers were ordered to remain at their usual cruising stations to the east of the gulf, though it was pre-arranged that they might be called on to make air strikes on retreating enemy ships at dawn. Also the scout planes on the battleships and cruisers were either stowed in the ships' hangars or flown off to safety. This was a wise precaution on Kinkaid's part since during the Battle of Savo Island on 9 August 1942, the American cruisers engaged had had their aircraft catch fire on the catapults with disastrous results.

Even without Sprague's assistance, Oldendorf had under him a total of six battleships, four heavy cruisers, four light cruisers and twenty-one destroyers. He had anticipated Kinkaid's instructions, so had already drawn up a preparatory battle plan. Now his staff under Captain Richard Bates made ready for the coming encounter. In the late afternoon Oldendorf held a conference on his flagship, heavy cruiser *Louisville* with Berkey and his battleship commander Rear-Admiral George Weyler. By 1725, all necessary decisions for the proposed annihilation of the enemy had been reached. Oldendorf reported to his chief that everything was ready. After the action, he remarked, somewhat ungallantly, that his motto was "that of the old-time gambler: 'Never give a sucker a chance'. If my opponent is foolish enough to come at me with an inferior force, I'm certainly not going to give him an even break."

The Admiral therefore drew up his heavy ships in an arc across the strait a little north of the destroyer picket-line. In the centre Weyler's battleships steamed east and west across the northern exit of the strait at a stately 5 knots, which was increased first to 10 knots, later to 15, as sightings of the hostile forces began to come in. Weyler's ships numbered the following:

West Virginia and *Maryland* both equipped with eight 16-inch guns.

Mississippi (flagship), *Tennessee, California, Pennsylvania*, all armed with twelve 14-inch guns.

The battleships were protected by Destroyer Division 'X-Ray' led by Commander Miles Hubbard in *Claxton*, with *Cony, Thorn, Aulick, Sigourney* and *Welles*. Their position gave ample sea room for manoeuvre, whereas the Japanese, approaching from the south, would be restricted by the shores of Leyte on the west or Hibuson or the larger island of Dinagat on the east. Also the battle line could be transferred to cover the eastern entrance to Leyte Gulf in a hurry should this prove necessary.

Extending the battleships' arc of fire were the cruisers on each flank. The left flank was stationed over two and a half miles south of the capital ships on the east of the strait. Oldendorf personally commanded this group comprising heavy cruisers *Louisville* (flagship), *Portland* and *Minneapolis*, light cruisers *Denver* and *Columbia*, and the screening destroyers of Captain Roland Smoot in *Newcomb* who commanded *Richard P. Leary, Albert W. Grant, Robinson, Halford, Bryant, Heywood L. Edwards, Bennion* and *Leutze*.

On the west of the strait, close under the bold shore of Leyte, were Berkey's right flank cruisers – his flagship *Phoenix* and *Boise*, both light cruisers and Australian heavy cruiser HMAS *Shropshire*. They were escorted by a division of Destroyer Squadron 24. Under Captain Kenmore McManes on board *Hutchins*, were *Daly, Bache, Killen, Beale* and the Australian destroyer *Arunta*. These ships were stationed about four miles south of the cruisers to ease the congestion in the main patrol area.

Despite the large number of vessels on hand, there were a few flies in the ointment. Every battleship was rather elderly. All but *Mississippi* had been present during the Pearl Harbour attack, suffering considerable damage. Indeed *West Virginia* and *California* had been sunk, but since they rested on even keel in the mud of the harbour, they were later salvaged. They had long since ceased to be regarded as useful for fighting naval battles, being relegated to bombardment in support of amphibious operations. This was the sphere in which they had gained experience – as indeed was true of Admiral Oldendorf. Since they were not expected to take part in ship-

The Action in Surigao Strait

to-ship fights, only *West Virginia, California* and *Tennessee* were equipped with the latest Mark-8 gunnery radar sets, the others having only the old Mark-3 radar with which it would prove difficult to locate targets.

Also it will be remembered that the American plans had been readjusted in a hurry. The battleships had been loaded for bombarding Yap. Consequently, they had filled their magazines mainly with high capacity (HC) shells, suitable for such activity. Only just over one-fifth of their ammunition was of the armour-piercing (AP) type which is essential for a fleet action. They had already expended over half their HC shells during the previous days' work, while some of their AP allowance had also been used against the stronger targets on shore. The heavy cruisers had only about one-third of their armament in AP shells. The destroyers had used up all but some 20 per cent of their 5-inch shells, which could not readily be replenished. No torpedoes at all were available to replace any used in the coming action although of course the destroyers' tubes were fully loaded when it began. Finally, all ships were low in fuel, the twenty-fifth having been scheduled as the date for taking on fresh supplies.

Fortunately the shortages in no way affected the issue but Oldendorf very understandably did not wish to waste shells in a lengthy running battle – especially since Captain Bates was insistent that provision must be made for a possible later encounter with Kurita should he succeed in eluding Halsey. Oldendorf therefore planned a short decisive action at close quarters where his battleships' "percentage of hits and their fire effect would both be high". It was decided that they would hold their fire until the range was down to 20,000 yards or less. The big ships were prepared to use AP ammunition for their first five salvoes, then change to HC if they found any small enemy vessels as targets.

On the other hand, Oldendorf emphasized that the geographical situation whereby the enemy was forced to run through the narrow strait with his power to manoeuvre vastly restricted, afforded a "wonderful opportunity" for his destroyers to deliver torpedo attacks. While Hubbard's division was to be held back to screen the battleships, the ships of first McManes, then Smoot, would speed south into the strait to launch their 'fish', afterwards retiring up the sides of the strait so as to deceive the Japanese radar as well as avoiding American shell-fire. These planned destroyer-strikes were, in practice to be preceded by a third.

The patrolling destroyers of Squadron 54 were not included in the original battle plan since technically they were under Wilkinson not Oldendorf. However, Captain Coward, a veteran of the Battle of Guadalcanal, had no intention of not participating. At 1950, he signalled to Oldendorf that in the event of contact with the enemy, "I plan to make an immediate torpedo attack and then retire to clear you." Oldendorf approved, so to Coward fell the honour of making the first destroyer attack.

However, even Coward was not the first opponent that the Japanese would meet. At noon, Kinkaid had ordered Commander Selman Bowling, Commander Motor-Torpedo-Boat Squadrons Seventh Fleet, to send all available craft (PT boats as the Americans called them) into Surigao Strait or the Mindanao Sea as far as 60 miles south-west of the strait's lower entrance. Of the forty-five PTs originally accompanying Seventh Fleet, six were inoperative due to defects resulting from their 1,100-mile voyage to the gulf, but the remaining thirty-nine, in thirteen sections of three, had all taken up their positions before nightfall with orders first to report all contacts of any kind, then to attack independently. Their primary function therefore was as long-range look-outs.

The strength of the defending forces was clearly sufficient to deal with the fleets of Nishimura and Shima, which even if combined would, it will be recalled, consist only of two old though modernized battleships, *Yamashiro* and *Fuso* each with twelve 14-inch guns, three heavy cruisers, one light cruiser and eight destroyers. Also the narrow approaches to the gulf as well as restricting manoeuvres, would reduce opportunities to take up favourable positions for torpedo attacks. Since Japanese radar was very poor, their ships would have to rely on searchlights in a night action – these the Americans had long-since abandoned as they inevitably presented fine aiming-points.

To add to the troubles of Admiral Nishimura who commanded the Van of the Southern Force, he learnt at about 1830 from Kurita that Central Force due to delays in the Sibuyan Sea would not be able to assist him by making a simultaneous attack on the gulf from the north. Morison remarks that "whether Nishimura imagined he could get through Surigao Strait without a fight we do not know", but in fact Nishimura could not possibly have been unaware of the formidable obstacles in his path for at 0200, heavy cruiser *Mogami* had launched a search-plane, which flying over Leyte Gulf in the freshness of dawn when details stood out clearly, reported a greatly-exaggerated number of transports, but also faithfully warned the Admiral of his opponents' six battleships plus supporting forces. Nevertheless, Nishimura

The Action in Surigao Strait

persisted in maintaining speed without waiting to combine his attack with that of Kurita or even that of Shima.

After the war, Commander Shigeru Nishino, skipper of lucky destroyer *Shigure*, stated that he believed Nishimura had deliberately avoided co-ordination with Shima. The two admirals had been classmates at the Japanese Naval Academy but although Nishimura, the elder, possessed a greater sea-going experience, Shima now had a six-months seniority in rank. Also apparently "a certain incident" in their careers had resulted in there being "a personal antipathy" between them. However, since Nishino based his statement on the ground that Nishimura increased his pace, whereas we now know he only maintained it, some other reason must be sought for his rash decision.

It seems most probable therefore that the Admiral who had been understandably alarmed by Davison's attack earlier since he had no aircraft protection at all, did not wish to wait until dawn for supporting forces because daylight would only bring further air attacks. Since Shima had not radioed his position to Nishimura, the Van Force's Commander probably did not realize how close he was – about 40 miles behind during the crossing of the Sulu Sea. There was some encouragement for Nishimura in the reflection that the Japanese Navy had in the past excelled at night-fighting, even on occasions overcoming worse odds than he was facing. The situation now, particularly in view of the American progress in radar, was very different but doubtless Nishimura determined to do his best, hoping against hope for a repetition of former successes.

Finally about 1900, Nishimura received Toyoda's signal that "all forces will dash to the attack". This must have brushed aside any doubts he may have had as to the correctness of his decision. He maintained course and speed.

Shima for his part was not at all eager to join forces with Nishimura or even notify him of his presence. Should he do so, then as has already been mentioned, by the rigid Japanese rules of seniority he would have been compelled to take command of both forces. This was just what he did not want – a further indication this, that Nishino's theory of bad blood between the admirals was unjustified. Shima had been detailed to support Nishimura only at the very last minute, learning of his colleague's mission only through an intercepted message while already at sea. Since he was not acquainted with the plans of the Van Force, Shima felt that his taking over could only lead to confusion. Further, since he was sighted only by a high-level bomber of which he was unaware, he believed that his fleet was unknown to the Americans. Therefore he maintained radio silence, planning to surprise his foes by bringing in his reinforcements without warning.

Thus the southern pincer came for Surigao Strait in two separate sections. Indeed when the Japanese were first encountered by the PT boats they were in three groups, for after dark Nishimura had sent *Mogami* with three destroyers – *Yamagumo, Asagumo, Michishio* – ahead on reconnaissance leaving only *Shigure* on guard with his battleships.

The night of 24–25 October was clear at first but a few minutes after midnight the moon went down leaving the sky pitch-black. The wind was slight with only a few of the usual rain squalls. Occasional flashes of sheet lightning lit up the strait while thunder growled in the islands' hills. The sea was smooth, without swells – perfect for the PT boats. Three sections of these were stationed out in Mindanao Sea as far as the south-east of Bohol Island, five more at the narrow entrance to Surigao Strait, the remaining five within the strait.

The little PT boats were woefully armed. They had no protection whatever against shell-fire. They carried only four torpedoes plus a miserable 37-mm gun. They were facing a strong enemy force, or series of forces, which included battleships and heavy cruisers. They were without experience in torpedo-attacks, apart from a practice before leaving for Leyte. In short their only advantage lay in a speed of 40 knots together with their considerable manoeuvrability. It is perhaps misleading therefore that due to subsequent events the best-known PT attack is one in Blackett Strait on the night of 1–2 August 1943, when fifteen PTs attempted to ambush a small enemy force of destroyers carrying troops. Morison describes the action thus: "They used torpedoes lavishly but made not one hit on enemy ships going or coming". As a culmination of this unsuccessful interception *PT109* commanded by a certain Lieutenant John F. Kennedy was deliberately rammed, not even fired upon, by an enemy destroyer while at slow speed. This encounter, which has attracted such admiration since, cost Kennedy his ship, cut clean in half, and two of his crew their lives, but Commander Hanami of *Amagiri* merely the tip of a propeller-blade. This was not a good example for the PTs off Surigao to follow.

First sighting came at 2236 when Ensign Peter Gadd picked up two large targets on *PT131*'s radar. Accompanied by *PT130* and *PT152*, he headed towards these at 24 knots. Since radar had warned the Americans where to look they saw the Japanese before being spotted

The Action in Surigao Strait

themselves. At 2250, the bulk of Nishimura's battleships came looming out of the darkness. Yet, as Kennedy among many others had discovered, in a competition for alertness the Japanese had few equals, an ironical contrast to pre-war propaganda that they suffered from poor night-vision. Their look-outs were not only specially selected and trained for this work but were equipped with huge, exceptionally powerful night binoculars. At 2252, the lynx-eyed watchers on destroyer *Shigure* sighted the approaching PTs. The action in Surigao Strait had begun.

As the torpedo-boats closed the range, the battleships sent up starshells, *Shigure* opened fire with 5-inch shells, the red and yellow tracers whipping over the PTs, and a searchlight beam also from *Shigure* brightly illuminated the attackers. It will be remembered that Kinkaid's orders had been that the PTs should first ensure that targets were reported as accurately as possible, with strikes against them a secondary consideration. However, the PTs' laudable ambition to deliver a blow with their torpedoes overcame the more important task. They pressed on through the barrage in an attempt to reach a favourable launching position.

Such was the fury of *Shigure*'s gunfire, however, that the little vessels were unable to carry out their intention. *PT131* was damaged by shrapnel from repeated near-misses which put her radio out of action. *PT152* received a direct hit which blew up her solitary gun, killing one man and wounding three. It also started a fire. As she turned away, a spout of water from a near-miss helped quench this. *PT130*, so far undamaged, got between *PT152* and the enemy, sending out smoke to protect her consort, while firing ineffectually at the searchlight. As she did this a 5-inch shell passed clean through her without exploding, the concussion knocking out her radio as well. All three PTs retired under the smoke-screen in safety, albeit still pursued by gunfire.

Now the PTs were in a quandary. As a result of their impetuosity none was able to signal their vital discovery. However, Lieutenant (jg) Malcolm of *PT130* ("using his head" commented Kinkaid) managed to contact *PT127* of another section which had not made a sighting. This vessel passed on the report to her tender *Wachapreague* about ten minutes after midnight. It finally reached Oldendorf at 0026 – his first news of the enemy's approach.

Apart from this first encounter, the fighting in or near Surigao Strait took place after midnight – hence on 25 October. There seems to be a tradition of fighting decisive battles in late October – Trafalgar was fought on the 21 October 1805; Alamein commenced on the night of 23–24 October 1942; but no day was more crowded with action than the twenty-fifth in 1944, which saw the culminating efforts made by the combatants in the war for the Pacific.

The first encounter of the day occurred 15 minutes after midnight when *PT146, PT151* and *PT190* attacked *Mogami* which in the darkness they mistook for a battleship, together with her accompanying destroyers. The first two boats each fired one torpedo before *Mogami*'s searchlight found them. *Yamagumo* opened fire – whereupon all three PTs retired under a smoke-screen. The port engine of *PT151* failed for three minutes but although frequently straddled not one of the torpedo-boats was hit. Nor did their torpedoes find their mark.

Some 25 minutes later, the two sections of Nishimura's force reunited. At 0100, their commander ordered approach formation with *Michishio* and *Asagumo* in the van. Next came *Shigure* and *Yamagumo* flanking *Yamashiro*, 4 kilometres behind the van destroyers. *Fuso*, then *Mogami*, followed at 1-kilometre intervals.

Pressing on in their new order the Van of the Southern Force reached the narrow entrance to Surigao Strait about an hour later, passing between Panaon and Sumilon Islands. At the same time a formation of three more PTs – *PT132, PT134* and *PT137* – which had been lurking off the southern tip of Panaon made the next attack. *PT134* under Lieutenant-Commander Robert Leeson, in tactical command of all boats, set a splendid example by racing in to close range despite being illuminated by star-shells and searchlights. Amidst heavy though luckily inaccurate fire, *PT134* fired three torpedoes at 0205, turning sharply to dodge out of the searchlight beam immediately afterwards. The torpedoes missed. The two other PTs also fired but also missed.

As the Japanese were engaged with Leeson's group, another section, consisting of *PT490, PT491* and *PT493* which were closing in from their original patrol line some 10 miles north, concentrated on the enemy destroyers. At 0207, Lieutenant (jg) McElfresh in command of *PT490*, fired two torpedoes at the leading destroyer while Lieutenant (jg) Thronson's *PT491* launched two more at another one. All missed. The Southern Force promptly turned its attention to this new threat. Searchlight beams found the PTs and furious gunfire followed. Thronson retired pursued by shells but McElfresh with his boat brightly illuminated continued through the spouts of near-misses to the desperately close range of some 350 yards from an enemy

The Action in Surigao Strait 101

destroyer, whence he sent two more torpedoes at his target without result. *PT490* also fired her gun; McElfresh later claiming that he knocked out his enemy's searchlight. He may have been over-optimistic; in any case, a second searchlight promptly found him. As a shell crashed home, McElfresh finally turned away.

While wounded *PT490* was retiring, Lieutenant (jg) Brown's *PT493* whose torpedoes had refused to launch, got between her companion and the hostile force in an attempt to provide cover with a smoke-screen. This succeeded, but Brown in turn was now caught by a searchlight. Three 5-inch shells struck his boat killing two men, wounding five and blowing a large gap in the bottom. Petty-Officer Brunelle, although previously regarded by his crew-mates as "a slight, sissified-looking boy whom no one expected to be of any use in combat", rose magnificently to the occasion by wedging his life-jacket in the hole. This enabled the shattered craft to stay afloat long enough for Brown to beach her on Panaon Island. Later *PT493* slid off at high tide, to sink in deep water, but the survivors of her crew were rescued shortly after sunrise by Thronson's *PT491*.

Meanwhile, immediately after the attack by McElfresh's section, *PT523*, *PT524* and *PT526* sighting the Japanese ships silhouetted by their own star-shells, also attempted to intervene. Each boat fired two torpedoes at a target they identified as a heavy cruiser. If they were correct, this could only have been *Mogami*, an incredibly difficult ship to account for as later events as well as previous ones proved. No hits were scored. Nor were the PTs damaged as they retreated under smoke amidst heavy fire.

In addition to their strikes, the various PTs had attempted to send news of the sightings to Oldendorf or Coward, although not all signals reached them while others were delayed in transmission. However, they received a fairly accurate account of Nishimura's progress. One last report came at 0225 from *PT327*. Patrolling about halfway up the strait north-east of Panaon, she observed Nishimura some 10 miles to the south. She promptly notified Coward who ordered the PTs to clear the area while he took over the attacks on Nishimura's Van Force.

The PTs action was not yet over, however. Admiral Shima's two heavy cruisers, one light cruiser and four destroyers were now approaching. These were spotted well out in the Mindanao Sea. Word first reached Oldendorf at 0038, this being his first intimation that he would have to deal with two widely separated antagonists. However, Shima was not attacked until he was entering the strait. The PTs were now scattered as a result of their encounters with Nishimura. Also that officer had twice signalled to Shima that he was fighting off torpedo-boats so the Commander of the Second Striking Force was well on the alert.

Finally at 0315, taking advantage of a convenient rain squall, Leeson's *PT134* located the new targets off Binit Point, Panaon. She duly fired torpedoes but had no success. At that stage, Shima's ships were in column, two destroyers ahead while the other two followed the cruisers which were led by Shima's flagship *Nachi*. Five minutes later with the squall past, Shima ordered speed increased to 26 knots, swinging his column first east to clear the Point then north up the strait, simultaneously ordering the leading destroyers to fall in astern.

As this manoeuvre was being executed, Lieutenant (jg) Michael Kovar commanding *PT137* seized the opportunity for a surprise attack. He launched a torpedo at one of the destroyers taking up its position at the rear of Shima's force. The 'fish' passed under the stern of the destroyer but found its mark in the radio-room of light cruiser *Abukuma*, flooding this, killing about thirty men and reducing the ship's speed to 9 knots. Down at the bow, too crippled to continue, she dropped out of the formation. Leaving her unescorted to limp away westward, Shima sped on towards Leyte Gulf. There was a considerable element of luck in this achievement since Kovar had not even sighted *Abukuma*, nor did he know he had hit her – but who will deny that the PTs had richly deserved a slice of good fortune. The enemy destroyers fired star-shells while the cruisers contributed gunfire but Kovar escaped unhurt.

This was the final effort by the torpedo-boats during the Japanese advance, though subsequently they also attacked retreating vessels. "The skill, determination and courage displayed by the personnel of these small boats" stated Nimitz later, "is worthy of the highest praise."

Including the subsequent attacks, the PTs fired a total of thirty-four torpedoes. Although they made numerous optimistic claims of hearing underwater explosions or observing flashes or fires breaking out on their targets, in reality the hit on *Abukuma* was the only one scored. This, however, reduced the ranks of the enemy by one ship at any rate. The remainder were not halted or delayed though the attacks probably helped to rattle their crews at least slightly. On the other hand the PTs performed according to Nimitz, "an invaluable service" by keeping Oldendorf and Coward notified of the arrival and progress of both Japanese forces – had those in the Guadalcanal campaign

The Action in Surigao Strait

been of a comparable standard several ships, not to mention countless lives, would have been saved. And somehow not one of the PTs was sunk by being rammed.

After the PTs' opposition, Admiral Nishimura enjoyed a temporary rest while his ships drove north at 20 knots; then came the next stage in his afflictions – attack by destroyers. First on the scene came Coward's Squadron 54. Leaving *Mertz* and *McNair* on guard between Desolation Point and Homonhon Island lest another enemy group attempt an approach by that entrance to the gulf, Coward split his remaining five destroyers into two sections with orders first to attack from either bow simultaneously; afterwards to retire close to the land-masses thus avoiding detection. All the destroyers were instructed to withhold their fire which would disclose their position without being able to inflict serious damage on their foes; in addition the Americans had learned in the Guadalcanal campaign that gunfire at night tended temporarily to blind the command and control personnel. The PTs' reports enabled Coward to plot his opponents' progress with considerable accuracy. At 0230, having previously notified Oldendorf of his intentions, he led his ships south at 20 knots.

As stated, the attackers formed two groups: *Remey, McGowan* and *Melvin* under Coward steamed east of the middle of the strait closing almost head-on to Nishimura; Commander Richard Phillips with *McDermut* and *Monssen* raced in on the west close by the shore of Leyte. All crews were tensely alert for action. "We are going into battle," stated Commander Bergin of *Monssen*, "I know each of you will do his duty. I promise you that I will do my duty to you and for our country." "Tonight" broadcast Commander Fiala of *Remey*, "our ship has been designated to make the first torpedo run on the Jap task force that is on its way to stop our landings in Leyte Gulf. It is our job to stop the Japs. May God be with us to-night."

Ten minutes later, the enemy had been picked up on Coward's radar. By 0245, his strength was correctly estimated as seven ships; "two battleships, one cruiser and four screening vessels". *Remey, McGowan* and *Melvin* increasing speed to 25 knots swept on towards these tempting targets.

In contrast with American radar efficiency, the Japanese were in a sorry state. Their radar was so poor that it gave no warning at all of the destroyers' approach; the screens were blurred; the 'pips' of the attackers lost in the haze. Fortunately, Japanese eyesight was as good

The Battle of Leyte Gulf

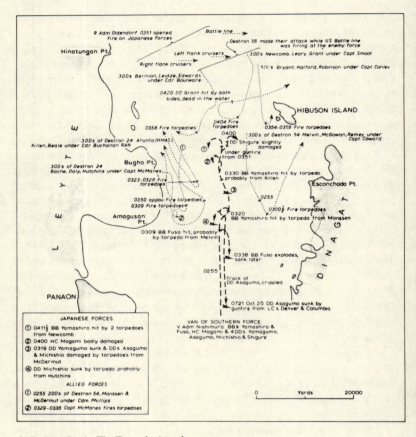

3 Surigao Strait: The Torpedo Attacks

The Action in Surigao Strait

as ever. At 0256, alert *Shigure* again gave warning reporting Coward's three vessels 8 kilometres to the north-east. *Yamashiro* tried to pick these up with her searchlight but they were still out of range. Two minutes later *Melvin*'s look-outs sighted the Japanese. Laying a smoke-screen behind which to retire, Coward's force increased speed again to 30 knots, swung to port in succession just after 0300 in the glare of *Yamashiro*'s searchlight which had now found them, and fired their 'fish'. Twenty-seven torpedoes streaked through the glassy waters.

As soon as they had fired, the destroyers continued their turn to port, retiring up the coast of Dinagat under their smoke, zigzagging independently, their speed building up still more to 35 knots. As they turned, *Yamashiro* and her escorting destroyers opened fire on them. The first salvoes fell short. Then brilliant, well-placed star-shells illuminated the Americans. Further heavy gunfire followed continuing for over ten minutes. Five-inch shells landed dangerously close, splashing water over the decks of the retreating destroyers. However, bad radar meant that night-gunnery was never Japan's strongest point. All Coward's ships escaped unhurt.

Apart from sheer stubborn persistence, Nishimura appears to have displayed few virtues from start to finish of the night's activities. Though it is scarcely creditable that he did not realize the destroyers had advanced for the purpose of firing torpedoes, he took no evasive action whatsoever. In consequence at 0309, a torpedo, probably from *Melvin*, found its mark on battleship *Fuso*; in fact it seems very likely that two torpedoes hit her for all the destroyers reported seeing or hearing at least that number of explosions.

In any event *Fuso* was fatally wounded. Although no one knows exactly what happened, it seems that the hit (or hits) caused damage to her engine room as well as starting fires, for she fell out of the line to starboard her speed decreasing rapidly until she came to a halt. Presumably the fires then spread, ultimately reaching the magazines. About thirty minutes later, a series of great explosions blew her literally in half; her two parts drifted slowly southward, each blazing furiously, for nearly an hour before first the bow, then the stern, disappeared. Strangely enough Nishimura knew nothing of this catastrophe, nor did any of his staff or the other ships of his formation think to notify him of it, for he remained in the belief that his consort was still in formation.

Meanwhile, Commander Phillips with *McDermut* and *Monssen* was approaching from the west. It appears that these ships remained undetected until 0308, when the Japanese opened fire on them, though they were not illuminated. Six salvoes landed all round though not on *Monssen*. Simultaneously the destroyers swerved towards their targets so as to reach their planned firing point. Three minutes later, twenty more torpedoes were speeding towards the luckless Southern Force. Phillips then turned sharply to starboard, retiring very close to the shore-line.

At this moment a bright green light mysteriously appeared in the direction of Leyte — probably a parachute flare from an enemy aircraft. The destroyers were silhouetted against this, a fact of which the Japanese took quick advantage. A searchlight picked up *Monssen*. Several salvoes followed, landing close enough to splash water over her after guns but again not hitting her. Skilful use of smoke coupled with an abrupt turn towards the enemy enabled *Monssen* both to mask the flare and to dodge out of the searchlight beam. *McDermut*, by promptly identifying herself, also managed to prevent two eager PTs, sighted near the beach, from attacking her.

This time Nishimura took evasive action in the form of two simultaneous right-angle turns but since these merely led his own destroyers straight into the path of the torpedoes, he cannot claim much credit for this. At 0320, a fearful destruction befell the Southern Force. A torpedo from *Monssen* struck Nishimura's flagship, battleship *Yamashiro*. Hasty flooding of two magazines prevented a further disaster; as Nishimura signalled to his fellow commanders the hit caused "No impediment to battle cruising".

The Japanese destroyers, however, suffered even more in this strike, for Phillips' *McDermut* achieved the most incredible success of hitting no less than three of these. *Michishio* and *Asagumo* both staggered out of the formation as *Fuso* had done earlier, to come to a halt, drifting uncontrollably according to a signal from Nishimura at the time, the former in a sinking condition, the latter minus her bow. The third destroyer *Yamagumo* blew up, illuminating the strait dazzlingly in one titanic explosion that was seen 20 miles away on Oldendorf's flagship *Louisville*. It is understandable that many authorities consider Phillips' effort the most able torpedo attack of the Pacific War.

Other attacks were soon to follow. Just after 0300, Admiral Berkey ordered Captain McManes with Destroyer Squadron 24 guarding the right flank, to head down the west side of the strait making smoke. This Squadron also advanced in two waves; the former consisting of *Killen, Beale* and HMAS *Arunta*; the latter of *Hutchins* (with McManes on board), *Daly* and *Bache*.

The Action in Surigao Strait

At 0317 the first section, under *Arunta*'s skipper Commander Buchanan RAN, was ordered to attack. Some six minutes later, having reached a good position on the enemy's port bow, *Arunta* fired four torpedoes, the U.S. destroyers following with five each. A torpedo, probably from *Killen*, scored a second hit on *Yamashiro* which caused her to slow temporarily to a mere 5 knots though she quickly built up speed again to 15 knots. The section retired to the north. As they did so, a salvo fell between *Killen* and *Beale* but did no harm.

Hard on the heels of this section came McManes with his three ships. *Hutchins* had a modern combat information room below decks enabling McManes to control the operation from there, "bent over the pale light of a twelve-inch radar-scope, an earphone clamped over his head, and looking" remarks Woodward, "more like a physicist in his laboratory than the captain of a fighting ship in the heat of battle". Despite this advantage, his section, tearing south close ashore, overshot their best firing position. Hastily they reversed course, each launching five torpedoes at about 0330. All missed. *Bache* also contributed gunfire. This of course drew the enemy's attention, 5-inch or 8-inch shells hurtling in the destroyers' direction, while star-shells were sent up in an attempt to illuminate them. Fortunately the Japanese fire, lasting some twelve minutes, was inaccurate though one salvo near-missed *Hutchins*.

Simultaneously, an enemy vessel fired torpedoes at McManes. It is not known from which ship these came but of those carrying torpedoes which were still afloat, *Mogami* did not launch them until later, while *Shigure* never fired at all. Therefore either *Michishio* or *Asagumo* must have been responsible. Both were in a good position to send 'fish' at Section 24, but it seems most probable that *Asagumo* was the aggressor since she was still partially under control whereas *Michishio*, still drifting helplessly, was probably too badly damaged. Also this action indicates a fine spirit which *Asagumo* was later to show in abundance in a fight with American cruisers and destroyers which will be described in due course. During that encounter incidentally she used gunfire only, not torpedoes, which seems an additional indication that she had already expended these.

At any rate, two torpedoes now crossed *Daly*'s bows. They were so close that there was no chance of evasive action, but clearly it was the Americans' lucky night for both just missed. This incident caused Commander Laning, captain of *Hutchins* to remark fervently that: "the enemy torpedo deficiency lies in his religion, not in his ballistics".

McManes now turned in a complete loop then headed north-east while his ships opened fire on *Michishio* and *Asagumo* after 0340. He had intended to press home his attacks on these cripples but nine minutes later Berkey ordered him to retire northward out of danger as the heavy ships were about to open fire. As McManes obeyed, *Hutchins* sent five more torpedoes at *Asagumo*. Since that destroyer was turning slowly at the time, these missed, but American luck was still in for *Michishio* now drifted into the line of fire. Several torpedoes hit her at 0358. She blew up, sinking instantly.

Despite these consistent blows, however, Nishimura with undeniable courage but also with a singular lack of skill doggedly kept heading for the gulf, calling on his ships (including *Fuso* of whose loss he was still unaware) to attack anything they might meet. He did not even try to take advantage of the protection of either shore but stuck in the middle of the strait. Nor did he signal the course of events to Shima, though in fairness he did not have much opportunity. His greatest ordeal was now to befall him.

Although Commander Hubbard's Division was screening the battleships, the nine destroyers of Captain Smoot's Squadron 56 from the left flank were available for one last attack. At 0335, this squadron in obedience to Oldendorf's command: "Launch attack – get the big boys!" sped south at maximum speed for a strike in three waves, one on each of the enemy's flanks with the third heading towards his starboard bow from immediately in front. Yet before any of these ships could get within range, the night was lit up with flashes as the American heavy ships opened fire.

Aboard their battleships or cruisers Oldendorf's officers had waited rigid with excitement as an unbelievable prospect became steadily more attainable. Clearly on their radar screens, they could detect Nishimura's ships, with Shima's well in the rear; both groups still pushing on towards them. If these enemies continued on course the Americans would be able to open fire simultaneously with full broadsides on the Japanese ships while steering across the head of the hostile column; whereas only the front guns of the advancing vessels would be able to reply.

This tactic, known for obvious reasons as 'crossing the T', had only once before been performed successfully. Then ironically the demonstrator had been Admiral Togo, 'the Nelson of Japan', who at the Battle of Tsushima in 1905 had all but annihilated the Tsar's fleet. At Jutland, Admiral Jellicoe had twice put his Grand Fleet into this tactical position but on each occasion his rival Admiral Scheer had

The Action in Surigao Strait

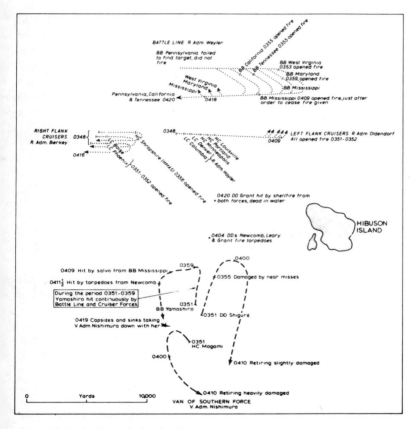

4 Surigao Strait: The Main Gunfire Phase

been able to break away from the trap, largely because he had practised a simultaneous Battle Turn-Away which, skilfully executed, saved the High Seas Fleet from apparently inevitable destruction. As he watched Nishimura's force get ever closer, Oldendorf must have thought that his opponent also would veer away at the last minute. On board the old battleships, dragged up from the mud of Pearl Harbour, the thrilling prospect of a fleet action, all hopes of which had previously seemed vain, was inducing a state of almost unbearable tension among the keyed-up crews. They even half-regretted the destroyers' successes in case these should deprive them of worthwhile targets.

Finally at 0351, when *Yamashiro* was 22,800 yards from the battle line and only 15,600 yards from *Louisville*, Oldendorf gave the long awaited order to open fire. Within a minute the 8-inch guns of *Louisville, Portland* and *Minneapolis*, plus the 6-inch guns of *Denver* and *Columbia* were blazing away at their targets, the first salvo from the flagship temporarily blinding Admiral Oldendorf with its flash since the over-eager gunners had neglected to buzz the usual warning signal. A total of 3,100 rounds was fired by this group of ships, no less than 1,147 of which came from the twelve guns of *Columbia*. Seconds later, the fifteen 6-inch guns mounted on both *Phoenix* and *Boise* of Berkey's group were also in continuous rapid fire, though later they slowed this rate to conserve ammunition.

Next at 0353, the first battleship opened up over the heads of the cruisers. *West Virginia* had the advantages of 16-inch guns and the new Mark-8 fire control radar, but on the other hand, reports Woodward, she had been manned shortly before the battle "by a new crew, the great majority of which — including two of her gun turret officers — had never been to sea before. The third turret officer had come from submarine duty and the fourth from small craft". None the less *West Virginia* led the battleships with a total of ninety-three shells fired. Two minutes later *California* joined in with sixty-three rounds of 14-inch, while *Tennessee* which had been ordered not to shoot until the flagship *Mississippi* did so, decided to mistake *West Virginia* for her, so added sixty-nine more 14 inchers to the weight of attack. Both the 14-inch gunned vessels, it may be noted, fired only in 6-gun salvoes in view of their shortage of ammunition.

Then at 0356, HMAS *Shropshire* which had been having trouble with her radar, added the strength of eight more 8-inch guns from the right flank, while finally at 0359, although *Mississippi* and *Pennsylvania* could not find a target, battleship *Maryland* managed to

The Action in Surigao Strait

locate one by ranging on the splashes from *West Virginia*'s shells; her eight 16-inch guns thereafter firing six full salvoes. The incredible thing is that this whole fantastic barrage lasted no more than eighteen minutes.

Under this "wall of gunfire" as it was called by Captain McManes who was in a good position to judge, the Japanese force, now reduced to one battleship, one heavy cruiser and one destroyer, was helpless. According to Captain Smoot also excellently though somewhat precariously placed to watch the spectacle as the shells roared over his head: "The devastating accuracy of this gunfire was the most beautiful sight I have ever witnessed. The arched line of tracers in the darkness looked like a continual stream of lighted railroad cars going over a hill. No target could be observed at first; then shortly there would be fires and explosions, and another ship would be accounted for." Six-inch, 8-inch, 14-inch, 16-inch shells crashed into *Yamashiro* and *Mogami*. Both vessels burst into flames.

Lucky *Shigure* in contrast suffered comparatively little damage perhaps because the Americans naturally concentrated on the larger targets. Even so Commander Nishino said that his ship underwent "a terrific bombardment". She received only one hit by an 8-inch shell that passed through her without exploding. However, she was straddled repeatedly by 6-inch or 8-inch salvoes. "The ship," reported Nishino, "was constantly trembling from the force of near misses." These put her gyro compass and radio temporarily out of action. They also damaged her rudder, making steering difficult. She had sheered to the east when the firing started so could not make proper contact with or receive orders from her fellow-warships. Her poor radar prevented her from finding targets for her torpedoes, but she fired aimlessly in the general direction of the gun-flashes, without any effect.

Finally just before 0400, *Shigure*'s skipper "decided to withdraw without receiving orders from anyone". The destroyer accordingly went south like a bat out of hell at 30 knots. Shortly afterwards Nishino had to slow down to repair his rudder but despite this carried out his retirement safely. The Commander was undoubtedly shattered by his experience – though in all fairness he had every excuse for this.

Yamashiro and *Mogami*, however, fired back at their torturers with despairing valour. A 14-inch shell near-missed destroyer *Claxton* screening the battle line but it was the only one that came near the battleships probably because the enemy's star-shells fell too short to illuminate them. The cruiser formations were silhouetted against the gun flashes of the battleships; yet although *Denver, Columbia* and

Minneapolis on one flank, and *Shropshire* on the other, were straddled by 14-inch or 8-inch salvoes, fragments of shell being found later on the decks of the first two named, not one hit was achieved by the Japanese.

Indeed more trouble was caused for the Americans by, typically, a misunderstood communication. Shortly after 0400, the battleships which had been steering east when the action opened, turned westward without ceasing fire. The order given was: "Turn One Five" which meant a turn of one hundred and fifty degrees. *California*, however, interpreted this as a turn of fifteen degrees with the result that she interfered with *Tennessee*'s fire for about five minutes. The latter ship narrowly avoided a collision by reversing all her engines at full speed. *California* shortly regained formation. Berkey's cruisers also reversed course to the west at about the same time.

Since these manoeuvres resulted in both groups concerned closing the range on the enemy, an even more accurate fire poured into Nishimura's luckless ships. His flagship swung away to the west burning brightly, apparently at least partially out of control. *Mogami* turned southward, firing her torpedoes by way of a last defiant gesture as she did so. A minute later a full salvo exploded on her bridge killing all the officers present including Captain Tooma. Almost certainly this came from heavy cruiser *Portland* which, despite the innocuous nickname of 'the Sweet Pea' bestowed on her by her crew, had a marvellous fighting record, especially in the Battle of Guadalcanal. Other 8-inch shells found *Mogami*'s engine-room and firerooms, but though she slowed almost to a halt for a time, she was still able to crawl away to safety.

Through the midst of this mêlée raced groups of U.S. destroyers, for while Squadron 56 was attacking, Squadron 24 was retiring up the strait. Commander Buchanan's section was shaken to hear itself described by one of the heavy vessels to the north as "three enemy ships". It retired in haste. Fortunately the error was detected in time.

McManes' three destroyers were able to add to the attacks on the Japanese ships as they raced past them. Their target was *Mogami*, already burning all along her deck. The destroyers hit her repeatedly, observing that "pieces of her superstructure were blasted into the air as each salvo landed". Then, passing on, they opened up on *Yamashiro*, an even more pitiable sight, shaken by great explosions, with gigantic flames rising so high above her whole length that her 5-inch gun mounts stood out clearly against them. Despite her damage she fired on McManes, near-missing *Hutchins* and *Daly*. Again

American luck was in. All McManes' ships came through without a scratch.

Captain Smoot's destroyers were less fortunate. As mentioned, the squadron attacked in three groups. Captain Conley in *Robinson*, with, *Bryant* and *Halford*, approached from the east against the background of Hibuson Island. The enemy fired on them as they advanced but the shots struck well short. Spurred on by Conley's command: "This has to be quick. Stand by your fish!" each destroyer fired five torpedoes at 0354. All of them missed. The section then retired close to the island pursued by further ineffective fire.

At the same time Commander Boulware's group, *Heywood L. Edwards, Bennion* and *Leutze*, came in from the west, firing their torpedoes at *Yamashiro* and *Shigure* three minutes later. Since these ships turned sharply shortly afterwards, Boulware thought his section made no hits. He was right. *Yamashiro* opened fire as the torpedoes were launched. Shell splashes chased the destroyers as they fled towards Leyte under a smoke-screen but yet again no more than near-misses were achieved.

Captain Smoot's own section – *Newcomb, Richard P. Leary* and *Albert W. Grant* – was the one to suffer. Smoot attacked down the middle of the strait aiming for *Yamashiro*'s starboard bow. When, at about 0400, the battleship swung to the west, Smoot's force turned right to parallel her.

Already heavy gunfire from *Yamashiro*, and perhaps from *Mogami* and *Shigure* also, was falling near *Leary* and *Grant*. Commander Terrell Nisewaner, captain of the last-named ship, described this experience as "slightly uncanny and terrifying. One could pick up a slight flash on the Japanese ships and then this pinpoint of light would get bigger and bigger until suddenly, with a roar like a freight train, it would pass close ahead and splash on the opposite side of the ship".

Four minutes later, five torpedoes were fired at the battleships by *Newcomb*, three by *Leary*, and five by *Grant*. Then all turned to zigzag northward while making smoke. This helped them escape the enemy's attentions, but since they were now coming up the middle of the strait not west by the shore-line as instructed, they were mistaken for hostile vessels by their own side. Shells from friend and foe landed all round them. *Newcomb* and *Leary* somehow escaped unhurt but *Grant* was hit nineteen times from the moment that she turned north; eight shells were enemy, probably from *Yamashiro*'s secondary battery, but eleven were 6-inchers from an American light cruiser – probably *Denver* was the unwitting villain of the piece. Heavy cruiser

Louisville also fired on *Grant*, no doubt being devoutly grateful that she scored only near-misses.

These hits reduced *Grant* to a shattered wreck. One shell struck a 40-mm gun, exploding its ammunition. Another knocked out a 5-inch gun turret. Three more hit the front funnel. Yet another burst against the mast, killing most of the radio gang and, as ill-luck would have it, wiping out an entire repair party specially trained for medical assistance. The M.O. Lieutenant (jg) Mathieu was also killed by one of the first hits. The entire after end of the bridge was blown off. A storeroom and the forward berthing compartment were flooded by a hit below the water-line. At least two shells knocked out the forward fireroom and forward engine-room, while smoke and scalding steam pouring from the latter necessitated the abandonment of the after engine-room also. "The situation definitely did not look good to us at this stage of the game," stated Commander Nisewaner. Fearing that the remaining five torpedoes might be exploded by fires or shells, he ordered them to be launched at the enemy, which was done successfully but without result. By 0420, *Grant* was dead in the water, flooding rapidly, with a bad list. All the ship's lighting except emergency circuits went out. All communications had been knocked out. Thirty-four of her crew lay dead, ninety-four more were wounded.

Now came the desperate fight to save her. Handicapped by the loss of key personnel already noted, *Grant*'s crew strove to drag wounded men clear of the threatening flames, to give first aid, to quench the fires and to check flooding. As usual a grim situation brought out the best in everyone. Groping in darkness amidst steam or flame, the damage control parties, somehow managing to overcome all difficulties, kept their ship afloat.

Commander Nisewaner set a splendid example. He seemed everywhere at once, encouraging or assisting his men. After making a tour of the after part of his destroyer, he entered the burning, flooding, steam-filled engine-room to help some badly-wounded men who were trapped there, throwing a heavy blanket from an emergency stretcher over his head to give some slight protection. "It was damned hot, but not utterly unbearable," he reported later. Inside he encountered Gunner's Mate Third Class Howard who on his own initiative had also gone to succour the casualties. Between them, Nisewaner and Howard dragged an injured fireman a rung at a time up the ladder to the safety of the main deck. They then returned, embarking on an agonizing struggle to pull up Fireman Second Class Rothe, a very big man who was too badly injured to move, having been "blinded by

The Action in Surigao Strait 115

steam which had seared his face and literally cooked his eyes and forehead". Inch by inch they crawled up to the hatch where other sailors pulled Rothe clear. Their efforts were in vain, however, for he died of his wounds next morning.

Finally Captain Smoot brought his *Newcomb* alongside *Grant*. The crippled destroyer was pulled clear of the danger zone. Later she was repaired, taking part, like *Birmingham*, in the Okinawa landings. Commander Nisewaner was awarded the Navy Cross; a just reward for his services to his ship and crew.

Meanwhile at 0409, Oldendorf, hearing that his own destroyers were becoming targets for U.S. shells, ordered "Cease Fire". All ships obeyed, but seconds later *Mississippi* at last located a target, landing a full salvo on *Yamashiro*, her gun crews in their excitement immediately reloading. The last shots of this stage of the action had now been discharged. An unearthly silence fell for the Japanese had also stopped firing.

Minutes afterwards, destroyer *Richard P. Leary*, then retiring north towards the battleships, had a narrow escape as four torpedoes, two on each side, just missed her on a parallel course. These were the ones fired by *Mogami* as she retreated. Although they found no victim, they were not wasted, for on receipt of *Leary's* report, Admiral Weyler ordered *Mississippi, West Virginia* and *Maryland* which were in the potential line of fire to turn due north, while the remaining battleships under Rear-Admiral Chandler, which were in some confusion at this time due to the near-collision of *California* and *Tennessee* described earlier, continued westward. These various events deprived the Americans of targets for when Oldendorf ordered a resumption of fire *Mogami* and *Shigure* had made good their escape.

Yamashiro had also turned south as her opponents' guns fell silent. Japanese ships were capable of taking immense punishment as *Yamashiro* demonstrated, for despite her ordeal she was able to increase speed to 15 knots. In the opinion of her senior survivor Lieutenant Ezaki, she could yet have made good her retirement; but less than three minutes later two torpedoes, probably fired by *Newcomb*, ripped open her port side. At 0419, she capsized, sinking instantly. Admiral Nishimura went down with his flagship and only a handful of her crew survived. When rescued, dazed but defiant, by the Americans next day, they refused to give any details of the end of their luckless though courageous "battlewagon".

The end of *Yamashiro* marked also the end of the old tactic whereby capital ships follow each other in a line of battle, combining their fire-power against a hostile force; a device already becoming increasingly rare as air-power made it impossible for ships to maintain station under attack. It was not admittedly the last time that battleships were seen in action for Japanese ones would be engaged later that same day, but these, to their own detriment, would fight as individuals not in battle line. Morison paints a delightful picture of the ghosts of all the great admirals, watching no doubt from Valhalla, from Sir Walter Raleigh who first suggested this tactic and De Ruyter to Togo and Jellicoe – all at the salute as battle line went into oblivion.

Admiral Shima, however, was still heading for Leyte Gulf. At 0400, his force (minus *Abukuma*) was speeding north at 28 knots with his four destroyers scouting ahead of *Nachi* and *Ashigara*. Ahead of him lay a dense cloud of smoke through which the flash of guns, the glitter of tracers and the glare of fires were intermittently visible. He had received previous messages from Nishimura but the last of these, sent just before Oldendorf's heavy ships opened up, had made no mention of the catastrophe to *Fuso*, while at that time of course *Yamashiro* was still fighting fit. Shima had thus had no inkling of the débâcle that had befallen the Van of the Southern Force.

In consequence one can picture his horrified surprise when he sighted the blazing halves of *Fuso* on his starboard bow. When he passed these at 0410, Shima concluded they were both *Fuso* and *Yamashiro*. The shock that this must have been can be better imagined than described. Immediately afterwards, he was further shaken to sight, first damaged *Shigure* then, the burning *Mogami*, appearing to be dead in the water though in fact still moving at low speed. Both these ships were correctly identified, thus increasing Shima's despair.

As the Second Striking Force loomed out of the darkness, *Shigure* challenged with her flashlight. "I am the *Nachi*" signalled Shima's flagship. "I am the *Shigure*" retorted Commander Nishino "I have rudder difficulties." It seems incredible that he should give no details of his squadron's fate, indeed no further information of any sort, but it scarcely mattered for by now Shima was only too aware that Nishimura had met with disaster.

At this inauspicious moment, *Nachi*'s radar picked up two objects ahead on the starboard bow. Shima's destroyers, however, which had been pressing on further northward than the cruisers could not find any targets so were unable to launch torpedoes. There is also some discussion about the nature of those located by *Nachi*. One unkind

The Action in Surigao Strait 117

suggestion is that they were Hibuson Island and a near-by islet. Most probably, however, Shima's radar was not quite as bad as that, and his potential victims were *Louisville* and *Portland*.

In any case, shortly after 0420, Shima swung *Nachi* and *Ashigara* in a ninety-degree turn east so that they could fire their torpedoes wide of *Mogami*, while avoiding the risk of being silhouetted against her flames. Each cruiser fired eight torpedoes. These had not the slightest effect, although a couple of them were later found on the beach at Hibuson – hence of course the probably incorrect assertion that Shima had attacked the island. He then recalled his destroyers, and was preparing to retire south when yet a further misfortune befell him.

When Shima had made his torpedo attack, he believed that *Mogami* was dead in the water, so his own ships would easily pass clear of her. However, the battered heavy cruiser was in reality moving at 8 knots, although in the dense smoke surrounding them, the Japanese cannot be blamed for not realizing this. *Mogami* attempted to join Shima's column, but as she was scarcely under control, she now yawed towards *Nachi*. By the time the torpedoes were launched – all officers on *Nachi*'s bridge having had their attention fixed on this task – the two vessels were almost on top of each other. In a frenzied effort to avoid collision *Nachi*'s wheel was put hard over and both her engines were stopped but amidst showers of sparks the cruisers met with a hideous grating of steel. *Mogami* suffered further bad damage. *Nachi* was holed in her port side near the stern; this caused flooding which reduced her speed to 18 knots. She retreated under a smoke-screen to investigate her injuries. *Ashigara* which had turned safely took up a position astern. *Mogami* after manoeuvring while she regained control, somehow managed to make sufficient speed to fall in behind. Shima's destroyers and *Shigure* also withdrew.

When Shima recalled his destroyers he informed his chief, Vice-Admiral Mikawa in Manila, that his force having delivered its attack was "retiring from the battle area to plan subsequent action". Of this Morison remarks: "Shima had unusual discretion for a Japanese Admiral" but here he may well be doing Shima an injustice for this signal was made before *Nachi* collided with *Mogami* and Shima probably did intend further attacks at that stage. Even after the collision, having assessed *Nachi*'s damage, at about 0500 he led his force – now including *Mogami* – northward again. On reflection, however, prudence soon asserted itself. As the first streaks of dawn began to appear, he finally changed course for the last time, heading for the safety of the Mindanao Sea.

Most authorities tend to deride Shima's exploits. Thus for example James A. Field in *The Japanese at Leyte Gulf: The Sho Operation* refers to his "tragicomic efforts in Surigao Strait". This also is unjust. Shima with only three cruisers, two of which were heavily damaged, plus his handful of destroyers stood no chance against the overwhelming American numbers. Nor did his knowledge of the movements of friendly forces give any comfort. He realized Nishimura's ships had been obliterated. He had had no recent information from either the Northern or the Central Force. Even if all went well for Kurita, he could not possibly arrive for several hours. Shima therefore was surely quite right in deciding it was futile to offer up his own vessels in a fruitless sacrifice.

Indeed it was just as well that Shima waited no longer, for shortly after 0430, Oldendorf, having detected his movements by radar, was on his track. Morison, among others, has criticized Oldendorf for not ordering a pursuit earlier as well as for proceeding with caution when he did so. This again seems unfair. It was in fact highly fortunate that he did not send ships southward earlier, since they might well have had an unpleasant encounter with Shima's destroyers then looking eagerly for targets for their torpedoes. As for the caution with which Seventh Fleet advanced, hindsight makes it clear that this was regrettable, yet Oldendorf was surely correct to ensure he did not mar the victory he knew was already won by incurring casualties through counter-attacking too recklessly. He could not know that there were no enemy destroyers lying in wait for a chance to deal out lethal vengeance on their pursuers. It is scarcely arguable that in the circumstances he was right not to risk this possibility.

Of Oldendorf's vessels, the cruisers of the right flank never made contact, ultimately turning back at about 0540. Commander Hubbard's 'X-Ray' Division of destroyers, the only one which had not fired torpedoes, now received orders to chase the retiring Japanese to remedy this. Unfortunately half-an-hour elapsed before the division could form up for the hunt. Hubbard then charged south at 25 knots but Shima had too good a start. At 0535, the 'X-Ray boys' were ordered to join the screen of Oldendorf's left flank cruisers.

Oldendorf's own group had been the first of the pursuers. Screened by Smoot's destroyers, less crippled *Grant* and her rescuer *Newcomb*, they advanced cautiously at 15 knots, but just before 0530, in a dim half-light, they sighted Shima's column. Most of the enemy ships increased speed but *Mogami*, unable to keep up with them, again became a target for American gunfire.

The Action in Surigao Strait

Louisville, Portland and *Denver* all now concentrated on the burning cruiser. All scored direct hits. *Mogami*'s fires blazed up again, spreading from bow to stern. From *Louisville* she appeared "burning like a city block". According to Captain Curts of *Columbia*, she was "completely ablaze and burning worse than the *Arizona* burned at Pearl Harbour" – *Arizona* incidentally had blown up! But nothing it seemed could stop *Mogami*. Japanese ships were notorious for the amount of punishment they could take but this one was quite exceptional. She continued steaming southward.

At the same time, another target which the Americans believed was a destroyer, was silhouetted against the cruiser's flames. Several ships fired on her. It was reported that she also burst into flames. Assuming this was not another case of wishful thinking, which seems improbable, this could only have been *Asagumo*, the destroyer that had lost her bow at the start of the action. None of Shima's destroyers were damaged. Further, it seems that all were well south of *Mogami* at this time. *Asagumo*, however, lay stationary very near the Japanese line of retreat. Also when encountered by the Americans in daylight, apart from her missing bow she revealed other damage in the form of heavy smoke pouring from her stern. This could only have been caused by Oldendorf's group, for though it is just possible that she received damage from McManes' gunfire earlier, he reported none – in any case it seems incredible that she had not yet been able to quench any fires started almost three and a half hours earlier.

At 0537, Oldendorf, still concerned lest his opponents counter-attacked with torpedoes, broke off the action to turn north. However, as light increased, reducing any chance of a successful ambush, he turned back again. The sun rose at 0630. Shortly afterwards, Oldendorf detached Admiral Hayler with light cruisers *Denver* and *Columbia* escorted by destroyers *Claxton, Cony* and *Thorn*, "to polish off enemy cripples".

Meanwhile the indefatigable PT boats were trying to do some polishing off on their own account. *PT321, PT326* and *PT327* attacked *Shigure* at 0455 without success. The destroyer fired on them, inflicting one hit but no damage on the first-named. All other encounters came after 0600, by which time the odds were heavily in favour of the Japanese since it was now light enough for them to see their attackers long before they came within range – not that that stopped the PTs keeping up the pressure.

Next sighting was by Lieutenant (jg) Thronson of *PT491* who had been well to the fore during Nishimura's approach. He located the battered *Mogami* now down to 6 knots, burning strongly aft — but it took more than a motor-torpedo-boat to daunt that fighting warship. She promptly concentrated 8-inch gunfire on Thronson as he trailed her endeavouring to signal his news in the face of attempts to jam his wireless. Some of the shells came very close, splashing water over the decks of the PT boat. She launched two torpedoes but, missing, retired — still chased by the fire of her formidable antagonist.

Shima also was spotted at about 0620 by a section consisting of *PT150*, *PT194* and *PT196*. The first of these fired a torpedo at *Nachi* without success. Shima returned the fire hitting *PT194*, seriously wounding three of her crew. The PTs were forced to keep their distance. Ten minutes later, *PT190* sighted Shima's force. Two destroyers immediately dashed at her, firing as they came, causing her to retire smartly under a smoke-screen. The Japanese then moved close to the shore of Mindanao, thereby avoiding further interference from their tormentors. Keeping destroyers *Ushio* and *Shiranuhi* with his heavy cruisers, Shima detached *Kasumi* to locate and assist *Abukuma*, limping home alone, and *Akebono* to protect *Mogami*.

That heavy cruiser had still not escaped the attentions of the PTs, but by 0645 when she was picked up by *PT137*, she had been able to put repairs in hand, enabling her to raise her speed considerably as she sought to catch up with Shima. Also *Akebono* was now guarding her. Both cruiser and destroyer fired on the PT boat, driving her off. *PT489*, *PT492* and *PT495* spotted *Mogami* five minutes later — the last sighting made by the little boats. They were unable to attack since she was heading for safety "at high speed".

By this time the ghastly flotsam left by the action was clearly exposed. Smouldering wreckage littered the strait. Great patches of oil dotted the surface of the sea. Among the debris large numbers of survivors were sighted, many badly injured, most covered with fuel. The American destroyers offered aid, as they did throughout the day, but true to their standards, most of the Japanese preferred to die rather than pass into captivity. *Claxton* saw an officer ordering his men not to surrender, but in fact they showed precious little inclination to do this without the need for any urging against it. When *Halford* came alongside a small boat, the survivors crowded aboard it promptly sprang over the side. Only a minute handful of men would accept the proffered assistance.

The slaughter was still not over. Two very gallant survivors of Nishimura's force were soon to perish also. *Asagumo*, unable to escape, was attacked by all five of Hayler's ships at 0707. She

The Action in Surigao Strait

returned their fire with her after turret, blazing back with magnificent spirit as the cruisers' fire crushed her. She sank by the bow at 0721, firing her last salvo as her stern disappeared under the waters.

No further targets remained for American gunfire, but their airpower was now to show itself again. When he had commenced his pursuit, Oldendorf, on notifying Kinkaid, had suggested an air strike be launched on the fleeing enemy. Seventh Fleet's Commander had anticipated such a demand, so even while *Asagumo* offered her last resistance, Avenger torpedo-bombers from Sprague's escort carriers were on their way with their covering fighters, bent on wiping out as many of her companions as possible.

These aircraft made their first raid shortly after 0830 — without result. About forty minutes later, however, another wave attacked. Two torpedoes at last inflicted fatal injuries on the incredible *Mogami*. Even then this great fighting ship performed her last service to her crew by remaining afloat for over three hours while they were taken off safely by *Akebono*, which then had to put yet another torpedo into the cruiser before she finally went down.

The end of *Mogami* may also be taken as the virtual end of Nishimura's command — only *Shigure* returned home. It was also the close of the fighting in or near Surigao Strait. No one would deny that the Americans had heavy odds in their favour, yet the use they made of their strength was spectacular. The PTs' contact reports; the shattering torpedo-assaults by the destroyers; the way the battle line so beautifully 'crossed the T'; the use of aircraft in the pursuit — all speak highly of the abilities of Admirals Kinkaid and Oldendorf, their officers and their men; "a perfect ambush and an almost flawless attack" was how Admiral Nimitz described their achievement. It was gained moreover at the cost of only a handful of lives, damage to one destroyer and the loss of one PT boat. Nobody knows how many Japanese died that night, it may well have been over 5,000.

At 0728, Kinkaid felt able to signal a typically simple though hearty "Well done!" to the victors. "Please" added the Admiral to correspondents crowding round him for his comments "don't say I made any dramatic statements. You know I am incapable of that." The southern arm of the Japanese pincers was irretrievably broken.

6

The Action off Cape Engano

Dawn on 25 October saw two further naval actions about to commence, each hundreds of miles apart from that in Surigao Strait and from each other. The first of these took place off the north-eastern tip of Luzon, Cape Engano — so named by a sixteenth-century Spanish navigator possessed apparently of second sight. To Cape Deception on the morning of the twenty-fifth, came Admiral Ozawa with his decoys. They were there to die for their Emperor and by their sacrifice to clear the way for the approach of Kurita's battleships. With the pitiful total of twenty-nine aircraft, mostly fighters, at their disposal, they could neither defend themselves adequately nor even have the satisfaction of hitting back at their attackers. Nor were they unaware of their prospective fate. "I expected complete destruction of my fleet," stated Ozawa after the war "but if Kurita's mission was carried out. that was all I wished." "Our ships would be sunk," carefully explained his Chief of Staff, Captain Toshikazu Ohmae "because we went too near [to Third Fleet] on purpose to lure your ships to the north. Surely we would be sunk; that was our mission."

During the night, Ozawa had steered various courses while maintaining roughly the same distance (some 200 miles) from Cape Engano. He did not want to sail too far south in order that he could pull Halsey as far as possible from San Bernardino Strait. By about 0700, he had been rejoined by Matsuda's advance force, which, since he had sent two picket destroyers home, put a total of seventeen ships under his command. The Northern Force now steamed north-east at 20 knots with the light cruisers and destroyers grouped in two circles, one centred on *Chitose, Chiyoda* and *Hyuga*, the other round *Zuikaku, Zuiho* and *Ise*. These positions were adopted as the best for anti-aircraft protection, for the Japanese were only too conscious that their enemies would not long delay their onslaught. Grimly but defiantly they awaited their executioners, for their only concern was still to entice the Americans ever further north — they must have been extraordinarily unselfish as well as intensely gallant men — it would be worse than unchivalrous to fail to acknowledge this.

With the poverty of the Japanese forces may be contrasted the opulence of those of the Americans. At 2345, Task Groups 38:2 and 38:4 then heading north joined up with Sherman's Group 3, after which Admiral Mitscher that past-master of carrier warfare who was now directed to take tactical command, had under him sixty-five vessels including six fine modern battleships, five fleet carriers and five light carriers. The carriers between them held 401 fighters, 214 dive-bombers and 171 torpedo-planes, (plus three survivors from *Princeton*). In addition, McCain's Group 1 containing three fleet carriers and two light carriers was ordered to rendezvous with Captain Acuff's tankers prior to steaming north to join in the attack on Ozawa also as soon as practicable. With this strength at his command Mitscher would have no difficulty in dealing with his opponent provided only that he could find him. At 0100, *Independence* launched five radar-equipped search-planes to do that. Forty minutes later she also flew off two night-fighters to deal with a Japanese 'snooper' that had appeared on the radar screen. This turned out to be a four-engined 'Mavis' flying-boat which the Hellcats promptly shot down.

First sighting came at 0208 when Matsuda's battleships were picked up heading north-east – although they were not correctly identified. Half an hour later, Ozawa's carriers were also observed proceeding on a converging course to that of the battleships with which they were reunited before 0700. At that time they were still 210 miles from Mitscher but, probably because of yet another fault in transmission, that officer believed that his prey was only some 90 miles distant.

Since this would mean that action might well be joined within two hours, Mitscher decided that battle line should now be formed. Halsey approved his recommendation, whereupon Mitscher promptly ordered Admiral Lee to form Task Force 34[1] taking station 10 miles north of *Lexington*, Mitscher's flagship. Mitscher also ordered a change of course from north-east to north so as to close the Northern Force more rapdily.

Task Force 34, thus finally constituted, consisted of all six

---

[1] It will be recalled that Mitscher originally believed that only two battleships would go north with him as a result of Halsey's message that Task Force 34 "will be formed". Later he had learned that all the capital ships were going north, and as described his staff had unsuccessfully urged him to advise Halsey that he should leave some of them guarding San Bernardino.

battleships, *Washington* (Lee's flagship), *Alabama, Iowa, New Jersey, Massachusetts* and *South Dakota*, escorted by heavy cruisers *Wichita* and *New Orleans*, light cruisers *Vincennes, Miami, Biloxi, Santa Fe* and *Mobile*, and eighteen destroyers drawn from all the task groups. They took some time forming up in the dark, so, to assist them, the carrier groups slowed to 10 knots. This delay did no harm, however, for of course the enemy carriers were not nearly as close as reported.

With Task Force 34 at last in being, it seemed that Lee's splendid fast 16-inch gunned battleships would now come into their own. The Americans' plan was that their airmen would strike at the Japanese over the heads of the surface vessels. Then these would hurl themselves upon any stragglers or cripples that the planes left, while also engaging *Hyuga* and *Ise* in a gunnery duel. Any two of Lee's battleships could outclass the Japanese battleship-carriers, and he had six under his command. Through the early morning hours, the big ships' crews waited eagerly for the chance of combat. On the carriers also an atmosphere of tense expectation prevailed. At 0430, Mitscher ordered them all to be prepared to launch combat air patrols plus a bombing-raid at earliest dawn. The deck crews at once commenced arming their planes; the air-crews tried to take a final rest before action. It appeared impossible that anything could prevent Halsey's objective – the annihilation of the Northern Force – from being attained.

Yet already irritating difficulties had arisen which although not ultimately harmful in themselves, prophesied graver troubles for the future. The scout from *Independence* that was trailing Ozawa was forced to return by engine trouble. A relief plane which was sent out, suffering difficulties with its radar, was unable to find the enemy, even reporting the American fleet as hostile. Other planes also sought the elusive Japanese carriers later, but in vain. Only one report came in and that was merely of two destroyers far to the north – presumably pickets *Fuyutsuki* and *Suzutsuki* on their way home. Mitscher therefore ordered that dawn searches be made, sectors for these being assigned west and north-west.

With the first streaks of dawn shortly before 0600, the carriers of all three task groups turned into the wind. An endless succession of aircraft roared off their decks; first combat air patrol; next search-planes from *Lexington*; finally the first strike group. Mitscher did not wait for the scouts to discover the enemy before ordering off this raid, since that would have cost too much time. Instead this force, numbering sixty-five bombers and fifty-five torpedo-planes escorted by sixty fighters, selected from all the task groups and including airmen from *Franklin* and *Enterprise* who had already attacked both Nishimura and Kurita, all under the control of Commander David McCampbell the all-time record-breaker of the previous day from *Essex* who was named as target co-ordinator, was instructed to orbit well ahead of Task Force 38 until the enemy vessels were again picked up. This scheme of course would only prove of value if the Japanese were spotted within a reasonable time. It can be imagined that Mitscher's anxiety increased as the minutes passed without his searches discovering anything in the expected position.

Two of Mitscher's intelligence officers, Lieutenants Cheston and White, meanwhile were insisting that the enemy were east of due north in a sector not previously covered. Fighters from combat air patrol were sent to reconnoitre this area. At 0710, one sighted Ozawa's reunited ships which had just turned northward, 145 miles from Mitscher.[2] It was a perfect flying day, there was a calm sea, a clear blue sky with just a few clouds on the horizon and a light breeze. McCampbell's airmen were at once directed to their victims.

Ozawa of course had been expecting this. He had watched the scout-planes for some time before the attack began – accounts vary but probably this was at about 0830. He sent a signal to Kurita that his diversion had succeeded but as usual communications were deficient – the message was never received. His gun crews were closed up, waiting. Because of his shortage of aircraft, they would have to be his main defensive weapon.

All the reports of his reconnaissance planes notified Halsey of his foe's weakness in the air – as he stated in his report, he was "puzzled by the fact that there were scarcely any planes on the decks of, or in the air near the enemy force, and no signs of 'bogeys' around our own force". However, it did not occur to him that the warnings of Lee and others might be confirmed by this; he believed instead that the Japanese had been taken by surprise. Indeed even after the war he preferred to be "still far from sure that Ozawa's force was intended solely as a lure" – regardless of the fact that Japanese records for months before, during and after the *Sho* operation make it quite clear that it was – as of course does his own description just quoted. MacArthur, Nimitz, Kinkaid, Mitscher, Sprague, Lee – all accepted that the Northern Force was merely bait, but Halsey resolutely refused to be convinced.

[2]McCain had also sent out search planes which located the Japanese later.

In reality, Ozawa who had also sent out searchers, had only fifteen Zeros manned by inexperienced pilots as fighter protection. Most of these were on board *Zuiho*. When the first raid was sighted this light carrier pulled out of formation to launch her tiny band. They rushed into the heart of the enemy squadrons, downing one Avenger and damaging others before the hordes of American fighters shot down at least nine of them. Presumably the others were also destroyed or else perished when their fuel was exhausted. There was no further interference from enemy fighters during the action off Cape Engano.

Now the attackers swarmed down on the luckless Northern Force. The Helldiver bombers struck first, closely followed by strafing fighters to draw the enemy's fire from the Avenger torpedo-planes releasing their torpedoes from close range. As they approached, the Japanese ships twisted and turned in desperate evasive actions while sending up intense, accurate fire, the bursts and tracers being coloured to identify the shooting of individual ships. *Hyuga* and *Ise* blazed away with their main batteries at long range and there was "a new shell that sent whirling spring-like brass wires into the air". Pilots also reported "white bursts of phosphorus with long tentacles". These undoubtedly came from the battleship-carriers which in addition to sixteen 5-inch and no less than one hundred and eight 25-mm A.A. guns each, also carried one hundred and eighty 5-inch rocket launchers, the rockets containing phosphorus and trailing long wires; these proved more impressive than effective, however. So thick were the bursts of gunfire that they left a heavy haze over the enemy vessels and made formations like cumulus clouds.

During the day the Japanese gunners claimed surprisingly few victims — only ten of Mitscher's aircraft were shot down by them, though many others were seriously damaged or returned with shell-holes in the wings, or minus a wingtip or an aileron. However, the fury of the barrage did much to prevent the Americans from obtaining that overwhelming destruction which constant massed attacks free from fighter opposition might otherwise have made certain. Comparatively the Third Fleet airmen did not inflict as much damage as their companions in the escort carriers of Seventh Fleet were to do, nor as much as their predecessors had done at Midway. On the other hand if Morison is right in claiming that the anti-aircraft fire of Ozawa's ships "especially *Ise*'s and *Hyuga*'s was perhaps the most deadly on either side in the Pacific War", the pilots had every excuse for allowing their aim to be spoiled.

The first attack, however, provided a fine beginning. As usual it is

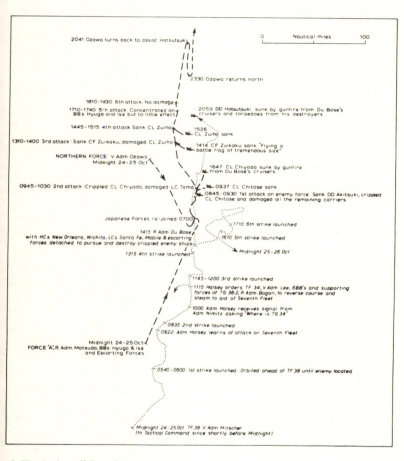

5 The Action off Cape Engano

impossible to determine who did what in the midst of the exaggerated claims made. Also the Americans' ship-identification was definitely not good. There is no doubt at all, however, that light carrier *Chitose* received several bomb-hits including three below the water-line. Since the dive-bombers from *Essex* claimed eight direct hits on a light carrier while *Lexington*'s dive-bombers claimed more on the same ship and the Avengers from *Essex* also (apparently incorrectly) thought they made two torpedo-hits on the same one, it seems that these were the planes that went for *Chitose* — reports that they attacked *Zuiho* must be considered inaccurate as only *Chitose* suffered mass-hits of this nature. Also since the ship thus attacked was reported as burning, exploding and listing, it could only have been *Chitose* for neither of the other light carriers was badly damaged in this raid. *Chitose* staggered to a halt, to sink at 0937.

Of her fellows, *Zuiho*, dodging several torpedoes, suffered one hit from the *Intrepid* dive-bombers which did not slow her down. *Chiyoda* may also have been damaged for McCampbell claimed that all four Japanese carriers were hit; if so her injuries were not serious either. Big *Zuikaku* was less lucky. The torpedo-bombers of *Intrepid* and *San Jacinto* which attacked her scored one hit aft that wrecked her communication system, gave her a slight list and so damaged her steering control that she became partially unmanoeuvrable, being steered awkwardly by hand. With her speed reduced to 18 knots, she nevertheless pushed on northward leaving a long trail of oil in her wake.

Of the smaller targets, destroyer *Akitsuki* was mysteriously sunk — one says this since none of the American accounts indicate what happened to her. It was reported, however, that "a violent explosion was seen on a light cruiser after a torpedo hit". Most authorities claim that this victim was *Tama* which certainly was hit early on. However, as will be seen, there were several claims for hits on light cruisers in the second raid of the day which all but merged with the end of the first attack — the Japanese considered them as one. Morison believes that *Tama* was hit in the second raid which is probably right in view of these claims — the more so since apparently she only fell out of formation after this attack, although admittedly the lapse of time was not great in any event. In this case the victim of the explosion could only have been *Akitsuki*. She was one of the large *Terutsuki*-class destroyers which pilots constantly mistook for light cruisers. This supposition seems confirmed by the Japanese accounts of the raid which state that *Akitsuki* was the first ship they lost and that she blew up —

Cape Engano: attack on Ozawa's carriers

Carrier *Zuikaku* under attack

Light carrier *Zuiho* under attack

Battleship *Ise* under attack

Samar Island: destroyer *Heermann*

Escort carrier *Kitkun Bay* launches Avengers

Escort carrier *Gambier Bay* and destroyers lay smoke

Gambier Bay and destroyers under fire

Gambier Bay dead in the water, shelled by a heavy cruiser on the horizon

Last sight of *Gambier Bay*, left behind to her fate

Kamikaze: attack on escort carrier *Sangamon*

Kamikaze: the end of escort carrier *St Lo*

with a "violent explosion" presumably.

Meanwhile the second raid was already approaching — a much smaller one this, consisting of only six Helldivers and sixteen Avengers escorted by fourteen fighters, the aircraft coming from *Lexington* and *Langley* of Group 3 and *Franklin, San Jacinto* and *Belleau Wood* of Group 4. Bad luck pursued this formation at the start for damage caused when launching prevented the five Avengers from *Langley* from dropping their torpedoes successfully. On the other hand, by arriving on the heels of the first wave the pilots were able to attack while the Northern Force was still in confusion and they were also able to receive useful advice from the returning airmen of the former strike by radio.

As these planes headed for their prey, Fukudome's land-based air forces made their only contribution to the action. A group of about twenty-five aircraft was sighted on the radar making for Davison's command. Fighters were sent out to meet them, whereupon the inexperienced Japanese turned back still some 80 miles from the carriers. No further interference from the air interrupted the slaughter of the decoys.

This continued as the second wave pressed home its attack around 1000. The Helldivers from *Lexington* and *Franklin* went for light carrier *Chiyoda*. Two hits set her afire, then a third disabled her engines, bringing her to a halt. Several torpedo-hits were claimed by the Avengers on light cruisers. One of these was almost certainly that which wounded *Tama*. A light cruiser was reported "dead in the water" after this raid — this was an exaggeration for *Tama*'s speed was reduced to about 10 knots but she continued her flight trailing oil. Several other hits claimed on carriers or battleships were mere wishful thinking.

Chiyoda, however, really was dead in the water. Ozawa, proceeding northward with his main force, instructed Matsuda with the battleship-carrier *Hyuga*, light cruiser *Isuzu* and destroyers *Shimotsuki* and *Maki* to take her in tow, or if that failed, to rescue survivors. These vessels therefore split away from the main body and, hovering around the crippled carrier, they made splendid potential victims for Task Force 34.

There was now a lull in the air attacks. Ozawa's staff took advantage of this to urge the Admiral to abandon his flagship since the damage to her steering and that to her communication system, which if it never seemed able to contact Kurita had at least allowed him to control the vessels in his own force, was preventing him from fully exercising his command. Ozawa was by no means certain that he wished this. "What is the good?" he asked bitterly, "All my vessels are destined to be sunk. Our task is accomplished. I want to die in the *Zuikaku*." Finally, however, he accepted the pleas of his staff, transferring by way of a small boat to light cruiser *Oyodo* at about 1100 hours. The crews of *Zuikaku* and *Zuiho* which between them had been present at every carrier battle of the Pacific War[3] were well aware that they at least had rendered their last service and were inevitably doomed; but in the true *Samurai* tradition they hoisted their battle-flags and prepared to die bravely.

Yet if there was bitterness on the bridge of the *Zuikaku*, by now there was a harrowing anxiety on *New Jersey* as the reason for the Northern Force's sacrifice began to become dreadfully clear. First intimation came at 0822 in a frantic signal from Kinkaid sent off at 0707. Japanese battleships and cruisers, stated this message, were firing on the most northern of the escort carrier units. The seriousness with which Seventh Fleet's Commander regarded the situation was shown by the fact that he had not allowed time to be wasted in coding the signal but had sent it in plain English.

The previous evening Halsey had been confident that he could "return in time" to relieve any "temporarily tight situation" in the south, but now that that situation had arisen with a vengeance he discovered that he was too far north – over 350 miles from Leyte Gulf – to do this. Yet ever consistent in his inconsistency, he apparently remained unperturbed by the news. "I figured," he stated later, "that the sixteen little carriers had enough planes to protect themselves until Oldendorf could bring up his heavy ships." This remark of course overlooks the fact that the escort carrier pilots were trained and equipped for ground-support and anti-submarine work, not for attacking an enemy fleet. But even if Halsey thought that the escort carriers would be able to hold off Kurita for a time, it still seems strange that he did not at once detach part of his own force to steam to their assistance. The results which would have followed had he done so will be considered later.

He did not do so. Indeed his next order was to Lee: "Close enemy at 25 knots" – the enemy in question being Ozawa not Kurita.

[3]*Zuikaku* had been at Pearl Harbour, Coral Sea and Eastern Solomons; *Zuiho* at Midway (though, fortunately for her, not in the Carrier Striking Force but with the supporting Covering Group); both had taken part in the Battles of Santa Cruz and Philippine Sea.

However, after a short delay, at 0848 he did cancel previous orders to McCain to join in the strikes on the Northern Force, instead instructing him to steam south-west at his maximum speed in order to launch attacks on Kurita as soon as possible. Task Group 38:1 was at that time still refuelling, some 260 miles south-east of Halsey. McCain seems to have appreciated the danger of the situation far more quickly than his superior, for he cast off from the tankers at once, to charge to Seventh Fleet's aid at 30 knots. Unfortunately, he was then rather farther away from Kurita than Halsey was. It would take him more than an hour and a half before his group could reach a position from which he could launch his planes even at their extreme range of some 340 miles; it would take another hour and a half before those planes could reach the target-zone.

Meanwhile as Task Force 34 sped onwards, pulling more than 20 miles ahead of Mitscher's carriers, a ceaseless flood of messages poured in upon Halsey's dismayed staff. Rear-Admiral Clifton Sprague commanding the unit under attack sent Halsey an appeal for help, reporting that he was under fire from battleships and cruisers. A whole series of signals, many in plain English, continued to come from Kinkaid who of course was responsible for the safety not only of the escort carriers but of MacArthur's army ashore. Again and again he called for assistance from Third Fleet: "Request Lee proceed top speed to cover Leyte; request immediate strike by fast carriers"; "Help needed from heavy ships immediately"; "Situation critical, battleships and fast carrier strike wanted to prevent enemy penetrating Leyte Gulf." Halsey also received the grim news that the enemy's strength amounted to four battleships and eight cruisers plus supporting craft while Kinkaid notified him that Oldendorf's capital ships were short of ammunition after their night encounter. Halsey replied that McCain was on his way to assist, yet his own command still raced north.

Then at 1000 came a message from Admiral Nimitz about which discussion still rages. The Admiral, it will be remembered, had believed like most other people that Task Force 34 would be guarding San Bernardino Strait. Amazed by the attack on Sprague, he "at length felt compelled to intervene". He sent a curt reminder to Halsey:[4] "Where is, repeat where is Task Force 34?" This message

[4]Some writers have maintained that this signal was merely "a query about the situation rather than an order" but this cannot be maintained in the face of Nimitz's own statement that it was "a prod" which Halsey recognized as such.

was in code, which was unfortunate because it was an American security procedure to add random phrases — 'padding' — at both ends of every signal to reduce the chances of the enemy breaking the cyphers by intelligent deduction of their contents. This 'padding' which was always separated from the text by double letters was supposed to be meaningless. Thus, before Nimitz's message as quoted above, the encoding yeoman at Pearl Harbour added "Turkey trots to water GG"; but after it he added "RR the world wonders".[5] The decoding yeoman on *New Jersey* tore off the first padding as orders prescribed but the latter seemed so plausible that, despite the double letters preceding it, he decided it was part of the message. In consequence, though Kinkaid to whom the signal was sent for information received it in its correct form with the last three words omitted, they were still included in the version sent to Halsey.

That fiery character was not pleased by the message even as originally worded. His anger was increased by Nimitz having addressed copies to Admirals King and Kinkaid. When he spotted the 'padding', he was furious, believing that he had received "a calculated insult" from his chief. He brooded over this, for almost an hour, receiving another appeal from Kinkaid in the meantime; then shortly before 1100, Nimitz's 'prod' with its implication that the Admiral was concerned for the safety of Seventh Fleet had its effect. Halsey ordered his battleships to change course to due south, informing Nimitz and Kinkaid of his decision shortly afterwards. At 1115, Task Force 34 turned away from Ozawa. At that time the group of cripples left by the second air raid were no more than 45 miles ahead.

Matters now went from bad to worse. The big ships steamed south at only 20 knots. As they passed Mitscher's carriers, still pushing northward, Halsey detached heavy cruisers *Wichita* and *New Orleans*, light cruisers *Santa Fe* and *Mobile* and ten destroyers for additional surface support for Mitscher, but in exchange he added Admiral Bogan's Group 2 — fleet carrier *Intrepid* and light carriers *Cabot* and *Independence* — to Lee's force in order to supply air cover. Thus ironically he finally divided his command in the very manner that Bogan and Lee had wished him to do when the Northern Force was first discovered.

This re-organization imposed a frustrating delay. Then at 1345, the

---

[5]It has been suggested that he had been reading Tennyson's "Charge of the Light Brigade" — if so it was appropriate reading for Balaclava had also been fought on 25 October, ninety years earlier.

The Action off Cape Engano

battleships slowed to only 12 knots so that they could refuel those destroyers that were especially in need of this. Since this caused a further delay of two and a half hours, Morison is of the opinion that Halsey should have proceeded at once to help Seventh Fleet, leaving these destroyers behind. This clearly would have been a risk, though less great than some that Halsey had previously taken as well as others that he would take in the immediate future.

After the battle, Halsey stated that his turn south was his "gravest error". He lamented that "I turned my back on the opportunity I had dreamed of since my days as a cadet". Yet it is doubtful whether this was in itself an error. The great mistake occurred on the previous evening when Halsey as a result of several misapprehensions had insisted on taking his entire strength in pursuit of Ozawa leaving Kurita with a trouble-free run through San Bernardino Strait — an action which has already been discussed in detail.

Part at least of this error could have been retrieved had Halsey immediately sent some of his forces south on his first receipt of the news of Kurita's attack on Sprague. Had he then steamed south at full speed instead of continuing northward for two and a half hours, he would have been nearly 150 miles closer to Kurita by 1115 when Task Force 34 finally did put about. As described, further time was then lost by refuelling. If Halsey had responded at once to the calls for help while also avoiding this later delay, he would, as it happens, still not have been a factor in rescuing the escort carriers — they saved themselves — but he would have been able to bring six battleships under Admiral Lee, the most experienced battle-squadron commander in the U.S. Navy, across San Bernardino, blocking the escape-route of Kurita, who was later to retire through this strait. In this position Lee could have 'crossed Kurita's T' thereby almost certainly ensuring the complete destruction of the Japanese force.

Then at 1622, when fuelling was finally carried out, Halsey made another extraordinary move. Having once abandoned "the time-honoured principle of concentration" in the name of which he had not left even a single destroyer to watch San Bernardino, he proceeded to split up his command still further. Task Force 34 was dissolved. In its stead Task Force 34:5 was formed under the command of Rear-Admiral Oscar Badger to whom were entrusted the fastest of the battleships, his flagship *Iowa* and Halsey's *New Jersey*. Escorted by light cruisers *Vincennes, Miami* and *Biloxi* together with eight destroyers, these dashed south at 28 knots, drawing some 40 miles ahead of Bogan's carriers. The other four battleships, Lee's

Washington, *Alabama*, *Massachusetts* and *South Dakota*, were left behind with Bogan.

This action appears quite incredible. Badger's force as Morison points out "was both too late and too weak for the work in hand. Supported by Bogan's Carrier Group it would doubtless have put up a good fight but it would have been seriously outgunned by Kurita's four battleships" − which of course included *Yamato*. Further if Halsey was not going to use four of his battleships at all it is astonishing that he did not think of leaving two of them to pursue Ozawa. That commander had with him *Hyuga* and *Ise* which were formidable opponents to the cruisers left under Mitscher, but American battleships easily outclassed them. As Fuller points out: "If two of them had been left with Mitscher, in all probability the Northern Force would have been annihilated and Halsey's aim attained". In fact the final result of Halsey's decisions was that the Third Fleet, with a strength in fire-power greater than that of the entire Japanese Navy, found itself outgunned in the north, and outgunned in the south.

Fortunately, however, the great American strength in the air was applied by Admiral Mitscher with his usual cool efficiency. The Northern Force having lost *Chitose* and *Akitsuki* had fifteen ships still afloat. A rough picture of these can be obtained from a report by Lieutenant Roberts, leader of a fighter-squadron from *Belleau Wood*, who, having plenty of fuel in hand after the second strike, remained in contact with the Japanese in order to describe their composition. However, since like all pilots he made many errors − he reported only fourteen ships not fifteen, stated that at least two destroyers were damaged when they were not, claimed that two light cruisers were trailing oil when probably only *Tama* had been hit and over-estimated the speed of the carriers − it would seem permissible if his findings are amended somewhat here.

As mentioned, one body of ships remained clustered near stricken *Chiyoda*. Japanese records − confirmed by later sightings − show that these were *Hyuga* plus one light cruiser (*Isuzu*) and two destroyers (*Shimotsuki* and *Maki*). Roberts reported all these as present, although almost certainly they were closer together than the area of 20 miles over which he said they were scattered − it will be recalled that there had been many previous wrong estimates of positions or distances by American airmen. Two other light cruisers were also with or near this body. One of these was *Tama* which, when hit, had been in company with *Hyuga*. The other was *Oyodo* which had slowed down in order to pick up Ozawa with his staff. Possibly also the Admiral had delayed catching up his carriers while he checked on the situation of the *Chiyoda*-group. One of the light cruisers was reported to be north of the rest of these ships. Probably this was not *Tama* as Morison and others believe but *Oyodo*, beginning to increase speed to join the carriers, which she did not long afterwards.

The other section of the Japanese fleet consisted of *Zuikaku, Zuiho, Ise* and presumably the remaining five destroyers although only four were reported. These would be the targets for Mitscher's third attack which he launched shortly before 1200 from the two task groups remaining to him. Over 200 aircraft took part in this, the largest raid of the day. One hundred and fifty of these, having taken part in the first strike, had had to be serviced and re-armed in great haste by the deckcrews. Commander Hugh Winters of *Lexington* took charge of this formation as target co-ordinator.

The pilots "quickly passed by" *Chiyoda*, according to Winters, but in fact some aircraft from *Franklin* did attack her consorts unsuccessfully. In any event, the appearance of this swarm of planes alone made it clear to Matsuda that he could not use *Hyuga* to take the crippled carrier in tow, thereby providing the Americans with a beautiful new target in the form of his almost stationary flagship. Escorted by *Shimotsuki, Hyuga* set course to join the major group while *Isuzu* and *Maki* tried to rescue *Chiyoda*'s crew — but because of air attacks they were not able to carry out this task. The little light carrier was abandoned with her men still on board. This may well have been their own preference; certainly Captain Jyo, who had advocated Kamikaze attacks even before Onishi, wished only to go down with his ship.

In the meantime, Winters had spotted his prey. "There was broken haze-cloud cover at around 6,000 feet which was perfect for our work," he recounted. "They couldn't see us too well until we broke through and then there were only two or three seconds left to get their guns on [target]." Mitscher ordered him to sink the undamaged carriers, so, since he had a very large force at his disposal, he delayed the attack by Group 4's planes, meanwhile dividing those from Group 3; the pilots from *Lexington* attacking *Zuikaku*, and those from *Essex, Zuiho*, while *Langley*'s attacked both enemy vessels.

Racing out of the convenient cloud at about 1310, ignoring the usual fierce anti-aircraft fire, the pilots lashed savagely at their victims. Several bombs hit *Zuiho* starting large fires. These, however, were quenched and her speed was not reduced. *Zuikaku* was hit by three torpedoes simultaneously, as well as by several bombs; she slowed to a halt.

Commander Winters now dived through the haze to check on the damage done. Since *Zuikaku* was listing badly to port, burning and smoking heavily, he rightly concluded that "she needed no more". He also noted with rueful appreciation that her anti-aircraft gunners were still firing accurately and he had shrapnel damage in his left wing when he regained altitude. Sending Group 3's aircraft back, he therefore concentrated the pilots from *Franklin, Enterprise* and *San Jacinto* against *Zuiho*. They scored several more hits on her, causing heavy damage. Her fires sprang up again, while her speed diminished. However, she was clearly another ship capable of taking heavy punishment, for as Group 4's planes turned away she was still limping northward.

As he waited for fresh reinforcements to arrive, Winters made a circuit to "keep tabs" on other vessels in the area, sighting *Hyuga* and her consorts catching up with the main section. Returning, he was just in time to witness the end of *Zuikaku* – a symbolic moment, for *Zuikaku* was a terrific ship with a wonderful record. At 1414, quietly without any explosion, the last survivor of the carriers which had bombed Pearl Harbour rolled over and went down. Winters, watching with triumph not unmixed with a strange sense of regret, observed that she flew to the end "a battle flag of tremendous size, perhaps fifty feet square", which her crew had hoisted to the mast-head as a last gesture of defiance.

Thirty minutes later, Winters directed to the scene the fourth raid of the day, consisting of about forty aircraft under the co-ordinating direction of Commander Malcolm Wordell from *Langley*. Four near-misses shook *Ise* but did little damage; but the main target of course was *Zuiho*. At least twenty-seven planes concentrated on her, scoring two more bomb hits, possibly more, and claiming two torpedo hits as well. At 1526, this gallant vessel which although only a light carrier had a record that could be matched by only a few fleet carriers of either side, followed *Zuikaku* to the bottom.

Winters now headed home, though his adventures were not yet over, but Wordell remained to handle the fifth attack which arrived shortly after 1700. This numbered about 100 planes from *Essex, Lexington, Langley, Enterprise* and *Franklin* all determined to make a kill. However, as most of the pilots had been in action twice before on the twenty-fifth, as well as on the previous day, they were now becoming

The Action off Cape Engano

very tired. Also over half the raiders were fighters, though most of these were armed with bombs.

By this time, the Northern Force was strung out in ragged groups over some 75 miles. Farthest north were *Ise* and *Oyodo* escorted by destroyers *Hatsutsuki, Wakatsuki, Kiri, Kuwa* and *Sugi*, some of which were manoeuvring to rescue survivors from the sunken carriers. Next came *Hyuga* and *Shimotsuki*, the latter incorrectly reported as a light cruiser, then *Isuzu* and *Maki*. About 20 miles away on *Hyuga's* port beam, *Tama* was limping back alone trailing oil. Far behind, *Chiyoda* floated forlorn and helpless.

Yet when the Americans arrived, these scattered ships put up their usual desperate defence, shooting down several of the attackers, whose skill, unlike their determination, had been blunted by constant action; they claimed indeed that they had wrought considerable havoc, but their weariness increased the exaggeration invariably caused by over-optimism. Several destroyers were strafed without result – one which was reported to have "disappeared" had not been sunk but had merely escaped detection for a time. Eight fighter-bombers from *Enterprise* attacked a light cruiser, probably *Oyodo*, but she was less "hopelessly damaged" than the pilots stated – not damaged at all in fact.

Obviously, however, *Hyuga* and *Ise* were the favourite targets. *Hyuga* had seven near-misses but Matsuda reported: "No damage". *Ise*, consistently assaulted, bore a charmed life. No torpedoes struck though many claims were made. One bomb found its mark but Captain Ohmae, Ozawa's Chief of Staff who inspected her later, recorded only "very slight" damage which "did not hamper navigation". An astonishing total of thirty-four near-misses shook her, hurling tons of water over her decks but causing only minor harm from splinters. *Ise* was certainly a dangerously capable opponent. She sent up an "exceedingly intense anti-aircraft fire" while her C.O. Rear-Admiral Nakase was apparently "an expert at evasive manoeuvring", which was probably just as well.

One final attack was made by thirty-six planes from Davison's Group 4 shortly after 1800. By this time darkness was closing in. The pilots were exhausted. Not surprisingly no damage was done. Night now ended the air strikes on the Northern Force but they were not yet out of danger. Submarines lay across their line of retreat, while a surface force had already been detached by Mitscher to crush any cripples or stragglers.

Shortly after 1400, the American Tactical Commander, deciding that his carriers were getting far too close to the enemy for safety, turned his main force eastward; but at the same time he proposed continuing the chase with a cruiser-destroyer group under Rear-Admiral Laurence DuBose. A very capable officer who had commanded heavy cruiser *Portland* splendidly at the Battle of Guadalcanal, DuBose was, nevertheless, anxious about the risks involved. He knew that if *Hyuga* and *Ise* encountered his ships, it would be "tough on the cruisers," but signalled to his chief that "if you think it possible, we will do it".

Now, however, a signal from Commander Winters stating that *Hyuga* and her supports were steaming north abandoning *Chiyoda*, was received. Over the voice-radio, Mitscher promptly ordered DuBose to carry out his mission taking with him heavy cruisers *New Orleans* and *Wichita*, light cruisers *Santa Fe* (flagship), and *Mobile*, and destroyers *Porterfield, Clarence K. Bronson, Cotten, Dortch, Cogswell, Caperton, Ingersoll, Knapp, Patterson* and *Bagley*. In addition to hunting enemy ships, DuBose was instructed to keep a look-out for 'ditched' airmen, four of whom were in fact rescued at various intervals by his force.

At this point the omnipresent Winters re-appeared on the scene. Having lingered to watch *Zuiho* share the fate of *Zuikaku* he was at last coming home when he flew over *Chiyoda*, dead in the water, smoking slightly. She promptly fired on him, but since at that moment he sighted DuBose's vessels approaching, he was able to retaliate by directing these upon the light carrier, reassuring them also that there were no enemy capital ships within striking-distance. He then spotted the fall of shot when his friends opened fire.

This occurred at 1625, when the two American heavy cruisers commenced shooting at a range of 20,000 yards. The light cruisers joined in shortly afterwards. *Chiyoda* tried to reply with her 5-inch anti-aircraft guns but her efforts were futile. As shells riddled her, she burst into a mass of flames above which towered a dense column of black smoke.

DuBose now ceased firing, commanding his destroyers to finish off the target with torpedoes. Destroyers were to suffer frustration throughout the evening, however, the first instalment thereof coming at this point, for at 1650, before they could launch their missiles, *Chiyoda* capsized, sinking almost immediately. The American ships regrouped to continue the northward pursuit. Commander Winters finally flew back to *Lexington*, happy with the memory of three enemy carriers going down within a matter of hours.

As darkness increased, DuBose was guided by two night-fighters from *Essex* towards his next prospective victims. These were described by the pilots as a light cruiser with two escorting destroyers. These ships had remained behind the main enemy force after *Zuikaku* and *Zuiho* had perished, circling the area in an attempt to rescue more survivors. In fact, all three were destroyers but one – *Hatsutsuki* – was of the big *Terutsuki*-class which the American airmen consistently misidentified.

Some American naval officers were shortly to compliment her still more by mistaking her for a heavy cruiser. When DuBose, who had located his enemy on his radar-screens at about 1840, began firing some ten minutes later, *Hatsutsuki* returned the fire with considerable vigour, at the same time getting between the Americans and the smaller destroyers, with the result that both the latter managed to escape northwards, soon drawing out of range.

Hatsutsuki continued her long, lone running-fight with the U.S. Cruisers. At 1911, she took two direct hits. Fires sprang up but as quickly were quenched. More hits were scored; another fire flared up only to die down – but nothing stopped *Hatsutsuki*, another of those tough Japanese warriors that knew how to take punishment. She still blazed back, near-missing but not hitting *Santa Fe* and *Mobile* more than once. Also she twice placed herself in a position from which she could launch torpedoes. Seeing this on the radar, DuBose on each occasion wisely ordered evasive action, but thereby lost further time.

Finally, under cover of the cruisers' gunfire, destroyers *Clarence K. Bronson, Cotten* and *Patterson* made a torpedo-attack of their own at 2012, thereafter also opening gunfire. The lethal 'fish' apparently did their work for flashes were seen while a heavy explosion was heard. *Hatsusuki*, though still shooting, slowed to about 10 knots. Thereupon, the Americans closed in to a range of 6,000 yards. *Santa Fe* illuminated the target with star-shells, while all the ships pounded the brave destroyer, reducing her to a burning, exploding, sinking wreck.

To finish the job, DuBose instructed destroyer *Porterfield*: "Request you put a 'fish' in him". At 2059, however, Captain Todd the screen commander who had already seen *Chiyoda* go down before he could torpedo her, signalled indignantly: "He has gone down. We were cheated!" "It breaks our hearts," replied the Admiral cynically.

A quick search failed to find *Hatsutsuki*'s companions, so after hearing from reconnaissance planes that all other enemy ships sighted were so far north that even at 30 knots he could not overtake them before daylight unless they slowed down or changed course, DuBose reformed his forces at 2130, heading south-east for a rendezvous with Mitscher next morning. He was undoubtedly correct in his decision as if he had continued his pursuit he would have come within range of Japanese land-based bombers from Formosa. Further, he was aware of the necessity of refuelling his destroyers. It is probably also fair to add that he was still conscious of the possibility that *Hyuga* and *Ise* might suddenly turn back to descend on him.

If so, he had every justification. *Hatsutsuki* had signalled details of her running-battle. Ozawa heard from her that she was being attacked at about 2040. He now had *Hyuga, Ise, Oyodo, Isuzu* and perhaps some destroyers reunited under his command. Although in the heat of action *Hatsutsuki* had mistaken the two American heavy cruisers for battleships, which if true would mean that his enemies could out-gun him, Ozawa at once rushed to help her, doubtless hoping that surprise would compensate for any lack of strength. Also it seems probable that having been under attack all day with no chance of retaliation, the fighting Ozawa was determined to strike back at his foes on any terms that would give even a remote chance of success.

Since DuBose in reality had no battleships, a rich reward might well have resulted from Ozawa's action. As Woodward points out "the battle had suddenly taken an ironic turn in its closing phase. The pursuer had become the pursued, the decoy the aggressor, and though they did not make the assumption, it was the Japanese and not the Americans who had the superior gun-power in the end." Luckily when the Japanese arrived on the scene the fighting had ended; continuing their search they passed to the east of their enemies, though later it was discovered that they did not miss their interception by a very wide margin. They pressed on south looking for trouble until 2330, when, unable to find any, they reversed course northward. There still remained the barrier of the U.S. submarines – but by this time most of these, like the surface-force, had already shot their bolt.

North-east of Luzon, two 'wolf-packs' of three submarines each had waited eagerly for their chance. *Haddock, Tuna* and *Halibut* under Commander Roach, and *Pintado, Jallao* and *Atule* under Commander Clarey, bearing the ferocious nicknames of 'Roach's Raiders' and 'Clarey's Crushers' respectively, had been lying quietly on station during the afternoon, checking torpedoes, occasionally hearing distant explosions, or in some instances listening over high-frequency radios to the excited conversations of the pilots who were

The Action off Cape Engano

trying to wipe out the Northern Force. As darkness closed in, however, their own chances of adding to the losses of such a clever, experienced enemy steadily diminished.

Lieutenant-Commander Ignatius Galantin, skipper of *Halibut*, was the only officer lucky enough to find a target in daylight. At 1742, radar reported a 'big pip' at 31,000 yards. Then the pagoda-like superstructure of *Ise* appeared on the horizon. Galantin sped in on the surface until he spotted an escorting light cruiser – *Oyodo* – and a destroyer, when he submerged to periscope depth. At 1844, about half an hour after sunset, *Halibut* sent six torpedoes at what Galantin supposed was *Ise*. Four minutes later, five separate explosions were heard. Then came other noises which the submariners hopefully thought "similar to a ship breaking up". They also believed that they could now hear only two sets of screws above them. There was no counter-attack.

When *Halibut* surfaced an hour later, Galantin sighted in the light of a brilliant half-moon, "a very large mound" which he considered was the hull of a capsized ship since no superstructure was visible. As the submarine moved towards this, it disappeared. *Halibut*'s delighted crew were confident that they had sunk a battleship.

Unfortunately they had not. Among the minor puzzles of Leyte Gulf is this attack by *Halibut*. What, if anything, did she hit? It was certainly not *Ise* which returned home untouched. More than one American authority credits the submarine with sinking *Akitsuki* – which the airmen had not identified as being among their victims. However, all Japanese sources, including Ozawa's report, agree that *Akitsuki* was their first ship to be sunk by air attack. As already shown, this seems correct; nor would there have been any point in pretending this were it not true. Since all other enemy ships lost were accounted for, Morison therefore concludes that poor *Halibut* sank nothing. The torpedoes presumably exploded prematurely, perhaps on striking the target's wake as did happen on occasions – but then what was the "mound"? No one knows. It can only be assumed that it was an optical illusion.

Elsewhere events went little better. *Halibut* later sighted other targets including *Hyuga* but since they were zigzagging to avoid attack, she was unable to fire on them. *Tuna* and *Atule* saw nothing at all. Commander Roach's *Haddock* headed towards *Hyuga* and *Ise* but could not locate them in the darkness. Roach watched gun-flashes and star-shells from the fight between DuBose and *Hatsutsuki*; later he observed two destroyers, probably *Hatsutsuki*'s late companions speeding away, but they were travelling too fast for him to be able to intervene, "Disappointment was a foot thick on this ship," he remarked afterwards.

In fact only one success was scored by submarines that night. At 2004, *Jallao* picked up a target on the radar. *Pintado* followed suit but Commander Clarey, her skipper, left the attack to his comrade. Peering through his periscope in the moonlight, Lieutenant-Commander Joseph Icenhower who had optimistically thought he was pursuing a battleship, sadly re-assessed his enemy as a light cruiser. It was – injured *Tama* limping home alone. *Jallao* fired three bow torpedoes. An explosion was reported but apparently this was a "premature" for *Pintado*, watching, saw no hits. At 2305, Icenhower fired four stern torpedoes. This time there was no mistake. Cheers broke from the sub's crew as three hits struck all along *Tama*'s side producing brilliant flashes. Five minutes later, the little light cruiser, surrounded by smoke, amid a welter of foam, went to the bottom with all hands.

The remaining ten ships of the Northern Force – *Hyuga*, *Ise*, *Oyodo*, *Isuzu* and six destroyers – despite the fantastic odds that had been brought against them during the day, made good their escape. Ozawa was sighted at about 0900 on 26 October by submarine *Trigger* but he was far too clever to let her get into an attacking position. On 27 October, he reached Amami-O-Shima where his exhausted crews enjoyed a two days rest prior to returning to the Inland Sea.

There is no doubt that Admiral Ozawa carried out his mission with skilful resolution and a considerable measure of achievement. Because of the radio-failure he was not able to notify Kurita of the extent of this, but, as will be seen, other information quite apart from his own unopposed passage through San Bernardino Strait should have told Central Force's commander this in any event. Everything that lay within Ozawa's own power was carried out with great efficiency in the most trying of circumstances. Not only did he give Kurita a splendid chance of success, he even managed to extricate the larger portion of his own decoy force. As Roskill puts it: "he carried out his part of the plan to perfection".

Yet for Ozawa, as he honestly admitted in his battle report, the action was a "bitter experience". It is said that he contemplated suicide but was dissuaded by fellow-officers who pointed out that of all the Japanese commanders he was the only one who successfully carried out his mission. Bitter indeed must have been his memories of this battle in which fate had forced him to "expend his beloved 'flattops' as bait". But to his eternal credit "he faced the situation without flinching, and" concludes Morison, "it may be some satisfaction to him in his honourable retirement that his former enemies, now friends, consider him the ablest of the Japanese Admirals after Yamamoto".

7

The Action off Samar Island

In sharp contrast to the overwhelming American superiority in the fighting off Cape Engano or in the Surigao Strait was their appalling vulnerability in the most vital of all the battles of 25 October — the action off Samar Island. In this the unlikely contestants for the United States were neither fast powerful fleet carriers nor massive battleships but the slow, unarmoured escort carriers of Rear-Admiral Thomas Sprague, which at the time were further weakened by being divided into three groups.

'Tommy' Sprague's own Task Group 77:4:1, known as 'Taffy 1' from its voice-radio call-sign, was the most southerly of these, some 90 miles south-east of Suluan Island. The Admiral who had previously commanded escort carrier forces during the Marianas operation, had under him:

Escort carriers: *Sangamon* (flagship), *Suwanee, Santee, Petrof Bay.*

Destroyers: *McCord, Trathen, Hazelwood.*

Destroyer-escorts: *Richard S. Bull, Richard M. Rowell, Eversole, Coolbaugh.*

A hundred miles to the north sailed the Middle Group or 'Taffy 2' whose leader was Rear-Admiral Felix Stump who had been C.O. of *Lexington* during the Gilbert and Marshall landings. This group's station was off the entrance to Leyte Gulf. Its composition was as follows:

Escort carriers: *Natoma Bay* (Stump's flagship), *Marcus Island* (flagship of Rear-Admiral William Sample), *Manila Bay, Kadashan Bay, Savo Island, Ommaney Bay.*

Destroyers: *Haggard, Franks, Hailey.*

Destroyer-escorts: *Richard W. Suesens, Abercrombie, LeRay Wilson, Walter C. Wann.*

Stump's command in turn lay 30 miles south-east of 'Taffy 3', which was steaming north at 14 knots some 60 miles east of Paninihian Point, Central Samar. This Northern Group was made up of:

The Action off Samar Island

Escort carriers: *Fanshaw Bay*; Captain Johnson, flying the flag of the group's leader Rear-Admiral Clifton Albert Frederick Sprague (no relation to his namesake).
Kitkun Bay; Captain Whitney, flagship of Rear-Admiral Ralph Ofstie.
St Lo; Captain McKenna.
White Plains; Captain Sullivan.
Kalinin Bay; Captain Williamson.
Gambier Bay; Captain Vieweg.
3 Destroyers:
Hoel; Commander Kintberger, in which was accommodated the officer in charge of the destroyer screen, Commander William Thomas.
Heermann; Commander Hathaway.
Johnston; Commander Evans.
4 Destroyer-Escorts:
Dennis; Lieutenant-Commander Hansen.
Raymond; Lieutenant-Commander Beyer.
John C. Butler; Lieutenant-Commander Pace.
Samuel B. Roberts; Lieutenant-Commander Copeland.

'Ziggy' Sprague as 'Taffy 3's' chief was mysteriously nicknamed, was a thorough, conscientious officer, forty-eight years old, whose modest, retiring manner disguised a devoted dedication to his profession. He was a qualified naval pilot who had commanded a squadron of patrol planes between the World Wars. Noted for his constant consideration for his airmen, he was the designer of a new arrester-gear for flight-decks which had proved of immense value. During the Pearl Harbour raid he had commanded seaplane-tender *Tangier*, the first naval vessel to open fire on the attacking aircraft. Later he obtained more war-like commands, being captain of carrier *Wasp* at the Philippine Sea. He was promoted to Rear-Admiral in August 1944, with command of 'Taffy 3' — but it was on 25 October that he was to have his greatest hour.

Nothing could have been further from his thoughts. Escort carriers did useful anti-submarine work in the Atlantic, but in the Pacific their main task was to provide air-cover for convoys or support for amphibious landings — tough, important, unglamorous work, carried out in over-heated, cramped, uncomfortable surroundings. *Sangamon, Suwanee* and *Santee* of 'Taffy 1' were large converted tankers. The remainder were of the 'Kaiser'-class, built during 1943–4 in great numbers to cope with the emergency of war. They were known by various uncomplimentary nicknames: 'Jeep Carriers' was the most usual; 'Baby flat-tops' the most polite. Their official abbreviation in naval circles was CVEs.[1] New recruits who came to serve on them were informed by the old stagers that these letters stood for "Combustible, Vulnerable, Expendable!"

There was considerable reason for such cynicism. The maximum speed of the escort carriers was only $17\frac{1}{2}$ knots, too slow to enable them to seek safety in flight from a superior opponent. Nor, with their single 5-inch gun astern and their thin unarmoured sides and deck, could they possibly hope to fight one successfully.

The 'Taffies' did have one great advantage in their aircraft – 235 fighters and 143 Avengers in all. Apart from *Sangamon* and *Suwanee*, the carriers possessed not Hellcats but the older more rugged Wildcats. In view of their role of supporting the beach-head, they were limited to nine to twelve torpedoes apiece. Their bomb allowance was also curtailed. The majority of their pilots had had no training in attacking warships. Nor could the CVEs launch or recover planes with the same ease as their big sisters.

The escorting surface-vessels were in a somewhat similar position. Although the fast, powerful destroyers with ten torpedoes and five 5-inch guns each were very capable of looking after themselves in action, the destroyer-escorts or DEs were small, slow vessels possessing only three torpedoes and two 5-inch guns, designed simply for anti-submarine warfare – one of their number, DE *England*, sank six Japanese submarines in the last twelve days of May 1944. They had never launched any torpedoes and they had never practised a concerted torpedo-attack.

Not of course that such lack of experience seemed relevant. The task of the CVEs was not to fight naval battles but to provide air patrols or anti-submarine flights over the beach-head area. Also they assisted the soldiers ashore by attacking enemy airfields, convoys, fuel concentrations etc. On the morning of the twenty-fifth, they were busy carrying out these routine patrols for which of course they were provided only with general purpose bombs or depth-charges, as well as various odd jobs; *Marcus Island* of Stump's group for instance sent off ten Avengers at 0545 to supply water and rations to 96 Division troops ashore. As seen, aircraft from 'Taffy 1' also attacked the retreating Japanese Southern Forces. The previous evening Admiral Kinkaid had ordered that all the escort carriers must be

---

[1] The fleet carriers were designated as CVs; the light carriers as CVLs.

The Action off Samar Island

prepared to load torpedoes at short notice for this work. This had the effect of further directing attention south not north, but it was to prove a vital factor in the struggle, for C.A.F. Sprague and Stump thus had several Avengers already equipped with torpedoes or 500-pound semi-armour-piercing bombs at the crucial moment.

At 0530, 'Ziggy' Sprague's Group 3 launched a C.A.P. of twelve Wildcats to protect ships in the gulf. Within the next half-hour, four Avengers plus two fighters were sent off for an anti-submarine sweep in the same area. The patrols to safeguard 'Taffy 3' itself were also sent on their missions. By 0630, the ships' crews having ended their morning alert secured from general quarters to settle down to breakfast. On *Fanshaw Bay*, Admiral Sprague[2] allowed himself the luxury of a second cup of coffee.

At this precise moment, just over the rim of the horizon, the most formidable surface fleet the Japanese had sent to sea since Midway Island was rushing towards the hopelessly ill-equipped Northern Group. Not even in the early days of the war had any American force been caught by surprise by such a vastly superior fleet as that now under the command of Admiral Kurita, whose mighty Central Force, despite the losses suffered in the Sibuyan Sea, still mustered the horrific *Yamato*, three other battleships, six heavy cruisers, two light cruisers and eleven destroyers.

Since passing through San Bernardino Strait, Kurita had first steamed cautiously eastward until 0300, when he wheeled his fleet to starboard to speed south-east down the Samar coast towards the gulf at 20 knots with his ships in four widely-spaced columns each 5 kilometres apart. To the east sailed Destroyer Squadron 10 – light cruiser *Yahagi* followed by destroyers *Urakaze*, *Isokaze*, *Yukikaze* and *Nowake*. Then came Cruiser Division 7 with heavy cruisers *Kumano*, *Suzuya*, *Tone* and *Chikuma*, followed at 5 kilometres distance by Battleship Division 1 – *Yamato* and *Nagato*. In the next column were *Haguro* and *Chokai* of Cruiser Division 5 followed at a similar distance by Battleship Division 3 consisting of *Kongo* and *Haruna*. Finally, nearest to Samar, came the remaining seven destroyers led by light cruiser *Noshiro* together forming Destroyer Squadron 2.

The sea was calm, with a gentle north-eastern wind of about 10

---

[2]C.A.F. Sprague. For future reference, he will henceforth be called 'Admiral Sprague', while his namesake the escort carrier chief will be referred to by his full name as 'Admiral Thomas Sprague'.

knots. Big cumulus clouds loomed overhead. Scattered rain-storms caused temporary losses of visibility. On the whole, however, this was by no means poor — yet not one sighting report was received of Kurita's armada until it was almost within view of 'Taffy 3'. Sprague was given virtually no warning whatever, so had no chance to prepare for the incredible action he would have to fight.

The primary reason for this potentially disastrous state of affairs was that Halsey had recalled *Independence*'s night-fliers when their carrier went north with the others after the Japanese 'bait', with the result that they could not keep track of Kurita. As no picket destroyer was left at the San Bernardino Strait, no warnings were given by surface-sightings either. In addition to the Third Fleet's errors, Admiral King remarked after the war that he had "regretfully concluded that the Seventh Fleet — notwithstanding its excellent performance in other respects — had failed to take the reasonable precaution that would have discovered the approach of the Japanese Central Force". With the advantage of hindsight one can see that Seventh Fleet should have made more searches but since its officers believed that Third Fleet's battleships were guarding the strait it is understandable that they saw no overwhelming need for these. Also in fact certain searches were ordered by Kinkaid, "mostly out of curiosity to find out what was going on".

One of the numerous disadvantages of the escort carriers was that their pilots were not yet trained in night take-offs or landings — though Stump among others was taking steps to remedy this. In consequence, Kinkaid did not order a night search from them but instead he detailed five 'Black Cats' — Catalinas equipped for night-flying — to take off from their tender in the gulf to search northwards although only three did in fact do so. These according to Kinkaid (confirmed by the pilots) "had quite a hell of a time because every U.S. ship they came near fired at them". "I imagine," added the Admiral "that their greatest concern was to avoid U.S. ships rather than to find Jap ships." Since the planes covered different areas, only one pilot, Lieutenant (jg) Sillars could possibly have sighted the enemy. After flying up the shore of Samar in order to locate any coastal shipping such as barges or sampans, he flew through San Bernardino Strait at about 2230, then south into the Samar Sea, finally returning through the strait shortly after daybreak. Unfortunately, his outward journey came before the Japanese reached the strait, while when he passed through it the second time, Kurita had already done so.

Also, at 0155, Kinkaid ordered Admiral Thomas Sprague to be prepared to fly off three dawn searches to cover San Bernardino plus

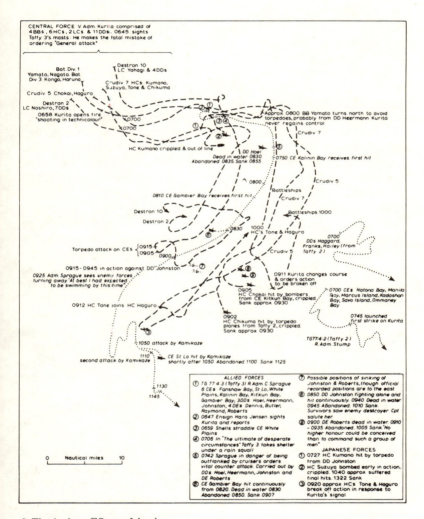

6 The Action off Samar Island

its eastern and western approaches as a routine precaution in support of Third Fleet. The usual communications trouble then intervened. At 0330 Thomas Sprague entrusted 'Taffy 2' with this task but it was an hour before the signal reached Stump. Half an hour later still, after checking the situation on each of his ships, the Middle Group commander detailed *Ommaney Bay* to carry out this mission. Ten Avengers were prepared, but this took time on the cramped, crowded, slippery, rain-soaked deck of the little carrier with the result that the planes only flew off shortly before 0700 – by which time their mission had lost all practical importance.

At 0637, the Combat Information Centre on *Fanshaw Bay* received the first warning of impending doom in an interception of excited Japanese voices on the interfighter director net – but this was believed to be the latest enemy attempts to jam the circuit, so little notice was taken of it. Eight minutes later, look-outs observed anti-aircraft fire to the north-west, while immediately afterwards Sprague's flagship picked up an unidentified contact on her radar.

A radar contact had also been made by Ensign Hans Jensen, on anti-submarine patrol from *Kadashan Bay*. Although this was not in the area for which he was responsible, he wisely investigated. To his horror he spotted what he described as a force of four Japanese battleships, eight cruisers and numerous destroyers – an estimate only too true – closing fast on 'Taffy 3'. These vessels fired on him; he replied by dropping two depth-charges at a heavy cruiser – he had no more suitable weapons – then radioed his sighting to Admiral Sprague. That officer promptly ordered "Check identification", believing that Jensen had really observed Lee's battleships. "Identification confirmed", came the strained reply, "ships have pagoda masts"[3] – an infallible indication of the older Japanese battleships. As everyone on *Fanshaw Bay* froze into horrified silence, Japanese top-hampers towered up over the northern horizon. Surprise was complete.

Yet Admiral Kurita was almost as shaken as the Americans. One of Japan's lynx-eyed look-outs sighted the CVEs before they spotted Central Force: "Masts to the south-east at varying distances" came the signal at 0644. Then Kurita observed Jensen making his attack. Shortly afterwards there appeared the high, flat hulls of aircraft carriers. These caused some consternation to the Admiral's staff who,

---

[3] The 'pagodas' in fact were not really 'masts' but towering superstructures including the bridge and control positions.

not knowing of the existence of the 'Taffies', had no photographs of the 'Kaiser'-class vessels. Some officers even urged that the ships sighted were those of Admiral Ozawa, although how even that doughty warrior could possibly have penetrated so far south, they did not pause to explain. Kurita, however, at once rightly identified the carriers as hostile.

The sight filled him with dismay. The constant strikes of the previous day during which he had watched the magnificent *Musashi* being battered to death had left him fearful of further encounters with carrier-planes. Since battle was now unavoidable, it seemed to him essential that his enemies be attacked before they could launch the aircraft they had aboard or before those out on missions could be recalled.[4] "We planned," he later stated, "first to cripple the carriers' ability to have planes take off and land, and then mow down the entire task force." Accordingly instead of immediately closing in on his targets, he swung eastward so as to stop the carriers heading into the north-easterly wind, thereby hampering the launching of their planes while at the same time preventing them from escaping to the open sea. He then intended to wipe out the vessels sighted, proceed to the gulf, shoot-up any transports or beach-head targets there, and escape through Surigao Strait. So intent was he to stay to the windward of his enemies that he not only did not at once reduce range but he ignored chance after chance of 'cutting corners' in order to reduce it later on.

However, it was probably his feeling that he must act immediately which caused Kurita to make his really fatal mistake. Instead of forming his battleships and heavy cruisers into a powerful, co-operating battle line while his light cruisers and destroyers came in to launch torpedoes, he ordered: "General Attack", which enabled each ship's captain to follow his own tactical inclination. To make matters worse, at the precise moment that 'Taffy 3' was sighted, the Japanese were in the middle of a complicated manoeuvre, changing from their formation in columns into the usual circular anti-aircraft one. The result was that each unit acted independently – which was in fact a mistake constantly made by the Japanese Army. "No heed was taken of order or co-ordination," lamented Koyanagi. The *Kongo* which was nearest to the Americans dashed off eastwards without relating her movements to those of her squadron-mate *Haruna*. The heavy cruisers, their alarm klaxons blaring, rushed forward without waiting

---

[4] Kurita believed that he had encountered one of Third Fleet's task groups and hoped that many of its planes would be away after Ozawa.

for the battleships. The light cruisers and destroyers were ordered to the rear.

In contrast to Kurita's lack of control, Sprague, though he had every cause for panic, kept a firm grip on events. Cool as ice, he made all the right decisions promptly. Sending out immediate calls for aid, he turned his ships due east which was sufficiently into the wind to allow planes to be launched while at the same time it avoided closing towards the Japanese more than was necessary. Increasing speed to $17\frac{1}{2}$ knots – all that an escort carrier could muster – he called on the CVEs as well as their escorting vessels to make smoke, and all aircraft to take off immediately. Planes began roaring off the little carriers' decks armed with whatever weapons they happened to have on board at the time.

As they hurtled down the flight-decks, great columns of water sprang into the air behind their ships with all the unexpected garish colours of the flowers on a cactus. "Look, look!" shouted a seaman on *White Plains*, "they're shooting at us in Technicolor!" To assist in spotting fall of shot, the Japanese shells were marked with dye of different colours. The shell-splashes from *Yamato*, a salvo from which opened the action, were coloured pink; those of *Kongo* were yellow; other ships had their missiles marked with red, green, blue, purple; one had no colour at all – the clear white pillars of spray from her shells contrasted with the vivid hues shown elsewhere.

The opening salvo was quickly followed by others rapidly coming nearer the escort carriers – particularly *White Plains* which was so unfortunate as to be closest to the enemy. Shells of several different colours and calibres crashed all around her hurling water over her bridge from 0700 onwards. In the next four minutes three 14-inch salvoes in quick succession straddled the CVE. The last of these came closest of all. Four shells landed "microscopically close" forward, and two more aft. Exploding underwater the great missiles shook *White Plains* so savagely that men were hurled off their feet. Steering control was temporarily lost. All electric power failed for several minutes. The starboard engine-room was damaged. A fighter on the flight deck was thrown out of its chocks and ripped some three feet out of another fighter's wing with its propeller. It was superb shooting by the Japanese gunners who for so many years had been dreaming of this sort of opportunity.

However, by this time, thick funnel-smoke pouring from *White Plains* began gathering in an increasingly dense cloud astern. Deceived by the very closeness of their shots, the Japanese believed she was on fire. They shifted their attention to *St Lo*. In turn she too was straddled. A near-miss to port flung water over her flight deck. Several bursts of shrapnel rattled against the ship causing some casualties. Splashes went up around some of her sister-ships also. "The enemy," remarked Sprague grimly "was closing with disconcerting rapidity and the volume and accuracy of fire was increasing. At this point it did not appear that any of our ships could survive another five minutes of the heavy-calibre fire being received."

Now, however, the destroyers and DEs were adding long trails of smoke (black from their funnels, white from the chemical smoke generators on their fan-tails) to those issuing from the escort carriers. Yet what really saved these from annihilation was a heavy rain squall which suddenly swept over them reducing visibility to less than half a mile. 'Taffy 3', still launching planes, plunged gratefully into its shelter. While so protected, Sprague turned his force south towards the gulf, whence he hoped help would be forthcoming. Kurita, determined on keeping the weather gauge, continued circling to the north of his targets. He ordered his ships to keep firing by radar but Japanese gunnery-radar was not good enough for them to do so accurately. The shell-splashes began falling ever wider during the fifteen minutes that the escort carriers were hidden in the rain.

Kurita also had other worries for by now aircraft were dashing in upon his vessels from all directions. First the local anti-submarine patrols attacked, strafing or dropping their useless depth-charges. Then planes from 'Taffy 3' joined in. Sixty-five fighters and forty-four Avengers took off from the ships under fire; but most of the bombers were not adequately armed for attacks on heavy ships; while fewer still carried their most effective weapons – torpedoes. *White Plains* and *Kitkun Bay* launched Avengers armed with bombs only but many aircraft were even less well equipped. *Gambier Bay*, for instance, sent up nine Avengers but torpedoes were carried by only two of these, one of which took off with practically empty fuel tanks, which caused her to 'ditch' within a few minutes. Of the others, three carried bombs, two had only depth-charges, while the remaining two had no weapons at all.

Furthermore the first attacks were made individually or by groups of two or three planes, often without fighter cover. At the start of the action, Rear-Admiral Ofstie, who later commanded a Fast Carrier Division in the Korean War, sent off the extremely able Air Group Commander of his flagship *Kitkun Bay*, Commander Richard Fowler, with orders to direct air strikes. Yet so hastily had the planes been launched, so confused was the situation, that Fowler was unable to collect enough aircraft together for a co-ordinated attack before 0830.

However, from the beginning gallant individual pilots swept to the attack dropping the dangerous 500-pound semi-armour-piercing bombs, 100-pound bombs incapable of inflicting more than superficial damage, or depth-charges. Fighters raced in low to strafe. The Japanese heavy ships were forced into avoiding actions which interrupted the pursuit. Machine-gun fire put the *Kongo*'s main rangefinder out of action. A bomb struck heavy cruiser *Suzuya*, reducing her speed to 20 knots. And hard on the heels of the aircraft came the first destroyer attack.

Destroyer *Johnston*, 2,100 tons with five 5-inch guns, had spent most of her brief but active life of almost exactly a year, at General Quarters – so much so that her crew nicknamed her 'G.Q. Johnny'. She had seen action at Kwajalein, Guam and Peleliu. She had helped to sink at least one submarine. And as luck would have it, her patrol sector in 'Taffy 3' lay nearest to the advancing enemy.

Johnston's captain, Commander Ernest Evans, had been in charge of her since she was commissioned. A short, sturdy, broad-chested man, he possessed Cherokee blood, and with it that reckless fighting-spirit which, rightly or wrongly, one invariably associates with the North American Indian. Ordering his crew to General Quarters with instructions to "prepare to attack major portion of Japanese Fleet", he turned his ship towards Central Force, laying a smoke-screen as he did so. This incidentally was his own decision without waiting for orders. Then as the Japanese heavy cruisers, aggressively led by Vice-Admiral Kazutaka Shiraishi, head of Cruiser Division 7, began outflanking the escort carriers to port, Evans, again on his own initiative, considered it his duty to turn these back by attacking them single-handed.[5]

Racing forward at 30 knots with her bow-wave curling outwards, *Johnston* opened fire at 0710 on Shiraishi's flagship, heavy cruiser *Kumano*; range 18,000 yards. Immediately a salvo from the cruiser straddled her. The other cruisers quickly joined in, for the angle of *Johnston*'s approach enabled them all to shoot at her without obstructing each others' line of fire. Battleships and light cruisers also

---

[5] Full details of *Johnston*'s part in the action may be found in an article written in the *Saturday Evening Post* on 26 May 1945, by Lieutenant Robert Hagen, her Gunnery Officer who was the senior survivor. This is entitled: "We Asked for the Jap Fleet – And Got It!"

opened up on her, splashes of half-a-dozen different colours rearing up all around her. Despite the concentration of fire, however, she was not once hit during her advance, while her own 5-inch guns blazed more than 200 rounds in rapid salvoes at *Kumano*; several hits were observed.

At 0716, Admiral Sprague ordered his destroyers to counter-attack with torpedoes. Commander Evans was already in a good position to oblige. When the range had decreased to 10,000 yards, he launched all ten of his lethal 'fish' at *Kumano*, then dodged back into the protection of *Johnston*'s own heavy smoke. While so concealed, *Johnston*'s crew heard the thunder of an underwater explosion; and on emerging from their cover they saw the gloriously satisfying sight of *Kumano* dropping slowly out of formation, blazing furiously astern.

This lone attack was only the start of *Johnston*'s activities – but it was a singularly effective beginning. *Kumano*, crippled, her speed reduced to 16 knots, fell out of the chase. Heavy cruiser *Suzuya* already slowed by her bomb-hit also dropped out in order to pick up Admiral Shiraishi and his staff. Having done so, further trouble befell her. No one knows exactly what did happen to *Suzuya* but it is unarguable that at some time she was hit again fatally, and immobilized. Since she never returned to the pursuit while the position where she was crippled was well to the north of the main scenes of action, it appears almost certain that she was struck fairly early on – presumably at about 0845, when, as will be seen, the first heavy strikes from 'Taffy 2' began to arrive. It also seems likely that she was disabled at about this time in view of the fact that she would then have been a reasonably easy target, being unsupported as well as travelling at a comparatively low speed.

None of the cruiser's misfortunes were known to *Johnston* however – she had more than enough worries of her own. Minutes after she had left her smoke-screen, the enemy again poured heavy fire at her. At about 0730, reported Lieutenant Hagen "this ship got it. Three 14-inch shells from a battleship followed thirty seconds later by three 6-inch shells from a light cruiser hit us. It was like a puppy being smacked by a truck."

These hits caused dreadful injuries. The destroyer's speed was cut to 17 knots. One of the heavy shells landed in the after engine-room wrecking it. The steering equipment was also knocked out, necessitating manual steering from aft. The gyro-compass was rendered useless. All power for three of the 5-inch guns was temporarily lost. The search-radar mast snapped off to come crashing down by the bridge. There were many casualties. On the bridge three officers were killed while Commander Evans had all his clothes above the waist blown off as well as two fingers from his left hand. Yet the stout little ship continued her fight.

Now a curtain of water fell across *Johnston*'s mangled decks as she found sanctuary in the rain-squall. Under its protection her crew made hasty repairs while at the same time coming to the aid of wounded companions. Enough power was restored to enable the three knocked-out guns to function again. On her remaining engine, the destroyer began her return journey to catch up the escort carriers, firing back at any target that opportunity offered as she did so.

As *Johnston* was entering the rain squall, the CVEs were emerging therefrom – in time to be confronted by the worst menace yet. The remaining four heavy cruisers – *Tone, Chikuma, Haguro, Chokai* – much more ably handled than were the battleships, were drawing level with 'Taffy 3' on the port quarter. Clearly their intention was to outflank the CVEs, in order to turn them back into the great guns of the capital ships. Destroyers were starting to close in to starboard. It was, remarked Captain Dennis Sullivan, C.O. of *White Plains*, "a perfect set-up to polish off this unit. We could only go in the direction the Japs wanted to go themselves, to Leyte Gulf." To Sprague it seemed that his ships were "surrounded by the ultimate of desperate circumstances". Counter-action was "urgently and immediately required".

But from where could aid come? Promptly on sighting Kurita, Sprague had sent a call to Kinkaid asking for help. "This," Kinkaid later reported "was the first indication that the enemy's Central Force had succeeded in passing through San Bernardino Strait." He at once sent off the series of signals to Halsey that have already been examined. After repeated pleas, plus urgings from Sprague and Nimitz, Halsey finally sent Admiral Lee's battle line to assist – but, as we have seen, far too late. Admiral McCain was also dispatched to Sprague's help, but again a long time would elapse before he could intervene.

This left it as Seventh Fleet's task to rescue their comrades – but Kinkaid was now in a hideous quandary. His primary responsibility was protection of the beach-head, the amphibious forces and the Army ashore. Whatever the peril to 'Taffy 3' this duty had to take precedence. Kurita was within three hours steaming of the many vulnerable targets still remaining in Leyte Gulf. Further, Kinkaid's main surface-vessels were now in Surigao Strait after repelling the

The Action off Samar Island

Japanese Southern Forces. Kinkaid shrewdly and rightly estimated that at least part of these had not been engaged, so might well seize the chance of re-entering the strait to attack the gulf from the south if the opportunity to do so was given by the withdrawal of Oldendorf's ships. Since Shima's two heavy cruisers which had indeed not been engaged were quite capable of upsetting the whole amphibious force if let loose among it, Kinkaid had to leave at least part of his gunnery strength on guard in the south.

To make matters worse, Oldendorf's forces were not at all well equipped to meet Kurita. It has been stated that the battleships were short of ammunition. This is true, but the shortage was not very serious. The light cruisers had indulged in such furious firing that they had only some 50-80 rounds of armour-piercing (AP) ammunition remaining and there were no supplies on hand to replenish the deficiencies. Most of the destroyers had expended their torpedoes – again no replacements were available. Many ships were now dangerously low on fuel. Even if Oldendorf reached Sprague, his battleships were some 5 knots slower than those of Kurita. The Japanese ships could well outrange and outmanoeuvre those of Oldendorf in a running fight until the shortage of shells did become serious. It would be better, as his Chief of Staff, Captain Richard Bates urged, if Oldendorf kept his ships inside Leyte Gulf to attempt another 'crossing of the T' against Central Force.

Regardless of all his problems, however, Admiral Kinkaid could not bring himself to leave his men in 'Taffy 3' to their fate. He tried to solve his various dilemmas at 0850, by instructing Oldendorf to lead his force back to the north of Hibuson Island, where it could cover both the southern and eastern entrances of the gulf. Then he ordered his battle line commander to take battleships *Tennessee, California* and *Pennsylvania*, heavy cruisers *Louisville, Portland, Minneapolis* and HMAS *Shropshire*, and *Nashville* which now that MacArthur had gone ashore was free to take her place in the fighting, escorted by two destroyer squadrons, 25 miles eastward where they would be in a position to sortie in support of the escort carriers. He also ordered ships from two more destroyer squadrons then escorting unloaded transports home, either to reinforce Oldendorf or to go direct to attack Kurita. These, however, were somewhat desperate remedies, for apart from the disadvantages already described, it was unlikely that Oldendorf's vessels could reach 'Taffy 3' before it was overwhelmed.

However, Kinkaid's main aid for Sprague came in the shape of aircraft. Immediately he heard of the enemy's approach, he instructed his Air Support Commander, Captain Whitehead, to detail all aircraft not at the time engaged in strikes on enemy forces, to rendezvous in Leyte Gulf prior to concentrating attacks on Kurita. Also the other two 'Taffies' were ordered to launch all available planes against him. This raised numerous risks as well. The absence from the beach-head of the usual air cover provided by the escort carriers, enabled Japanese aircraft to make twelve attacks during the morning, destroying a warehouse and a concrete dock at Tacloban and sinking two LSTs. Nevertheless, Kinkaid rightly persisted in sending every possible plane to assist Sprague.

Yet once more there was an inevitable delay before help could come. 'Taffy 1' was 130 miles south, with its planes already in the air pursuing Shima. It would take time then before Thomas Sprague could join in the fighting. Felix Stump's 'Taffy 2' was nearer at hand. On *Fanshaw Bay* the voice of 'Taffy 2's' commander came clearly over the TBS urging Sprague to keep calm, "Don't be alarmed Ziggy – remember we're back of you – don't get excited – don't do anything rash!" But as Stump spoke, so his voice rose to a positive shriek of anxiety for his friend and his friend's unit. Stump indeed did everything possible to help but many of his planes were out on routine missions. Also although deck-crews broke their own practice records for preparing aircraft in many cases, delays in making rendezvous or locating the enemy meant that an hour and a half elapsed from the start of the action before the powerful weight of 'Taffy 2's' strikes was brought to Sprague's aid.

During this period, Sprague was thus compelled to rely on his own tiny, ill-equipped force to defend itself against its vastly superior opponent. It was as if the fates had determined that an American victory in this most crucial part of the whole mighty battle would depend not on their larger numbers, not on their command of the air, but on the courageous resolution of those of their ships which were most out-numbered and least suited for a close-range mêlée.

The moment had now come for the escort vessels to fight a rearguard action covering the escape of the CVEs – but before following the savage, complicated encounters that resulted, certain factors must be kept in mind. First, the clouds of smoke drifting over the sea combined with the frequent rain squalls to reduce visibility drastically. Indeed *Heermann* the southernmost destroyer in the formation had not even seen an enemy ship up to the time that she went in to launch her torpedoes. The battle took on much of the

The Action off Samar Island

nature of a night-action, with ships suddenly looming out of the murk to attack each other. Near-collisions were frequent occurrences, *Heermann* especially having more than her fair share of these.

In consequence, confusion reigned supreme, with no one ship ever having a clear view of the action as a whole. Also large numbers of events took place more or less simultaneously. Although an attempt will be made to show the changing course of the fighting in some sort of chronological order – though times given are only approximations or at best majority-opinions – so much was going on at once that it should be appreciated that several of the encounters related overlapped each other and the constant use of the word "meanwhile" is quite essential.

The chaotic circumstances plus the bad visibility – though the latter provided welcome protection – also made it exceptionally difficult for the escorts to combine against their foes. When the screen-leader Commander Thomas was ordered by Sprague to attack with torpedoes, he at once passed the word to Commander Leon Kintberger in command of destroyer *Hoel*, but she had to attack by herself since *Heermann* was too far away, while *Johnston* was already in action with the enemy cruisers.

Kintberger first made for the Japanese battle line. While *Johnston* was firing her torpedoes at *Kumano*, *Hoel* was racing towards an even more formidable foe – battleship *Kongo*. Shortly before 0725, at a distance of 14,000 yards, she opened fire with her 5-inchers on her massive opponent. The enemy fired back, almost at once hitting *Hoel* on the bridge destroying all her voice-radio communications. Other hits followed in quick succession, but the destroyer, ignoring them, as the range decreased to 9,000 yards, sent five torpedoes at *Kongo*, which the battleship dodged by turning sharply to port.

Hoel was also swinging away when a frightful barrage of 14-inch shells from the furious *Kongo* fell on her. The heavy cruisers also poured fire in her direction, but it was two 14-inchers, striking practically simultaneously, that knocked out her after fireroom and port engine. Others ripped through her decks causing heavy casualties as well as so much damage that Kurita watching from *Yamato* thought that *Hoel* had blown up. Her rudder jammed hard right causing her to head straight for *Kongo* for two perilous minutes before steering-control was shifted aft, when the destroyer was able to turn slowly away. White-hot steam pouring from burst pipes in the engine room rendered one of her 5-inch guns unusable; a second was jammed by a very near miss; a third had half its barrel shot off by a direct hit; yet the remaining two guns continued firing.

Then at 0742, Sprague ordered another torpedo-attack — the most important of all since it was directed against the group of cruisers threatening to turn the carriers back into the battleships' guns. Unless these vessels could be held off until the promised air attacks from 'Taffy 2' could arrive, Sprague's ships were doomed. Despite her damage, *Hoel*, using one engine only, steering by hand, led this attack. Fortunately on this occasion she had the support of three other ships as determined as herself.

As mentioned earlier, destroyer *Heermann* lay south of the carriers, farthest from the Japanese. Commander Amos Hathaway, her skipper, accordingly made a dash right through the formation to launch his attack. "It was rather difficult threading through the carriers as the shell splashes were heavy in some spots," he later reported nonchalantly — he was to prove himself a master of this style throughout his description of the battle. Also visibility varied drastically from 100 to 25,000 yards due to rain or smoke. However, *Heermann* raced safely past the carriers, only to have to swerve wildly in order to avoid a collision with destroyer-escort *Samuel B. Roberts*, which was laying smoke between 'Taffy 3' and Central Force. Another near-collision followed almost immediately as *Heermann* charged up to *Hoel*. Not appreciating that her squadron-mate's speed was badly reduced she had to back her engines' emergency full speed to miss her. She then fell in behind *Hoel* to support the latter's attack.

Meanwhile Lieutenant-Commander Robert Copeland of *Roberts*, having seen Hathaway roar past, was determined to join in the fray himself. The tiny DE, of 1,350 tons with only two 5-inch guns and three torpedoes and a speed of only 24 knots, had no right to be in a naval battle — nor was she designed for one. Most of her crew were reservists with an average of less than one year's service. Yet Copeland at once signalled to Commander Thomas to ask if the 'Little Wolves' as the DEs were called were to attack with the 'Wolves' — code-name for the destroyers.

The screen leader replied that the destroyer-escorts should form up for a second assault — but since they had never delivered a concerted torpedo-attack even in practice, Copeland preferred to combine with the more experienced destroyers. In addition, since *Roberts* was the nearest 'Little Wolf' to the Japanese, he did not wish to waste time seeking the other DEs on the far side of the formation as the situation was far too urgent for any such delay. As he headed north for the Japanese line, Copeland gave his crew over the loud-speaker

The Action off Samar Island 161

system a fair assessment of their position: "a fight against overwhelming odds from which survival could not be expected, during which time we would do what damage we could". It made no difference to them. In went little *Roberts*.

At about the same time, wounded *Johnston* was quitting the shelter of her rain-squall as she limped back towards the carriers. As visibility improved, her crew sighted *Hoel* and *Heermann*, followed at about 3,000 yards distance by *Roberts*, tearing past for their attack. No one could seriously imagine Commander Evans being left out of this sort of brawl. "We'll go in with the destroyers and provide fire support!" he roared. Her torpedoes already spent but her guns blazing, *Johnston* turned back to join her comrades. For all their vast preponderance of power, the Americans were forced, in this the most crucial moment of the battle, to rely on the skill of three destroyers, two of which were damaged, plus one destroyer-escort.

Their hopes were in good hands. *Hoel*, first to assault the Japanese cruisers, was already badly hurt. She suffered further damage as she approached but at about 0745 — estimated times vary widely — she hurled her remaining five torpedoes at *Haguro* leading the enemy line, reporting gleefully that "large columns of water were observed to rise from the cruiser at about the time scheduled for the torpedo run". Unfortunately Japanese records show that these torpedoes missed. Since there were not at this time any bombers attacking the cruiser which might have raised the water-spouts with their near-misses, it can only be that the torpedoes (or some of them at least) either blew up prematurely or else exploded on hitting the ship's wake.

After the attack, the destroyer attempted a retirement to the south-west but because of her lost engine was unable to raise enough speed to do so. With the heavy cruisers on one side and the battleships on the other, she became the focal point for an almost unbelievable volume of fire. Although she manoeuvred desperately it was quite impossible to escape. Sixteen-inch shells from *Nagato*, 14-inch from *Kongo* and *Haruna*, 8-inch from the heavy cruisers, 5-inch from the destroyers; over forty hits struck home on *Hoel*. She stayed afloat only because the major-calibre shells were armour-piercing, which, although ideal for use on heavy ships, went right through the lightly-built destroyer without exploding. But they put so many holes in her that her engineering spaces flooded while she listed twenty degrees to port. All the time, her two remaining guns roared out, pumping some 250 rounds each at various enemy vessels.

Finally at 0830, an 8-inch shell put her starboard engine out of action, bringing her to a halt. More salvoes found their mark as she lay dead in the water. She began to sink by the stern. At 0835, Commander Kintberger ordered "Abandon Ship". Twenty minutes later, with enemy gunfire still tearing into her, *Hoel* fell over on her port side, to sink stern first. Loss of life was very heavy but both Kintberger and Commander Thomas, the latter badly wounded, were saved.

The other three American ships were – at least for the time being – more lucky. *Heermann* also selected *Haguro* as her target. Attacking amid continuous shell-splashes, she fired 125 rounds at her opponent before launching seven torpedoes at her as well. The heavy cruiser dodged these, retaliating with several salvoes which might otherwise have been aimed at the escort carriers. All of them missed.

In contrast to *Heermann*, *Roberts* withheld her fire during her approach. Thanks to this, in combination with clever use of smokescreens laid by the destroyers or by herself, she closed undetected to the suicidal range of 4,000 yards from the cruiser formation. Here she sent three torpedoes at *Chokai*, whereupon "fire, smoke, and a column of water were seen to rise from the water line of the target ship". The presence of the first two would suggest this was not a case of premature explosion, and although Japanese records do not indicate a success, *Chokai* was to go down later with almost her entire crew so it is possible that a hit on her would not be known, particularly since the hit, if scored, does not seem to have resulted in any great damage. But in any event the torpedoes were not wasted, for, like those of the destroyers, they caused the enemy ships to keep sheering away from the pursuit. Several cruisers began firing on the destroyer-escort; but *Roberts*' lack of size was an asset now, and she nipped in and out of the shell-splashes like a terrier while her two 5-inch guns spat back their defiance.

Johnston also was in action, firing at the cruisers in a bid to hold them off the carriers. As she and *Roberts* retired, still keeping between the Japanese ships and 'Taffy 3', the enemy captains who believed they were a heavy cruiser and a destroyer respectively – implied compliments richly deserved – were compelled to concentrate upon them rather than on the CVEs. Also by now the time had been gained for two other destroyer-escorts as well as numerous aircraft to reach advantageous positions from which to assault the flanking cruisers.

The Japanese battleships were also in trouble. As *Heermann* was sending torpedoes at *Haguro*, 14-inch shells from *Kongo*, sighted at

The Action off Samar Island

this time by the Gunnery Officer Lieutenant Meadors, began landing all round her. Behind *Kongo*, loomed *Haruna*, then *Nagato* and *Yamato*. Yet, unperturbed by these fearful odds, Commander Hathaway at once changed course to engage them. He raked *Kongo*'s superstructure with his guns – with some effect apparently since he reported the gunfire was "a joy to behold". There was other gunfire claiming his attention which was less pleasant. Big yellow splashes from *Kongo*'s shells were rearing up all round the destroyer, while other battleships also added their contributions, but miraculously *Heermann* suffered only slight damage from shell fragments. She steamed on through the towering jets of water until at 0800 with the range 4,400 yards, she let fly her remaining three torpedoes at *Haruna* before swinging abruptly away.

Hathaway believed that one of his missiles struck its target. Instead, they all missed – but they achieved far more important results than one hit on a battleship could ever have done, especially since the depth setting of the torpedoes had been only six feet and there had been no time to change it. The colossal *Yamato* now found torpedoes racing at her. It has been suggested that these may have come from *Hoel*, but it is clear from *Heermann*'s account that when she attacked *Yamato* was still in full pursuit, so had not already turned back as she would have done in this case; admittedly the Japanese records state that *Yamato* reversed course before *Heermann* fired but all times given during the whole action are wildly contradictory, while Japanese accounts throughout give earlier times than American ones. Further, the relative positions of the battleships and cruisers at the moment of *Hoel*'s attack on the latter were such that her torpedoes could not possibly have reached *Yamato* without changing course; quite apart from which, as we have seen, it appears likely that several of them exploded prematurely.

It thus seems highly probable that the 'fish' which threatened Kurita's flagship came from *Heermann*. In fact it is said she was confronted by two separate spreads, sugesting that either the Japanese doubled the number of torpedoes sighted in their anxiety or a few aircraft had also chosen to send some at the largest target on hand. In any case the result is unarguable. Kurita changed course, first to port, then almost due north, to evade. This was the worst possible action he could have taken, for the battleship now found the spreads chasing her from astern, forcing her to flee north for almost ten minutes before the torpedoes ran their course. *Yamato* then turned back but since she never caught up with the running fight, Kurita never regained control of his forces — which was perhaps the most important single factor of the whole action.

Heermann was also retiring, but in the opposite direction, firing as she went, laying smoke, and "chasing salvoes". This risky technique involves steering for the splashes of an enemy broadside on the assumption that the foe will correct his error, thus missing again, but it brings with it the hazard of steaming right into a subsequent broadside. However, *Heermann* escaped this sad fate, reaching the shelter of the starboard quarter of the carrier group, which, since Sprague had meanwhile swung round to the south-west, meant that she was now on the opposite side to the flanking cruisers.

They, however, were still under pressure. First destroyer-escort *Raymond* attacked alone aiming for *Haguro*. The cruiser promptly near-missed her with a full salvo; in all firing fifteen such at the DE. Equally discouraging was the sight of *Roberts* under heavy fire, surrounded by a curtain of splashes, though still blazing back at the enemy. Yet Lieutenant-Commander Beyer, undaunted, closed to 6,000 yards before firing torpedoes. Unluckily, just as he did so, aircraft also dropped 'fish' at *Haguro* which, turning to avoid them, escaped *Raymond*'s as well. *Raymond* then retired, firing, pursued by shell splashes.

Lieutenant-Commander Hansen of *Dennis* also attacked individually. On her approach, *Dennis* was near-missed by gunfire, as well as by torpedoes presumably from either *Chokai* or *Chikuma* since *Haguro* and *Tone* disclaim credit. At 8,000 yards she fired her 'fish' at *Tone* but missed her. She then retired as well, after exchanging fire with the enemy ships for some seven minutes while somehow escaping being hit.

The escorting vessels had now shot their bolt, at least as far as torpedoes were concerned, for although *John C. Butler* was to join in the fight later, she was never able to use the three in her tubes — "The situation is getting a little tense, isn't it?" remarked a humorous radioman on *White Plains* when the news came through. The little ships returned towards the carriers, still firing, still laying their smoke-screens, still offering themselves as targets for Japanese gunfire.

Indirectly, they achieved another success by their very presence. At 0800, *Haguro* which had been concentrating on shooting first at *Johnston* and *Roberts*, then at *Raymond* and *Dennis*, was caught by surprise by some of Sprague's Avengers. A bomb put her Number 2 turret out of action. As a result of this, plus the other air or surface

The Action off Samar Island   165

attacks on her, she fell back together with her squadron-mate *Chokai*. *Chikuma* now took the lead, followed by *Tone*. As the escorts retired, these pressed in towards the CVEs, their shells falling steadily nearer.

By this time, the 'baby flat-tops' were making their maximum $17\frac{1}{2}$ knots in their flight to the south-west. In the front of the formation was *White Plains*, closely followed by *Kitkun Bay* and *Fanshaw Bay*. The other three were trailing but *St Lo* on the starboard flank was screened by smoke from *Heermann, Johnston* and some of the DEs which as 'Taffy 3's' course changed, had now fallen astern. The smoke from neither escorts nor carriers, however, provided much cover for *Gambier Bay*, or *Kalinin Bay* which were on the port flank, for the wind was blowing it the wrong way — a fact of which the cruisers were quick to take advantage. These, reported Captain Walter Vieweg of *Gambier Bay*, were "in an excellent position to pour in a rather heavy fire on *Gambier Bay* and *Kalinin Bay* which they proceeded to do without delay".

As the shell splashes loomed closer, Admiral Sprague, preserving his sense of humour even in these trying circumstances, ordered: "Open fire with the pea-shooters when the range is clear". Even before this some of his ships were already using their solitary 5-inchers; a futile defence, yet strangely comforting, although one old Chief Petty Officer on *St Lo* was heard to growl: "They ought to fire that thing under water — we could use a little jet propulsion right now!"

First to take an 8-inch hit was *Kalinin Bay* at 0750. About fifteen minutes later, a second 8-inch shell also found its mark. Quite undaunted, the escort carrier fired back, at 0825 scoring a direct hit on one of *Chikuma*'s gun turrets, followed immediately by another one just below the first which caused a quick burst of flame to hide the turret temporarily.

Gambier Bay was also lucky — for a time. The Japanese salvoes according to Captain Vieweg were "about a minute and a half apart and not particularly large". This gave him the opportunity for some exceptionally neat salvo-chasing, as well as time to get in three hits from his "pea-shooter" on a cruiser — presumably *Chikuma*. In his own words:

> One could observe that the salvoes would hit some distance away and gradually creep up closer and from the spacing on the water I could tell that the next one would be on if we did nothing. We would invariably turn into the direction from which the salvoes were creeping and sure enough the next salvo would land right in the water where we would have been if

we hadn't turned. The next few salvoes would creep across to the other side and gradually creep back and would repeat the operation. The process lasted for, believe it or not, a half hour during which the enemy was closing constantly.

At 0810 when the range was down to 10,000 yards, this dicing with death ended abruptly as *Chikuma* found the range, landing a hit on *Gambier Bay*'s flight deck aft which started fires. Thereafter the CVE took repeated hits which killed or wounded several of her crew. But it was a near-miss which did the most vital damage. Exploding very near the forward engine-room it blew a hole about four feet square below the water-line. Flooding was so rapid that five minutes later the engine room had to be abandoned. *Gambier Bay*, slowing to 11 knots, fell astern of her colleagues. *Chikuma* continued pouring fire into her, while *Tone, Haguro* and *Chokai* concentrated on her also. Light cruiser *Noshiro* which had now come within range joined in as well, as did at least one destroyer.

Once again the screening vessels risked everything in an attempt to save their charge; *Johnston* as before showing the way. At 0830, Commander Evans sighting *Chikuma* shelling *Gambier Bay*, which by now was burning amidships and listing heavily, ordered his Gunnery Officer: "Commence firing on the cruiser, Hagen. Draw her fire away from the *Gambier Bay*." Hagen did his best by making at least five hits on his enemy from 6,000 yards range but without much effect for *Chikuma* refused to be diverted from her victim.

To *Johnston*'s aid came her comrade-in-arms *Heermann*. Since he had, as we saw, been on the wrong side of the carriers, Commander Hathaway rushed through the middle of them at full speed, amidst smothers of rain, smoke, and shell-splashes. At 0835, the great bulk of *Fanshaw Bay* towered up in front of the destroyer. *Heerman*'s log records vividly how she "backed emergency full to avoid collision"; however *Fanshaw Bay* had other matters to think about and her log merely notes: "Destroyer crossed our stern".

Five minutes later *Heermann* had another narrow escape as *Johnston*, which as Hathaway noted was "having steering difficulty", appeared out of the gloom. Again *Heermann* sent her engines into reverse at full speed, missing her sister-ship "by about three inches" whereupon both crews in affection and encouragement cheered each other on. Immediately afterwards Hathaway also used his 5-inch guns against *Chikuma*. Apparently he also scored hits for the cruiser now turned some of her guns onto *Heermann*.

The Action off Samar Island

Further help was on the way. Sprague again ordered the destroyer-escorts to help fend off the Cruiser Division. *Roberts, Raymond* and *Dennis* gallantly responded, being reinforced by *John C. Butler* which had steered through the formation laying smoke as she went. *En route*, she became involved with the near-collisions between *Heermann, Fanshaw Bay* and *Johnston* already described, but Lieutenant-Commander Pace managed to steer clear of these dangers.

Arriving at the battle-zone, *Butler* at once attempted to launch her torpedoes at *Chikuma*. Unfortunately her speed was not great enough to let her reach a suitable firing-position unless the cruiser conveniently changed course towards her. Since Captain Norimitsu was not so stupid as to oblige, *Butler* never did get her torpedoes away. She made up for this by turning such a continuous fire onto various enemy cruisers that she came close to exhausting her limited supply of ammunition.

Her consorts were firing away equally enthusiastically. *Raymond* closed in until she was only some 5,900 yards from the cruiser line. *Dennis* had her Number 2 gun rendered useless by a broken breech-operating spring but she continued in action with her remaining gun. *Roberts* sent off some 300 rounds from each of her two guns. She concentrated on *Chokai* obtaining "a great many hits". It was claimed that these "knocked out their Number 3, 8-inch gun turret, demolished their bridge and started fires aft under their secondary control tower". Even allowing for exaggeration it is clear that *Roberts'* "rapid and continuous fire" did do considerable damage.

Yet all the efforts of the escorts could not save *Gambier Bay*. Eight-inch shells poured in upon her – Captain Vieweg estimated that "we were being hit probably every minute". A shell which landed near the island structure knocked out all steering-controls. Another found the after engine-room, tearing a ten-foot hole below the water-line. The sea rushed in. With all power lost, the escort carrier came to rest, dead in the water. The flooding rose steadily and the ship's list increased while flames continued to rage in many areas and the tanks of aircraft began to explode violently – yet still the shelling persisted at short range. At 0850, Vieweg ordered "Abandon Ship". At 0907, *Gambier Bay* capsized and sank.

The destroyers indeed had put themselves in a position where they were likely to share the escort carrier's fate. At least four ships concentrated on *Heermann*. Splashes in several different colours drenched her to such an extent that Hathaway wished for "a periscope with which to see over the wall of water". At 0845, an 8-inch shell struck the pilot-house, killing three men and fatally wounding the steersman; but Chief Quartermaster Millay, although wounded, took over the wheel to carry out the orders of his skipper who was still "chasing salvoes". Hathaway's sense of humour remained unshaken. "Everything looked rosy," he commented "but only because the splashes were coloured red by the dye-loads."

Johnston, in contrast, was taking on only one ship, but since she had now turned to attack battleship *Kongo* sighted some 7,000 yards away on her port beam, she also had her hands full. She sent 30 rounds at her huge antagonist in 40 seconds, estimating that at least half of them hit. "As far as accomplishing anything decisive, it was like bouncing paper wads off a steel helmet," admitted Lieutenant Hagen, "but we did kill some Japs and knock out a few small guns. Then we ran back into our smoke. The battleship belched a few 14-inchers at us, but, thank God, registered only clean misses."

The destroyer-escorts were not so lucky. *Raymond* was near-missed but suffered only slight damage from shrapnel. *Butler* had four salvoes land close by her as she manoeuvred madly among the spouts of water. Shortly afterwards, Sprague ordered her to move forward to give better smoke-cover to the front of the carrier formation since the Japanese now had a clear line of fire to this. *Dennis* at 0850, was hit by an 8-inch shell – probably from *Tone* – which, penetrating her deck, went clean through to the opposite side without exploding. Ten minutes later, *Tone* hit her twice more, one shell landing on her after 40-mm gun director, while the other found her remaining 5-inch gun turret, killing or wounding the crew, thereby rendering the gun useless. Her fire-power thus quenched, *Dennis* retired behind *Butler*'s smoke-screen.

Also at 0850, *Roberts*' almost miraculous immunity from harm – due in part to luck but mainly to the skill of Lieutenant Commander Copeland – finally ended disastrously as an 8-inch hit below the water-line knocked out a fireroom. Her speed falling below 17 knots, she dropped behind her companions. As had happened to *Hoel* and *Gambier Bay*, she at once became the target for every hostile ship within range. A continuous flood of shells crashed into her, knocking out one gun and riddling her with some forty holes.

Finally at 0900, three 14-inch High Capacity shells from *Kongo* found their mark with a "tremendous explosion". Appalling havoc was caused. A giant hole 30 to 40 feet long and about 10 feet wide was blasted in *Roberts*' port side by the water-line. Fires were started on the fan-tail. An engine-room was wiped out. All power and communications were lost. The little ship came to a halt, still under fire, her after part "an inert mass of battered metal".

Yet the crew of Number 2 gun, who reported Copeland "as a crew distinguished themselves throughout the entire action", loaded, rammed, aimed and fired by hand. Each man must have realized the deadly risk involved. Without power, there was no compressed air to clear the bore of the burning fragments from previous charges. There was thus the perpetual hazard of an internal explosion in the gun. Nevertheless the risk was accepted. Six shots they fired at a heavy cruiser. The seventh blew up in the gun before the breech closed, killing or mortally wounding all but three members of the gun crew, two of whom died later on rafts. A Petty Officer who was the first to enter the turret found Gunner's Mate Third Class Paul Carr, the gun captain, holding a shell weighing 54 pounds above his head. Although his body was "completely torn open" from his neck to the middle of his thigh by the explosion, while "his intestines were splattered throughout the inside of the mount", his only thought was to ask for help to fire his gun. The Petty Officer took the shell from him, then dragged an unconscious man from the mount. When he returned, Carr was again trying to get the shell into the shattered breech. Several sailors pulled him to safety – but he collapsed, and died five minutes later.

Then came the order to abandon ship, but this took some time since the wounded had to be given first aid and placed on the life-rafts despite continuous fire. *Roberts* rendered her last service to her men by staying afloat despite her shattered state for an astonishing time. One of the largest rafts was pushed along the ship's port side by four men. The force of water rushing through the vast hole in the DE's side carried this, together with its guides, inside the burning, flooding, oil-soaked engine-room. Somehow they managed to push it back through the hole against the full force of the water. Still *Roberts* stayed afloat.

At last all the survivors had pulled themselves clear. Only then did *Roberts* roll slowly onto her side, to sink by the stern at 1005. Her epitaph and that of the three officers and eighty-six men who went down with her was given by Copeland, who with four other officers and eighty-four men survived. He recalled his estimate of the situation, "a fight against overwhelming odds from which survival could not be expected", then continued: "In the face of this knowledge the men zealously manned their stations wherever they might be, and fought and worked with such calmness, courage and efficiency that no higher honour could be conceived than to command such a group of men."

The remainder of 'Taffy 3' continued their flight south. As the escorts were sunk or crippled or their fire-power reduced, so the heavy cruisers were able to press ever closer towards the five remaining escort carriers. These fired back desperately with their 5-inch guns. *Fanshaw Bay* believed she scored five hits on *Chikuma*, one of which brought smoke from the superstructure. *White Plains* quite certainly put six shells into *Chokai*, "one of which appeared to decommission a forward turret". The cruiser's speed was also affected, and she temporarily ceased firing.

However, these forms of resistance were not going to save Sprague's ships. The ability to do so decisively lay, as Kurita feared, with the Air Groups of the escort carriers. As already mentioned, individual attacks were made by aircraft from 'Taffy 3' plus a few from 'Taffy 2' that were in the area on patrol, immediately the fighting commenced. Although in the confusion existing it was impossible for a co-ordinated attack to be made for some time, while the majority of planes were unsuitably armed in any case, they did do a surprising amount of damage, as witness that to *Kongo*, *Suzuya* and *Haguro* previously recounted.

'Taffy 3's' fighters also performed manfully in the face of severe anti-aircraft fire which caused quite heavy casualties. Sprague explained

> The Wildcat pilots were given a free hand to strafe, with the hope that their strafing would kill personnel on the Japanese warships, silence automatic weapons, and, most important, draw attention from the struggling escort carriers. Sometimes two, or four Wildcats would join up for a strafing run. Again, a Wildcat would join up and run interference for an Avenger. Then, likely as not, it would turn out that the Avenger had no torpedo or bomb and was simply making a dummy run. When their ammunition gave out, the fighters also made dry runs to turn the pursuers.

These 'dummy runs' could not stop Central Force but they did badger and harass the Japanese commanders, causing their ships to become still less co-ordinated as they swerved to avoid torpedoes — real or imaginary. For example Lieutenant-Commander Huxtable, the Air Group Commander from luckless *Gambier Bay*, who had exhausted even the ammunition in his machine-guns, was able by "flying down a line of cruisers, to divert them from their course and throw off their gunfire for a few precious minutes". Huxtable attacked the enemy for two hours without a round in his guns – nor was he the only American pilot to behave in this manner.

Time was also being gained for the aircraft away on missions to come to 'Taffy 3's' aid. Captain Whitehead was able to collect six Avengers and twenty fighters from the gulf area as the first reinforcements. "Improperly fuelled, improperly armed, but itching to get a crack at the Jap", these planes arrived at the scene of the action at about 0830. There the strike leader, Lieutenant-Commander Jackson from *Savo Island*, sighted a 'Jake' reconnaissance float plane launched from *Yamato*. This he promptly sent down in flames. Then he led his pilots together with a few from 'Taffy 3' in the first combined attack from the air on the cruisers of Central Force, although as his aircraft were armed only with 100-pound bombs or rockets, they could not have inflicted very great harm on their targets.

As well as aircraft coming from the gulf, there were several heading for it. As 'Taffy 3's' planes ran out of fuel or suffered damage they flew to the Tacloban airfield in Leyte which Army engineers had put into a state just suitable for receiving them. Some, unable to reach the field, 'ditched'. Others, watched "with aching heart" by MacArthur and General Kenney, crashed on landing. Yet the majority miraculously landed safely. *Kitkun Bay*'s Wildcats refuelled, collected some 500-pound bombs, then rushed back to join in the assaults on Kurita's ships. Four pilots from *St Lo* landed at Dulag. There they became involved in fighting Japanese ground forces then staging a counter-attack. Finally, however, after refuelling mainly by means of buckets, they succeeded in getting airborne again.

Other airmen sought shelter with Stump's 'Taffy 2' where they were rapidly supplied with fuel and ammunition. The crews of Stump's carriers surpassed all previous anticipations by carrying out these tasks with incredible speed, despite appalling conditions. The sheer volume of assistance they gave to the planes of their sister-groups was impressive enough in itself. *Manila Bay* for instance alone serviced and launched eleven visiting planes. At one point she had aircraft from *Sangamon* (of 'Taffy 1'), *White Plains, Kitkun Bay* and *Gambier Bay* all on her flight deck at the same time.

All this of course was in addition to the raids by her own airmen which 'Taffy 2' sent at the enemy. Starting at about 0745, Stump launched forty-three Avengers and thirty-six fighters in three strikes – or perhaps it would be better to regard it as one strike which went in in three waves, the first two, as a result of delays in joining up or locating targets, at about 0845, the third some ten minutes later by which time it had been joined by another sixteen torpedo-planes escorted by eight Wildcats which took off at 0833.

Stump's first double-wave arrived at a crucial moment, when the Japanese ships were ferociously battering the screening vessels as a prelude to getting at Sprague's remaining carriers. The pilots were unpractised in attacks on ships. Their aircraft were often equipped only with rockets or the useless 100-pound bombs. Yet, well knowing their companions' danger, they threw everything they had into the fight and their efforts indeed compare by no means unfavourably with the results of the attacks by Mitscher's crack pilots against Ozawa. Commander Otani, Kurita's Operations Officer, confirmed after the war that: "The bombers and torpedo-planes were very aggressive and skilful and the co-ordination was impressive; even in comparison with the many experiences of American attacks we had already had, this was the most skilful work of your planes."

Stump also avoided the error made by Halsey in the Sibuyan Sea. He ordered his airmen not to concentrate on one or two ships but to ensure they crippled as many as possible. In consequence they spread their efforts widely. As mentioned earlier, it seems that it was in these raids that *Suzuya* was fatally crippled. *Chikuma* was also attacked but in her case any damage she received could only have been minor. Other aircraft sent salvoes of rockets crashing into bridges or control positions. Fighters flew low, strafing. Destroyers *Hayashimo* and *Hamanami*, damaged, began to fall astern of the chase.

'Taffy 2' had a very personal interest in the successes of these strikes, for at about this time, it seemed probable that this group also would fall into the jaws of Central Force. Japanese look-outs had by now sighted Stump's carriers, for these had been steaming on a converging course during most of the action in order to fly off their planes, so their distance from 'Taffy 3' had now decreased considerably. *Kongo* and *Haruna* now began to take an interest in Stump. Fourteen-inch shells from the former began rising close by destroyers *Haggard*, *Hailey* and *Franks* which under Stump's screen commander, Captain Reynolds, had taken up station at the rear of 'Taffy 2' to guard against a possible destroyer raid.

This diversion of attack was greatly to the assistance of Sprague but less attractive in the eyes of his fellow commander who turned some of his planes against *Kongo*. Lieutenant (jg) Miller from *Ommaney Bay* had not been able to release his torpedo during the raids by 'Taffy 2's' planes just described. He therefore circled to gain height, then made a single-handed assault on *Kongo*, to drop his torpedo at about 750 yards range, pulling out amidst clouds of anti-aircraft shells desperately close to the battleship's stern. He believed his torpedo found its mark. He was wrong but his attack – so typical of the pilots' endeavours in these encounters – succeeded in its main objective. *Kongo* turned away, breaking off her attack.

Sprague's ships were still the main targets, however – particularly *Heermann* which was in between the escort carriers and the flanking cruisers. *Chikuma* now bombarded her with 8-inch shells. One of her guns was knocked out. A hit forward tore a jagged hole in her hull, flooding the forward magazines. The fore part of the destroyer began to sink lower until, remarked Hathaway, "it seemed as if the ship would dive headfirst beneath the surface". But remembering the fate of those ships which had slowed down only to become a target for massed gunfire, he kept on at full speed, his damage-control parties somehow managing to keep *Heermann* afloat.

Amidst all the destruction and agony, one gloriously amusing incident was recalled gleefully later by *Heermann*'s crew. One of the shells struck a big storage locker full of dried beans, which were reduced to a hideous brown paste. Another shell hit the uptake from the forward boiler with the result, stated Hathaway, that "the bean paste was sucked up by the hot blast of the uptake and thrown in the air". An unfortunate officer, Lieutenant Rutter, who was standing by the stack was "nearly buried in the stuff" – and what a beautiful coincidence that he should be the supply officer!

However, at the time it seemed unlikely that anyone on *Heermann* would survive long enough to enjoy the joke. Her position was still perilous in the extreme, with *Chikuma* pouring salvoes at her, while other vessels were also joining in. Then suddenly at 0902, *Chikuma* "turned sharply to her port, and retired to the eastward. At this time a large fire was observed on her fantail." Admiral Stump's second double-wave was now breaking on the enemy.

These attacks, in which the Wildcats supported the Avengers superbly, had immediate effect. *Chikuma* was the first victim. Caught by surprise as she fired on the vessels of 'Taffy 3', she was struck by two torpedoes – possibly launched by the Avengers from *Natoma Bay* which claimed to have inflicted such hits on a heavy cruiser. Already much battered by destroyers' gunfire as well as having possible bomb-hits from 'Taffy 2's' earlier attacks, *Chikuma* had now suffered more damage than she could take. Heeling out of formation, she limped to a halt, then began to sink, slowly but relentlessly.

Stump's airmen also unleashed a heavy raid on *Tone*. Captain Mayuzumi who had had plenty of practice in evading air raids in the Sibuyan Sea, manoeuvred his ship madly to escape. He succeeded in remaining unhit but in the process lost valuable distance. He ultimately fell in astern of *Haguro*, after which he joined her in keeping up the pursuit of the fleeing escort carriers.

Almost simultaneously with the attacks from 'Taffy 2' came the most effective of 'Taffy 3's' own air strikes. At the start of the shooting, *Kitkun Bay* sent off six Avengers escorted by twelve Wildcats under the leadership of Commander Richard Fowler who was the officer entrusted with the task of co-ordinating the strikes against Kurita. These aircraft flew towards the enemy force and encountered heavy anti-aircraft fire which shot down one Avenger. Another had to 'ditch' as a result of engine-trouble, while the fighters lost contact in the drifting rain-clouds. As related earlier, they flew to Tacloban where they collected some bombs in order to re-enter the action.

This left Fowler with four Avengers armed not with torpedoes but with the next-best weapons — 500-pound semi-armour-piercing bombs. Thick clouds plus his responsibilities in organizing other people's attacks, prevented Fowler from bringing his own planes in to the assault until about 0905, when, choosing his moment perfectly, he swung his formation out of the sun through the cloud bank upon heavy cruiser *Chokai*, also engaged in shooting at 'Taffy 3's' carriers. Fowler's men took her completely by surprise, meeting no anti-aircraft fire.

The results of this attack were spectacular. "We completed all dives in about 35 seconds," reported Fowler. In that time, *Kitkun Bay*'s pilots landed two very near-misses by *Chokai*'s stern, one direct hit astern, three direct hits on her bow and five more amidships. The bomb which found her stern sent the fatally wounded heavy cruiser turning sharply away from her column, while several successive explosions hurled clouds of steam and black smoke high in the air. She too drifted to a crippled halt, blowing up and sinking not long afterwards.

Yet despite these heartening successes, Sprague's position seemed as hopeless as ever. Stump and Fowler, temporarily at least, had now shot their bolt, although there were still individual aircraft buzzing about overhead, strafing enemy ships or making 'dummy runs'. Two of the flanking cruisers, *Tone* and *Haguro*, were still afloat, in a position to riddle the surviving escort carriers. Astern the rest of the

The Action off Samar Island

Japanese ships were still firing. The two remaining cruisers closed remorselessly to a range of 10,000 yards, their shells flinging up gouts of water all around their victims – or causing the dull red glare of hits.

Casualties mounted. *Kitkun Bay* though not hit was frequently damaged by shrapnel from near-misses. Part of a 6-inch salvo, presumably from *Noshiro*, fell on *White Plains*. In addition she was shaken from end to end by near-misses. Everything loose crashed to the decks, while soot and dust filled the engine-room. Many of the crew thought that their vessel was fatally hurt but all stuck to their tasks. *Fanshaw Bay* took four 8-inch hits plus two very near-misses. Of the shells that found their mark, one holed her below the water-line – fortunately not too badly; one exploded in the flag office wrecking it; one smashed the anchor windlass; and the fourth landed on the flight deck causing heavy damage. Three of the crew were killed and twenty more wounded.

Worst harmed of all was *Kalinin Bay*. Already damaged by two 8-inch shells early in the action, she was now struck by at least eleven more, to say nothing of one 14-inch hit. She was holed repeatedly below the water-line, but fantastic efforts by her damage-control parties, working among clouds of scalding steam or amid the choking stench of burning rubber, saved her. Her main steering control was knocked out, necessitating steering by hand. One shell, plunging through the flight deck, hit her forward elevator where it exploded, completely wrecking the elevator platform. Undoubtedly she survived mainly because the armour-piercing missiles the Japanese were using went clean through her thin hull without exploding in most instances – but neither she nor her sister-ships could long continue to bear this sort of punishment.

As if the situation of Sprague's carriers was not already bad enough, there also occurred at this time the most serious potential threat of all. In towards the starboard flank of the formation raced Destroyer Squadron 10. Rear-Admiral Susumu Kimura had determined to carry out a torpedo attack and he had light cruiser *Yahagi* (his flagship) plus destroyers *Urakaze, Isokaze, Yukikaze* and *Nowake* with which to do so. Each of these ships carried eight 'Long Lance' torpedoes – fearful killers which, propelled by liquid oxygen, could carry a war-head twice the size of that of their American equivalents for 44,000 yards at 36 knots or for 22,000 yards at 49 knots. A single one of these underwater horrors could easily sink an escort carrier.

But from one of Sprague's screening vessels this new danger was recognized. Suddenly, reported Kimura: "Enemy destroyer plunged out of smoke screen on our port bow and opened gunfire and torpedo attack on us." This was the battered *Johnston*. Commander Evans turned his guns – he had no torpedoes left in fact – on *Yahagi* scoring an estimated twelve hits, although *Johnston* was also hit by the Japanese destroyers in the process. *Yahagi* then sheered sharply away allowing Evans to switch his fire onto the leading destroyer. Thereupon to his amazement all four destroyers also turned away. At 0905, *Yahagi* fired her torpedoes; at 0915, the destroyers fired theirs; but harassed as they were, they all did so at very long range.

The result was that by the time these dreadful missiles caught up with the fleeing carriers they were slowing down and coming to the surface. As one approached the wake of *Kalinin Bay*, an Avenger pilot Lieutenant (jg) Leonard Waldrop returning to his ship *St Lo* after making 'dummy runs' on the enemy cruisers, sighted it. Diving down, he strafed the torpedo, exploding it about a hundred yards astern of *Kalinin Bay*. This warned the escort carrier of her danger. She began firing with her 5-inch gun depressed as far as possible at another torpedo coming perilously close. One shell burst ten feet ahead of this, causing it to veer off to port. All other torpedoes missed by a wider margin. The greatest of all threats had been diverted successfully.

However, a bitter price for her achievement had now to be paid by *Johnston*. *Yahagi* was still in trouble for apart from the hits from *Johnston* she was now strafed by aircraft, probably from 'Taffy 2', which killed one officer on the bridge and wounded several others. But the destroyers turned in fury on *Johnston*. *Tone* and *Haguro* were also firing at her as in the words of Lieutenant Hagen she "engaged first the cruisers on our port hand and then the destroyers on our starboard hand, alternating between the two groups in a somewhat desperate attempt to keep all of them from closing the carrier formation".

As hits riddled *Johnston*, her damage became unsupportable. Her mast was shot away, dangling over her superstructure. Fires raged amidships exploding the destroyer's own shells. A hit knocked out one forward gun and damaged the other. The bridge became unusable. Commander Evans was forced "to shift his command to the fantail, where he yelled his steering orders through an open hatch at the men who were turning the rudder by hand". Dead or wounded men lay on all sides.

Finally, as Destroyer Squadron 10 came still nearer, "an avalanche of shells" knocked out *Johnston*'s remaining engine and fireroom. All

The Action off Samar Island

power was lost, as were all communications. Only Number 4 gun was still firing — by local control. At 0940, *Johnston* came to a halt, whereupon the hostile destroyers formed a tight circle round her, shooting as they went — "like Indians attacking a prairie schooner" was Hagen's description.

Five minutes later, the order was given to abandon ship. One enemy destroyer closed in to finish the fight with a final full salvo at point-blank range. At 1010, 'G.Q. Johnny' rolled over to sink with the loss of 186 of her complement of 327 — including, alas, Commander Evans. She was not unhonoured in two countries for as she took her final plunge, the American sailors on their rafts or swimming nearby saw the Japanese destroyer captain at the salute in instinctive recognition of an exceptionally valiant foe.

By this time it seemed that nothing could possibly save 'Taffy 3' from annihilation, after which 'Taffy 2' already dangerously close would be overtaken, while only 45 miles away now was Leyte Gulf with its vulnerable beach-heads where frantic preparations for defence were being made. Admiral Sprague expected he would be swimming very shortly. Then at 0925, he heard one of his signalmen yell "Goddamit, boys, they're getting away!" *Tone* and *Haguro* with the range only 10,000 yards swung sharply to port breaking off the action. The whole enemy force, responding to a signal sent by Kurita at 0911, reversed course northward. The surface fighting off Samar was over.

"The failure of the enemy main body and encircling light forces to completely wipe out all vessels of this task unit," reported Sprague later, "can be attributed to our successful smoke-screen, our torpedo counter-attack, continuous harassment of the enemy by bomb, torpedo and strafing air attacks, timely manoeuvres, and the definite partiality of Almighty God."

8

Admiral Kurita Changes Course

Why did Admiral Kurita break off the action? Why did he not continue his advance towards Leyte Gulf? It is now known that these were two different decisions, the latter made over three hours after the former, but together they were of vast importance, for they made up the second really crucial error of the battle, compensating for Halsey's mistake in proceeding north. Thereby they ensured that final victory would fall inevitably to the Americans.

As for the reasons for the step thus taken, it is not easy to reach an indisputable solution, for the only person really qualified to explain was Kurita. Woodward is on record as stating that the Japanese commander "had difficulty in answering the question in two days of interrogation by American naval officers. He gave his reasons to be sure — perhaps too many reasons. But he left enigma as thick as a smoke screen in the wake of some of them." It should of course be remembered that matters which were clear afterwards appeared in a quite different light to Kurita at the time and that his actions were made in a position of great tension and uncertainty.

There seems no argument from any responsible Japanese officer that the first decision, to break off the pursuit of Clifton Sprague, resulted from Kurita having lost control of the ships under his command which had become widely scattered as the fighting progressed with *Yamato* lagging at the rear of the chase. Coupled with the earlier loss of his communications personnel, this meant that the unfortunate Kurita was unable to appreciate just how critical was Sprague's position. His Chief of Staff, Rear-Admiral Koyanagi, when questioned after the war, admitted that he had never realized that *Tone* and *Haguro* has closed to almost point-blank range of the CVEs when they were recalled. On the contrary, because the manoeuvring necessitated by the perpetual air or surface attacks had stopped the Japanese ships from catching the little carriers, Kurita had concluded that they were travelling at 30 knots — not far short of twice their

Admiral Kurita Changes Course

maximum speed – so that it would take a long stern chase before he overhauled them.

In view of Stump's heavy air strikes, this was a prospect that Kurita did not relish. It has also been suggested that he was worried about his vessels running low in fuel. Some of his destroyers were indeed beginning to go short though not seriously so. Yet Kurita was to state later that lack of fuel was not the cause of his action. However, according to Field, he was by now "anticipating that he would soon be subjected to increasingly heavy air attack". Since he had no fighter protection whatever, he knew that only if his force was concentrated would it be able to put up the mass gunfire needed for defence against such assaults.

Accordingly, Kurita determined that he would re-unite his command, re-establish his grip on proceedings, attend to his damaged cruisers which were careering about out of control and thereafter resume his advance on the gulf with his ships in a tight, orderly formation. As already seen therefore, he signalled to his widely-spread units that they were to converge on flagship *Yamato*. Clifton Sprague, still unable to believe it, found himself free from pursuit.

As the Japanese swung away from their targets, orders were given to assist the four heavy cruisers that had fallen victims to Sprague's destroyers or the 'Taffies'' airmen. Of these *Chokai*, torn apart by explosions, soon went down. *Chikuma* and *Suzuya*, fatally hurt, lingered on for some time, while destroyers *Nowake* and *Okinami* respectively stood by to take off their crews. Only *Kumano* could be saved. She withdrew at slow speed accompanied by destroyer *Hamanami*. Even allowing for these losses, Kurita still had a very strong force under his orders, consisting as it did of *Yamato*, three other battleships, two heavy and two light cruisers and some six to eight destroyers all fit for action. Yet instead of heading south with these as he stated he intended, he allowed his vessels to mill about on various courses for some three hours without their making any real attempt to proceed towards the gulf, or for that matter to return home; they simply manoeuvred aimlessly in the same waters they had been in when the fight was broken off.

During this period, so Koyanagi explained later, "we were assembling and assessing the information and taking account of the situation". The length of time that elapsed before any decision was reached, however, does suggest that Kurita was procrastinating. Having paused in his charge for Leyte Gulf, he was becoming filled with doubts as to whether he would be wise to continue it.

The first point for Kurita to worry about was that now he had given Sprague's carriers a respite, their aircraft would be on the alert, much more capable than before of pouncing on his ships if they again closed the range. This seemed the more serious to him since he judged Sprague's strength to be very much greater than was in fact the case — a belief founded in the confusion of the action off Samar for which the poor visibility, coupled with the resolution of the U.S. ships, was mainly responsible. The Japanese believed that the CVEs of 'Taffy 3', as well as those of Stump's command which they had also spotted, were large fleet carriers crammed with planes. The destroyers were reported as *Baltimore*-class heavy cruisers, which were similar in profile and the DEs were considered to be destroyers. Numbers were also exaggerated. Koyanagi believed that at least ten heavy cruisers were present and perhaps one or two battleships as well. Having been beaten back by this force once when he had taken it by surprise, Kurita was not eager to try conclusions with it a second time.

Such information as Kurita received from his own forces was not encouraging. Prior to engaging Sprague he had heard from Shima that he was withdrawing from Surigao Strait. Kurita rightly concluded that this indicated he would have no support from the Japanese Southern Forces. This, it might seem, could not have been a vital factor, for Kurita had pushed on long after this signal came through. He claimed later that the defeat of the Southern Forces in no way affected his decision. On the other hand Koyanagi flatly stated that it did.

It appears that the Chief of Staff may well have been correct. Shima's signal while it suggested that the Japanese had been repulsed, did not indicate the extent of the frightful losses the vessels under Nishimura's command had suffered. This, however, was made only too clear by a signal sent to Kurita as well as to Toyoda at 1018 by Commander Nishino, whose ship was the sole survivor of that command: "All ships except *Shigure* went down under gunfire and torpedo attacks". It is not known exactly when Kurita got this message but it was certainly during the period when he was debating whether or not to retire; it is inconceivable that it did not influence him.

From Admiral Ozawa, as a result of the constant communications troubles, Kurita had heard nothing at all, so he was not aware of the success with which the decoy-force had met. Yet surely the fact that he had broken through San Bernardino Strait completely unhindered must have told Central Force's leader that some at least of the Third Fleet strength had been diverted. Also at about 0945, he received a mysterious signal probably from Second Air Fleet in Manila which suggested an American Carrier Group was north-east of Samar. Although the position given was totally false – there was no such force so close to Kurita – he believed this might be Halsey. In this case it is hard to understand why he did not accept this as confirmation that Halsey had gone north. If it also inaccurately indicated that Halsey was now closing fast as he raced south to the rescue, did this not merely stress the need for Kurita to cease his manoeuvres and proceed to the gulf at maximum speed?

It should also be recalled that there had been no further orders from Kurita's chief, Admiral Toyoda, whose last command had been to continue with the mission. Indeed remembering Toyoda's "Divine Assistance" message, to say nothing of the desperate nature of the whole plan, it would appear that Kurita had been given no choice but to go on to the gulf in any event.

Yet this Kurita was increasingly reluctant to attempt. Although the horizon was empty, he felt that at any instant enemy forces would converge on him from all sides, while his anxiety was strengthened by his inability to check on his foes' movements. *Yamato* had launched two aircraft to scout in the direction of the gulf. One of these was sent down in flames by Lieutenant-Commander Jackson the strike leader from *Savo Island*. The other also failed to return, perhaps falling prey to an American pilot who did not live to tell of his success. A reconnaissance pilot from *Nagato* did report at 1235 that there were thirty-five transports in the gulf but Kurita believed that his long delay would have given these a good chance of escaping – which of course merely emphasizes how unwise that delay was.

Of one factor at least, Kurita was already unpleasantly aware; that the air attacks showed no sign of stopping. Sporadic raids continued to harass the Japanese Admiral throughout his hours of indecision. 'Taffy 3', recovering from its ordeal with amazing swiftness, flew off Avengers which there had not been time to launch during the action. *Kitkun Bay* sent off five at 1013, while a few minutes later *White Plains* sent off two more. Other Avengers arrived from Admiral Thomas Sprague's Group 1; these because of the distance they had to fly – which also resulted in casualties from loss of fuel – had not been able to intervene while the fighting was at its height. Those bombers from 'Taffy 1' which had attacked the retreating Southern Forces, landed at Tacloban to refuel. Having done this they learned of the situation off Samar, so promptly took off again to add their weight to the strikes against Kurita.

Of course Admiral Stump's tireless 'Taffy 2' was not left out of the fight. At 0935, regardless of a dangerous cross-wind, eleven Avengers, one armed with a torpedo, the rest with four 500-pound bombs apiece, took off from the CVEs accompanied by an escort of eight Wildcats. About half an hour later, 'Taffy 2's' planes fell on Kurita, claiming three bombs hits on already-damaged heavy cruisers. It seems very probable that it was a hit from this raid which finally finished off *Suzuya*, which, although the first enemy heavy cruiser to be crippled, was in fact the last to go down – as she finally did at 1322.

All these events were very depressing and as if they were not enough it seemed to Kurita that the number of air attacks would mount as he continued to the gulf, where furthermore he felt: "I couldn't use the advantage that ships had of manoeuvring whereas I would be a more useful force under the same attack with the advantage of manoeuvre in the open sea". Also he had intercepted messages from Commander Whitehead suggesting that the CVE planes make landings at Tacloban. Not realizing that this was an expedient based on desperation, not knowing the state of the Tacloban air-strip, he imagined that this would be fully operational, crowded with aircraft ready to strike him from all sides as he entered the gulf.

Other intercepted American signals proved equally disheartening. Kinkaid's plain-language transmissions to Halsey were picked up, as were some of his commands to his own forces to prepare to intervene in the fighting. Kurita later admitted that this knowledge did influence his decision for he thought that Halsey and Oldendorf would be closing in on him to trap him between them.

"Thus," writes Morison, "partly from what he knew but still more from what he imagined, Kurita, reached the conclusion that his prospects in Leyte Gulf were both thin and grim and that he had better save the rest of his fleet, possibly to fight another day." To this, Roskill adds that of all the factors, influencing Kurita, "it was probably the lack of Intelligence, combined with failure of his own resolution, which contributed most to the loss of the greatest opportunity to come the way of the Japanese Navy since Pearl Harbour; for a determined drive into Leyte Gulf might well have played havoc among the invasion shipping".

At 1236, Kurita finally made up his mind and signalling to Toyoda that he was abandoning his planned "penetration of Leyte anchorage", he irrevocably turned his back on those vital, vulnerable beaches, which, had he but known, offered such a rich prize, and for

Admiral Kurita Changes Course

which so many casualties had already been suffered. It was the decisive moment of the battle.

Kurita offered various excuses for his turn-away, designed to 'save face' by suggesting that it was not really a withdrawal but the commencement of a new mission. First he stated that he had "concluded that it was best to go north and join Admiral Ozawa". Since Kurita like everyone else had previously confirmed that Ozawa had been a decoy only, this observation was greeted with polite incredulity by American intelligence officers. Thereupon, Kurita changed his story; his intention, he now stated, has been "not primarily to join Admiral Ozawa but to go north and seek out the enemy" — by which he meant the phantom fleet reported north-east of Samar.

Again it seems unarguable that this was merely an excuse. There is no question that the Japanese Commander believed that he would have to do battle with this force. He is said to have preferred action with enemy carriers to that with transports — though his behaviour when confronted by 'Taffy 3' scarcely supports this. More to the point, if he did engage this foe, he would be in the open sea not in the cramped waters of the gulf. He would be well away from the American airfields on Leyte, but on the contrary, near the Japanese bases in Luzon, from which he could call on air support. In practice, it may be mentioned that large forces of Japanese aircraft were sent out by Fukudome, probably at the insistence of Toyoda, in an effort to combine with Central Force in an attack on the Americans, only to find that there were no targets for their bombs — not that it seems likely that they would have done much damage in view of their ineffectiveness of the previous day. Two bombers, however, completed Kurita's misery by attacking him — fortunately unsuccessfully.

Yet while Kurita was willing to fight any vessels encountered, it is apparent that this was not his main objective. When he signalled to Toyoda his intention to retire he stated that after attacking the enemy to the north, he would "pass through San Bernardino Strait". It seems clear from what followed that this was his main aim and if he had engaged any American force north of him, it would have been because this blocked his route of escape.

Thus, Kurita's course along the coast of Samar back towards San Bernardino was almost the same as his route south to the scene of his encounter with Clifton Sprague. He made no attempt to go north of Samar to seek out his elusive enemy. The question of his fuel supply which he had stated did not affect his decision not to proceed to Leyte, he now felt had become "a very important consideration", though the majority of his ships did not experience any real difficulty in this respect.

Indeed the genuine motive for the retirement northwards became quite clear from Kurita's remarks when being interrogated after the war when he stated bluntly: "Secondarily or over-all, I wanted to be at San Bernardino at sunset to get through and as far to the west as possible during the night." When questioned as to whether this was more important then engaging his enemy, he replied: "I won't say which was more important, because if I did not get into the Strait by night, the next day was hopeless for me, because I could be brought under attack by land planes and by this force."

There can be no real doubt therefore that Kurita had lost his nerve — and once this is accepted, who would fail to understand or even to withhold sympathy? The strain on the Admiral had been almost unendurable. On the twenty-third, his flagship, heavy cruiser *Atago*, had been blown out of the water by *Darter*'s torpedoes, forcing him to swim for safety. There had followed the continuous air raids of the twenty-fourth when he had seen the magnificent 'unsinkable' *Musashi* being battered to death — a fearful blow to morale. The tricky passage of San Bernardino although successful must have tried him still further mentally. Then came the encounter with 'Taffy 3' which cost him four more heavy cruisers sunk or crippled. Strafing, shell-splinters, bomb-splinters; all had inflicted their toll on Central Force's remaining vessels, only one destroyer, *Yukikaze* — a ship with a charmed career throughout the war which indeed she survived — being entirely undamaged. The news of Nishimura's annihilation and Shima's retirement were further blows to his spirit. And the air attacks which were still continuing relentlessly, would in his opinion grow steadily heavier as his foes closed in on him.

Thus when Kurita made his vital change of course he was not really capable of considering the matter in a dispassionate frame of mind, nor indeed could this be expected of him. "I have no doubt," Admiral Kinkaid later remarked understandingly "that Kurita was physically exhausted after three gruelling days." Perhaps Sir Winston Churchill gave the fairest assessment of Kurita's action: "Those who have endured a similar ordeal may judge him".

That ordeal was not ended by Central Force's withdrawal for even as Kurita made his signal to Toyoda, yet another raid launched by the indefatigable Admiral Stump was preparing to attack him. These attackers consisted of thirty-five Avengers with about the same number of Wildcats, including not only aircraft from 'Taffy 2' but also several from the other 'Taffies' notably the Avengers from *Kitkun Bay* which had landed on *Manila Bay*, re-armed with four 500-pound S.A.P. bombs each and were more than ready to get back into action. The indomitable Commander Fowler acted as strike co-ordinator.

The airmen sighted Central Force at about 1220; their arrival was apparently an additional reason why Kurita now finally determined to retreat. Passing over sinking *Suzuya* with destroyer *Okinami* standing by, Fowler attacked Central Force's main strength at 1245, half his pilots under his own command coming in from the port side out of cloud clover, while the remainder under the leadership of Lieutenant-Commander Dale, head of the Air Group from *Kadashan Bay*, took the starboard side.

Despite heavy anti-aircraft fire which put over thirty holes through Fowler's own plane, the Americans caused considerable damage. One bomb went right through the bows of battleship *Nagato* to explode in the water. Another struck heavy cruiser *Tone* which had become the latest flagship of Vice-Admiral Shiraishi in succession to *Kumano* and *Suzuya*, temporarily putting her steering gear out of commission — even so this fighting ship was more lucky than either of her predecessors. There were several near-misses, and if there was any slight chance that Kurita would yet return towards Leyte before this attack, there was certainly none at all after it. Central Force sped north at top speed, while their tormentors sought the safety of their own or other carriers; Dale for instance was unable to get back to 'Taffy 2', so landed on *Kitkun Bay* instead.

Half an hour later, aircraft swept in upon Central Force from the north-east. The carriers of Vice-Admiral McCain's Task Group 38:1 had been rushing towards Samar ever since their commander had intercepted Kinkaid's first call for help, an action subsequently confirmed by Mitscher. At 1030, *Hornet* launched six Hellcat fighters to scout for Kurita. Fifteen minutes later, *Hornet, Hancock* and *Wasp* sent off a strike numbering thirty-three Helldiver bombers and nineteen Avengers escorted by forty-eight Hellcats. Two of the Helldivers crashed on launching but the remaining aircraft were soon on their way to the aid of Seventh Fleet.

Unfortunately McCain was still at an extreme range of some 335 miles from Kurita. Also, since no information was available to him as to whether or not his planes could land or refuel at Tacloban, he had to make arrangements ensuring that they were able to get back to his carriers. This meant that wing tanks had to be fitted to provide the necessary extra fuel, while no torpedoes could be taken because the additional weight would have made it impossible for the aircraft carrying these to return. Despite this, two crews volunteered to fly Avengers loaded with torpedoes on the raid, a request which naturally was refused.

Happily the weather was clear, but because the pilots had such a lengthy flight in front of them, they were already tired when they attacked. Also the air-groups from the different carriers attacked separately instead of in co-ordination. The Japanese, in contrast, reacted with considerable vigour. Six Zeros, presumably part of the force sent by Fukudome from Luzon, attacked but of these two were shot down while the rest were driven off. Kurita had now re-established control over his ships, which manoeuvred well together while pouring out an intense, accurate anti-aircraft barrage that knocked down three of the attackers and damaged others. Of all the bombs dropped, only one scored a hit – on heavy cruiser *Tone* – and this did not explode.

There followed a desperate flight back to the safety of Task Group 38:1, a perilous undertaking which resulted in many cases in a nightmare experience of watching fuel-gauges falling well past the danger-margin. Some aircraft went down short of their carriers. Others could not attempt the return flight because of damage, so went to 'Taffy 2' or Tacloban. Losses were high. Of the twelve Helldivers from *Hancock* for example, flak got one, loss of fuel forced down two more, two others landed at Tacloban one being wrecked in the process, and four more landed on Stump's CVEs. Only three returned to their parent ship.

At 1500, another group of McCain's airmen – twenty fighters, twenty Helldivers and thirteen Avengers flying 320 miles from *Hornet* and *Hancock* – attacked Kurita. This raid also was not well co-ordinated as the planes had become separated during their long haul to the targets. No hits were scored. Again there followed the ghastly return trek. In the two strikes, fourteen of McCain's aircraft were lost, a figure which does not include those which failed to return to the task group but found safety elsewhere.

A few minutes later, Kurita suffered his final attack of the day from the CVEs of 'Taffy 2', reinforced by a few aircraft from *Kitkun Bay* – in all twenty-six Avengers escorted by twenty-four Wildcats. This was Stump's seventh raid and by now his pilots were all but exhausted. Also though some Avengers had torpedoes, most carried little more

Admiral Kurita Changes Course

than anti-personnel bombs since supplies were now extremely low. Perhaps not surprisingly therefore, this strike had no success either.

Kurita might yet have faced a more powerful foe before he could reach San Bernardino Strait, for it will be remembered that Rear-Admiral Badger with battleships *Iowa* and *New Jersey*, light cruisers *Vincennes, Miami* and *Biloxi* and eight destroyers, had been detached by Halsey to cut off Central Force's retreat. However, the various delays before Halsey sent his forces south which have already been recounted, resulted in Badger being unable to get to San Bernardino before Kurita did — although since Halsey had left only two battleships on hand for an engagement while the Japanese had four, all fit for action even if their crews were rapidly approaching exhaustion, this may well have been fortunate rather than otherwise.

Be that as it may, the main body of Kurita's force, leaving a long trial of oil from several damaged vessels, was able to avoid further fighting. At 1727, Kurita signalled to Toyoda that he was heading for the strait, which he did at 24 knots followed by some stragglers and damaged vessels. At 2140, a scout from *Independence* reported him entering the strait with his ships in single column. By the time Badger was able to cover the entrance, Kurita had already made good his escape.

There was still a chance that Badger's Task Group 34:5 might be able to mop up some stragglers, indeed an *Independence* plane was able to give warning of one such at conveniently close range. This was the unlucky destroyer *Nowake*, which, having stood by the sinking *Chikuma*, had been unable to catch up the main body. Accordingly Badger detached Rear-Admiral Whiting in *Vincennes* with *Miami, Biloxi* and destroyers *Miller, Owen* and *Lewis Hancock* to intercept this target, while the battleships with the remaining destroyers turned away to clear the line of fire.

The resulting quick destruction gives some idea of the magnitude of Clifton Sprague's success by supplying a graphic example of how quickly even light cruisers when properly handled can wipe out a large destroyer. *Vincennes, Miami* and *Biloxi* commenced firing at 0054. Within minutes the target, already on fire, had slowed to 13 knots. By 0103, she lay dead in the water, burning from end to end. Destroyer *Owen* fired five torpedoes at her but apparently without result. Then *Owen* and also *Miller* came in to close range, pouring rapid, accurate fire upon their victim, now too damaged to reply. Showers of sparks came from the Japanese destroyer, which finally "flared up in a tremendous explosion that sent flaming debris high in the air and illuminated the whole area". After this the flames died down, only to burst up again in a second titanic blast after which "the target disappeared from view and from all radar screens". That was the end of poor *Nowake* and the loss of life must have been very heavy for she was packed with the survivors she had rescued from *Chikuma*.

Even so, this was a poor consolation for the men of Third Fleet. Task Group 34:5 continued down the east coast of Samar searching for other opportunities to use its guns – but in vain. The remainder of Kurita's ships had already escaped. The final result of Halsey's impulsive move north, plus his subsequent delay in turning back, had been that the great American battle fleet had raced about fruitlessly during the most crucial hours of the battle leaving inferior forces to deal with the enemy in two areas. Nimitz was later to sum up the fiasco as follows: "The fast battleships of the Third Fleet had steamed 300 miles north and then 300 miles back south between the two major enemy forces without quite making contact with either."

As a crowning misfortune, Badger's ships did not come across the survivors from those vessels of 'Taffy 3' that had been sunk in the surface action, although they did rescue nine airmen from the escort carriers as well as six seamen from *Suzuya* who for a change were willing to be saved. Clinging to rafts or even bits of floating wreckage, the men from *Gambier Bay, Hoel, Johnston* and *Roberts*, remained drifting helplessly far from aid.

For almost two days from the time of the sinkings, no help appeared. Friendly planes flew over at intervals but did not drop supplies to assist their comrades. The Leyte beach-head was under air attack for most of the time and the Catalinas often used in rescue work were busy saving airmen from 'ditched' planes – Seventh Fleet in fact was too occupied to send out much in the way of an air-search.

Surface craft had been dispatched but the original estimate given by the 'Taffies' of the position of the survivors was well south of their actual location. Also they drifted westward towards Samar on the prevailing currents. Destroyers sent out from 'Taffy 1' were unable therefore to discover a single man from the sunken ships.

As the second day went by without aid, great numbers of men began to die from exhaustion, exposure or wounds. Some became delirious, being prevented from injuring themselves or others only with difficulty while others had to be stopped by force from drinking sea-water. From *Johnston*'s complement of 327 alone, 186 were lost. Of these, only 49 were killed directly by the enemy. Forty-five more died on the rafts from their wounds. The other 92 were seen alive in the water but later disappeared. Among those who perished in this manner was the destroyer's heroic captain, Commander Evans.

Many of those who were lost in the water may have fallen victims to sharks, for as a final horror, these great fish appeared. One man from *Gambier Bay* and one from *Johnston* were quite definitely killed by them but according to Morison a veteran Gunner's Mate from *Johnston* was "bitten twice by a shark which then let go, evidently not relishing his salty flavour — leaving this ancient mariner with a row of shark-tooth imprints on his right thigh to exhibit to the incredulous". In fact these lacerations might possibly have been caused by the shark's rough skin rasping against the man; this has often been known to inflict similar injuries. In either case, one feels that the sailor in question had an unpleasantly narrow escape.

Meanwhile Admiral Kinkaid had personally initiated another surface search by two patrol craft and five LCI gunboats under the leadership of Lieutenant-Commander Baxter. After hunting all day on 26 October, finally at 2229, they sighted signal flares. Shortly afterwards, they located survivors from *Gambier Bay*, whom they commenced to rescue. Next day, rafts from the sunken escort vessels were also sighted. By 1000, Baxter had taken on board his ships over 1,150 survivors. These were treated with such capable skill and care that not another wounded man died. Early the following morning, the rescued sailors were transferred to hospital ships.

Even so, the cost in American lives was heavy. The total U.S. losses off Samar — which includes those suffered in subsequent air attacks to be described later were 1,130 dead and 913 wounded. Yet it might be argued that it was a miracle that casualties had not been vastly higher. Certainly Seventh Fleet had paid a comparatively cheap price for their astounding achievement of turning back the most powerful Japanese surface fleet ever to engage an American force.

9

Kamikaze

The retreat of Kurita by no means ended the ordeal of the escort carriers. Even while 'Taffy 3' was suffering the full might of Central Force's assault, 130 miles southward, Rear-Admiral Thomas Sprague's own 'Taffy 1' was experiencing the first onslaught of a totally new and in many ways far more terrifying form of attack. At 0740, as the CVEs – *Santee, Suwanee, Sangamon* and *Petrof Bay* – were busy launching or recovering planes, four Zeros, each carrying a 300-pound bomb, suddenly burst out of the low clouds. The anti-aircraft fire blazed up. The vessels swerved desperately. At long last, the pent-up fury of the Kamikaze unit was about to break upon the American Navy.

The deliberate sacrifice of life automatically involved in a suicide attack is something which in its dreadful disdain for death appears all but incomprehensible to Europeans or Americans. Yet in many respects the motives behind the use of such tactics were quite logical ones.

They arose originally from the growing Japanese losses, coupled with a great fall in the standards of the replacements, on the one hand, and the growing American efficiency as exemplified in their superb Hellcat fighters and their even more lethal proximity-fused shells on the other. As we have already observed, the Americans were able to inflict fearful losses on their opponents in the Philippine Sea, off Formosa and in the actions off Luzon on 24 October, while their only fatal casualty in all these encounters was light carrier *Princeton*, sunk by an exceptionally gallant individual attack. The strength of the defences was such that it was rare for a conventional bomber to get near enough to an American warship to have even a chance of hitting it. The prospects of an attacking pilot living to return from a raid were scarcely less remote.

On the other hand, the tactic of ramming an aircraft into its victim, while making it quite certain that the pilot would not survive, did have the advantage of vastly increasing the likelihood of a hit. However badly the plane was damaged, even if the pilot was killed before the moment of impact, the momentum of the plane's dive would often be sufficient to carry it through to its target. The only really certain way of stopping such a dive was to blow up the attacker in mid-air, which, needing a direct hit in the right place, could not easily be achieved.

Also the constant Japanese shortage of petrol, with its resultant loss in pilot ability, could be offset in part at least by the new form of assault. A Kamikaze pilot required far less experience or training. His indoctrination for the new corps often lasted only seven days. Throughout there was far less concern with flying ability than with matters relating solely to the attack such as the best height for approaching a target, the most effective angle of dive, or the point of aim – the elevators on a carrier were most favoured. Although the first Kamikazes were very experienced airmen, the later ones in many cases were not – in fact the more capable, less expendable pilots were usually detailed to fly the escorting fighters whose job it was to see that the Kamikazes were not intercepted *en route* to their victims.

Similarly, obsolete types of aircraft such as the older Val dive-bombers could be used in these raids. During the Okinawa campaign, even antique 'wood-and-canvas' biplanes were employed – for an obsolete aircraft was less vital than a modern one but the impact of the former would very probably do much the same kind of damage to a vessel as the impact of the latter.

Thus, although the suicide-raids came about only in a desperate situation, they were not a mere reckless waste of life as certain American (and even Japanese) writers have stated. They could and did inflict far greater losses on the United States forces than any amount of conventional bombers. The inevitable death of the pilot was often more than compensated for by the damage he caused or in the destruction of scores of lives on the ship he struck. It seems certain that the Japanese leaders had a good idea of the potential effectiveness of such attacks. Although the presiding founder of the corps, Vice-Admiral Takijiro Onishi, at first definitely planned only an offensive to cover the period of the Leyte Gulf action, it is inconceivable that he did not foresee at least the strong probability that the raids would have to continue even after the battle; indeed there had been discussion about the prospect of such tactics since the beginning of the year, long before the *Sho* plan came into being.

It is, however, one thing to state coldly that logically such attacks would prove more profitable from a strict military point of view than orthodox bombing; it is quite another to understand how any pilot could calmly embark on such a mission, knowing that whatever his achievement, his own life would be terminated. Even to attempt an explanation requires a journey back through the history of Japan. A convenient point at which to start is the event from which the 'Special Attack Corps' took its name.

In 1281, the Mongol Emperor Kublai Khan, whose armies had overrun all Central Asia, China and Korea, determined on the destruction of Japan. He had previously sent six successive embassies, insisting Japan acknowledge herself as a tributary state, but these demands were rejected scornfully, several of the envoys being executed. A Mongol raid in 1274 was defeated by a combination of stubborn defence and bad weather, but seven years later Kublai massed together a vast force with the help of his Chinese and Korean tributaries. His armada which descended on the coast of the Japanese island of Kyushu is said to have carried 150,000 warriors.

For fifty-three days, a continuous, savage struggle took place as the invaders slowly enlarged their beach-head. Despite all the preparations of the defenders, despite their desperate courage in fighting to the death without a thought of surrender, as they were to do in a more recent conflict, the Mongols gradually began to attain the upper hand. However with astonishing ineptitude Kublai had failed to foresee the intervention of the elements, although the summer months in Japan during which the invasion took place are notorious for their storms. On 15 and 16 August 1281, a typhoon of fearful dimensions obligingly fell upon the Mongol fleet, literally blowing it to fragments. Many vessels went down in the open seas with dreadful loss of life, others ran ashore on the mainland and yet others crippled and harassed by Japanese light craft were wrecked on the coast of Kyushu. The troops ashore, cut off from their supplies, were slaughtered in their thousands. The Mongol threat was lifted – forever as it transpired – and the Japanese people gratefully acknowledged the typhoon as a gift from the Gods. It was therefore called 'Kamikaze', meaning 'Divine Wind'.

The society to whose aid the Divine Wind came, lived under what is usually called a 'feudal' system – a term which has now become little more than a vaguely abusive epithet. In practice it denotes an extremely complicated political organization, the basis of which is the holding of land in return for service, mainly military service. With this system in Japan, went a code of behaviour which later became known as *Bushido* (The Way of the Warrior). This emphasized not rights but

Kamikaze

duties, chiefly those owed by the warriors or *Samurai* towards their lords.

Foremost among such duties was the obligation of the warrior to do battle for his lord, sacrificing his own life without question if the need arose. The most dreadful breach of this duty was the act of surrender. A *Samurai* fought to the bitter end. If he surrendered, his shame was such that he became an object of contempt, unworthy of consideration as a human being. This outlook was summed up in the saying: "Death is lighter than a feather, while duty is weightier than a mountain"; an attitude which was invariably shown by the Japanese in the Second World War – at Tarawa for instance only seventeen men surrendered out of a garrison of 4,500 – and which explains in part why Allied prisoners received such disgusting treatment at the hands of their captors.

It might also be remembered that in contrast with the disgrace suffered by a prisoner, the warrior who fell fighting would, so he firmly believed, have consolation after death. The Shinto religion of Japan holds that the souls of the dead continue in close association with the living as well as with each other. In the case of the warrior, since his sacrifice would wipe out any faults, his spirit would return directly to the Yasukuni shrine near the Imperial Palace where the souls of the warriors consort in eternal friendship.

Since death was unimportant while survival as a prisoner was almost unthinkable, it was not surprising that numerous Japanese fighting men threw away their lives in order to achieve the success of their missions rather than attempting to save themselves, especially in conditions where they would fall into enemy hands. On 7 December 1941, the first day of the war, came the first such sacrifice. Lieutenant Fusata Iida deliberately flew his damaged Zero into an aircraft-hangar. This type of gesture was repeated on numerous occasions especially in the actions round Guadalcanal. Planes rammed American ships and fighters rammed American bombers. These were unplanned, spontaneous acts, but the spirit behind them could easily be adapted to organized suicide-sorties.

As well as the determination to succeed literally at all costs, there were two further factors motivating the Kamikaze raiders. In the event of failure, in other words, of inadequate performance of his duty, a warrior almost invariably would atone for his disgrace by suicide, usually in the hideous ritual of *seppuku* (abdomen-slitting) also less frequently, because more vulgarly, termed *hara-kiri* (belly-cutting). So when the Japanese armed forces saw their dreams of domination in the Pacific fade away before America's might, they were morally obliged to kill themselves in expiation thereby wiping out the stain of failure. What better way to make good their fault than by ending their own lives, while by the same act bringing benefit to their threatened country?

The final strand in the Kamikaze philosophy is, however, the most easy to understand. A member of the armed forces of any country knows that if the worst happens, he may be called upon to lose his life. On numerous occasions, Allied airmen perished unflinchingly while trying to save the lives of companions – pilots who remained at the controls of blazing bombers so that their crews might parachute to safety for example.

This total unselfishness was practised instinctively by the Japanese with their scorn of death. In the Battle of the Philippine Sea for instance, there came a sublime example of this. Warrant Officer Sakio Komatsu had just taken off from carrier *Taiho* in his Zero fighter, when he spotted the track of a torpedo heading straight at his ship. Without hesitation he dashed his plane onto it, aircraft and torpedo disintegrating together in one vast explosion.

To the Kamikaze pilots, operating in the desperate conditions of the Leyte operation, or in the still more perilous circumstances surrounding the fighting in Luzon, Iwo Jima or Okinawa, it seemed that they were protecting not a ship but their homeland and their God-Emperor. They were devoted patriots to whom these were all-important. Nowhere is this made more clear than in the pilots' last letters home.[1]

Thus Ensign Teruo Yamaguchi, a university graduate, writes:

> The Japanese way of life is indeed beautiful, and I am proud of it, as I am of Japanese history and mythology which reflect the purity of our ancestors and their belief in the past – whether or not those beliefs are true. That way of life is the product of all the best things which our ancestors have handed down to us. And the living embodiment of all wonderful things out of our past is the Imperial Family which, too, is the crystallization of the splendour and beauty of Japan and its people. It is an honour to be able to give my life in defence of these beautiful and lofty things.

Similarly, another university graduate Ensign Heiichi Okabe states:

---

[1] These letters were collected by a Mr Ichiro Ohmi after the war in the course of a study lasting four-and-a-half years. Some were later published in the book *The Divine Wind* by Captain Inoguchi and Commander Nakajima with Roger Pineau.

"We shall plunge into enemy ships cherishing the conviction that Japan has been and will be a place where only lovely homes, brave women, and beautiful friendships are allowed to exist"; while Lieutenant (jg) Nobuo Ishibashi sums up this attitude in one short sentence: "I think of springtime in Japan while soaring to dash against the enemy".

These "wonderful things" were now threatened. It was obvious that a miracle was needed if the tide was to be turned. A new 'Divine Wind' to sweep away the enemy fleet was essential. This would be provided by the warriors of Japan who would balance the physical might of their foes by what they believed was their spiritual superiority. "I feel confident of my ability in tomorrow's action," claims Cadet Jun Nomoto, yet another graduate, "Will do my utmost to dive head-on against an enemy warship to fulfil my destiny in defence of the homeland." "I shall be a shield for His Majesty," says Flying Petty-Officer First Class Isao Matsuo "and die cleanly along with my squadron leader and other friends. I wish that I could be born seven times, each time to smite the enemy."

As these varying motives came together, they produced a great upsurge of enthusiasm in the airmen who were to take part in the attacks. That this was no mere temporary emotion is shown by the fact that sometimes weeks or even months elapsed before the pilots went on their one-way missions, yet during this period morale remained at its peak, there was no gloom or depression, and the airmen constantly attended lectures designed to ensure that their attacks would do the greatest possible damage, even spending many hours working out the most profitable way in which they could terminate their lives.

Indeed the one thing that worried the Kamikaze crews was that they might prove unworthy of the great task before them. Ensign Tatsuya Ikariyama who refused to join a celebration because "I am going on a suicide attack tomorrow and want to be in top condition" provides a typical example of this attitude. In the course of attacks, pilots might make more than one run against a victim so as to be certain of striking home in a vital place, or might scorn a smaller vessel in order to dive on a carrier.

In contrast, they had no fear of death. They volunteered in their thousands. Pilots whose planes could not take off due to some mechanical defect, were inconsolable. Officers were besieged by men demanding to be sent on a suicide mission as soon as possible, because they regarded this as the highest honour that could befall them. When it was necessary to select certain men only for such a mission, as a result for instance of a shortage of planes, there would be shouts of "Unfair!" from those who were left behind, while their comrades who were detailed for the raid screamed: "Thank you for choosing me!" to their operations officer as their aircraft hurtled down the runway.

It could of course be argued that these descriptions come from commanders who ordered such attacks, so naturally would be insistent that no pressure was put on their men. However, once again the pilots' letters confirm these statements. There is no hint of regret, only a complete unselfishness. Thus Cadet Nomoto, reporting that one of his fellows has been dropped from the list of those destined to take part in an attack, writes: "Cannot help feeling sorry for him". "The training and practice have been rigorous," reflects Ensign Okabe, "but it is worthwhile if we can die beautifully and for a cause" while Ensign Susumu Kaijitsu remarks cheerfully: "I have never felt better and am now standing by, ready for action."

Indeed exultation appears to be the airmen's first reaction. "Dear Parents: Please congratulate me," calls Petty-Officer Matsuo, "I have been given a splendid opportunity to die." "Please do not grieve for me, mother," asks Lieutenant (jg) Ishibashi, "It will be glorious to die in action. I am grateful to be able to die in a battle to determine the destiny of our country." Apart from requests to look after relatives, the pilots' one concern is that they shall carry out their mission: "We are sixteen warriors manning the bombers," comments Petty-Officer Matsuo, "May our death be as sudden and clean as the shattering of crystal."

Thus as the outriders of the suicide forces hurtled towards 'Taffy 1', the main emotion of the pilots was neither rage nor despair. Still less, as has often been stated, was it a kind of apathetic fatalism, unlikely surely to appear in young, ardent men who as we have seen, had had in most cases a considerable education. Instead it was exultation. This was their greatest moment. Without hesitation, three of them plunged towards their targets.

The first plane, achieving complete surprise, fell upon *Santee* before she could fire a shot in her own defence. Strafing as it came, it crashed into the flight-deck on the port side forward and plunged through this into the hangar deck. Its bomb exploded as it struck, blowing a hole 30 feet long and 15 feet wide in the flight deck and starting fires on both decks which the fuel from the aircraft's tanks helped to spread. Planes on the flight-deck also burst into flames.

Amidst fire and smoke the damage control parties with fearless skill and determination fought the flames, jettisoned depth-charges or dragged away wounded men, some of whom had their clothing ablaze. In the immediate vicinity of the flames were eight 1,000-pound bombs. Had these exploded the CVE's fate would have been sealed, but miraculously they did not and the fire was brought under control by 0751, eleven minutes after the aircraft hit – however sixteen dead men plus twenty-seven wounded marked the first success of the Kamikazes.

Both the other planes which attacked at this time were hit by anti-aircraft fire. Trailing smoke, they continued to roar down. One which was heading for *Sangamon*, came under heavy fire from that ship as well as from *Suwanee* which it had previously circled round astern. Just as it seemed certain to strike home, *Suwanee* managed to hit it with a shell from her solitary 5-inch gun. This flung the plane to one side, causing it to crash just off *Sangamon*'s port bow. As it struck the water, the aircraft's bomb exploded, the shrapnel slightly damaging *Sangamon* and killing one luckless seaman on the forecastle. The third plane which headed for *Petrof Bay* was also riddled by anti-aircraft fire; it near-missed the escort carrier without causing damage. The fourth Zero remained aloft, circling in the clouds while it awaited its opportunity.

As all eyes were trying to locate this menace, a periscope appeared off *Santee*'s starboard side. At 0756, a torpedo from Japanese submarine *I56* hit the escort carrier amidships, flooding several compartments, thus causing a slight list; but the sub had chosen the wrong target, no doubt having been tempted by *Santee*'s fires. *Petrof Bay* would have been a far more suitable victim, for such a blow would have doomed a 'Kaiser'-class CVE, whereas *Santee* being a converted tanker with multiple subdivisions of her hull, was able to keep her place in the formation with the aid of some emergency repairs. Nor did she suffer any casualties. Destroyer *Trathen* counter-attacked with depth-charges but the submarine escaped unharmed.

The appearance of *I56* was not part of a clever plan by the Japanese to use submarines and suicide-planes in combination, it was purely fortuitous. It was, however, extremely disconcerting for the Americans for it diverted attention from the remaining Kamikaze which now seized its opportunity. Two minutes after the torpedo explosion, it emerged from the clouds, dodged a Hellcat fighter attempting to intercept it and came straight down towards *Suwanee*.

Once again every gun blazed away at the diving Zero. It was hit, smoke streaming behind it, but this time nothing stopped the pilot. He struck the flight-deck of *Suwanee* about 40 feet forward of the after elevator, slightly to the starboard side. Tearing a 10-foot hole in the flight deck, the Zero plunged through onto the hangar deck, where its bomb went off ripping a great 25-foot hole. The plane's engine penetrated as far as the main deck. A fire started on the hangar deck, while the blast from the explosion knocked crew-members over the side, temporarily put the CVE's steering out of action and jammed the after elevator.

As in the case of *Santee*, however, *Suwanee*'s damage-control teams worked wonders. The fire was promptly put out thanks partly to William Brooks, Chief Ships Fitter, who opened the valves controlling the water curtain and sprinkler system thereby preventing the aircraft in the hangar from catching fire – an action he was destined to repeat next day under even grimmer circumstances. Repairs to the flight-deck were carried out so speedily that within two hours planes could land again on it, though the after elevator remained out of action. Yet the first suicide-raid had proved frighteningly destructive – and far worse would soon occur.

Apart from strafing attacks by groups of three or four fighter-bombers just before and after noon which caused a few casualties, Thomas Sprague's 'Taffy 1' had no further air attacks on the twenty-fifth, but to the north Clifton Sprague's 'Taffy 3' had just begun to recover planes after the running battle with Kurita, when the Kamikazes made another impressive appearance. At 0725, five Zeros from Mabalacat, Luzon, took off on their one-way mission. At 1049, having escaped detection on Sprague's radar by approaching at a very low altitude, then climbing sharply when at close range, they hurled themselves at 'Taffy 3's' five surviving CVEs.

So sudden was the onslaught that Sprague's fighters were unable to intercept; the attackers were met by the ships' gunfire only. One, strafing as it came, aimed for the bridge of *Kitkun Bay*, just missed it, crashed into the port catwalk, then bounced into the sea off the carrier's port bow; but the bomb it was carrying exploded as it hit, causing fires and other damage.

All the other four attackers were caught in a desperate cross-fire from 40-mm machine-guns. Two of them, trying to get to *Fanshaw Bay* were hit in time, falling blazing into the sea. The other two began a dive on *White Plains*. At an altitude of 500 feet, they pulled out, turning to port. Then they separated, one swinging away for a run on *St Lo* while the other circled, then charged again at *White Plains* from astern, "with the apparent intention" says Woodward "of landing on the after end of the flight-deck and crashing forward the length of the ship". *White Plains* turned hard to port in evasive action, her guns pouring shells into the Zero which weaved until just astern, when it rolled over, narrowly missed the port catwalk and exploded in the air, covering the flight-deck with shrapnel as well as gruesome remains of the pilot, doing some damage and injuring eleven men.

The second member of this pair meanwhile was bursting through the protective fire onto *St Lo*. Although smoke poured from it, nothing could stop this plane, flown according to the Japanese records by Lieutenant Yukio Seki the group-leader. It struck the flight deck squarely, bursting through into the hangar deck, where its bomb exploded, hurling debris and blazing fuel over the flight-deck. The bombs and torpedoes in the hangar then began to detonate also; first a minor explosion which sent up clouds of smoke; then a bigger one splitting open a large section of the flight-deck; then a really huge blast which blew the forward elevator high out of its shaft to land upside down on the deck.

By now the fires were raging furiously. Several men were driven over the side by these, others were blown overboard. More vast explosions rang out, flinging great parts of the flight-deck, not to mention entire planes, hundreds of feet into the air. The flames spread from one end of the ship to the other while she began to heel over to port. At about 1100, Captain McKenna having stopped the engines, ordered: "Stand by to abandon ship!"

Despite further heavy explosions from below, one of which apparently tore out a large section of the hull for the carrier shifted from a list to port to a sharper list to starboard, the evacuation was carried out with great precision. Large numbers of wounded were lowered carefully into the water; some 400 of these including 75 stretcher-cases were picked up later by *Heermann*. The ship was abandoned only just in time. At 1125, under a dense cloud of smoke, *St Lo* which had successfully defied the 18-inch guns of *Yamato*, sank by the stern. Up above, three more Zeros which had provided the fighter-escort for the attackers, flew off to Cebu where they reported the first – but emphatically not the last – sinking achieved by the Kamikazes.

While the explosions still rocked *St Lo*, a group of fifteen Judy bombers appeared at 1110. The Combat Air Patrol managed to get among these in time but even so some still broke through. One of these attacked *Kitkun Bay*. All the CVEs opened fire at the plane, shooting its wings off – barely in time, for it crashed only just short of *Kitkun*

Bay, its bomb missed by about 25 yards, and debris from the aircraft landed on the carrier's forecastle, causing minor damage.

Kalinin Bay which had survived such a hammering from Kurita's guns faced an assault from four Kamikazes. Two were shot down at a safe distance. A third, approaching from astern smoking from hits, crashed on the port side of the flight-deck, damaging it badly, though several fires which it started were quenched in less than five minutes. The fourth, attacking from the starboard quarter, was set on fire by the ship's gunners but it still came on, smashing into the after part of the superstructure a large portion of which was wrecked. *Kalinin Bay* stayed in formation. By this time her damage-control parties doubtless felt that they could cope successfully with anything.

Admiral Sprague now steered slowly southward, leaving *Heermann, Butler, Dennis* and *Raymond* picking up *St Lo*'s survivors, which they did for another four hours. Having rescued 754 men, including many wounded as previously stated, Commander Hathaway the senior officer present set off after his escort carriers, but because of the damage to *Heermann* and *Dennis*, the squadron's speed was limited to 15 knots. At 1625, Hathaway sent *Butler* and *Raymond* on ahead to rejoin Sprague before dark. Also destroyers *Sproston, Hale* and *Picking* which had been detached by Admiral Kinkaid from escorting transports to Manus, joined 'Taffy 3' at 2000 hours. However, 'Taffy 3' had had no screen whatever for eight hours which as Sprague admitted was "a desperate expedient", but, he added, "we had been through so much by then, that it didn't seem to matter whether we had escorts with us or not".

'Taffy 3' then bowed out of the fight. *Heermann* and *Dennis* went to Kossol Passage for repairs. *Butler* and *Raymond* went to Leyte Gulf to refuel and land badly wounded survivors. The escort carriers with their three new protectors headed for a much-needed recoupment at Manus. 'Taffy 1', however, was still in trouble.

First submarines made another attempt at the force's destruction. At 2237, destroyer-escort *Coolbaugh* spotted the periscope of *I362*. All vessels promptly made an emergency ninety-degree turn, which was only just in time for two torpedoes passed one each side of *Petrof Bay*. Had they hit her she would almost certainly have been lost. *Coolbaugh* counter-attacked but without success. Next morning, 26 October, destroyer-escort *Richard M. Rowell* chased off another submarine endeavouring to reach a favourable position from which to launch her 'fish'.

The Kamikazes were an even more dangerous proposition. About noon, they reappeared. Some six Zeros were picked up by radar while still 35 miles away; later they were sighted flying at about 10,000 feet. The Combat Air Patrol shot down three of them but it seems that these were escorts not suicide-planes. Three genuine Kamikazes evaded the fighters but one was engaged by a torpedo-bomber returning from its anti-submarine patrol; it crashed astern of *Petrof Bay*. The other two attacked in the usual terrifying dives, one on *Suwanee*, one on *Petrof Bay*.

Petrof Bay was again the lucky one. She turned sharply to port in an attempt to throw the Zero off her track, but the pilot rolled over thereby keeping his alignment on her. When only 500 feet above the deck, however, the enemy's tail was knocked off by the ship's gunners. The Zero went into a spin but was still coming on when a terrific concentration of fire ripped it apart. It crashed just astern without causing any harm.

The Zero diving on *Suwanee* was also damaged, but the whole point of the Kamikaze tactic was that an attacker could be hit continuously yet still find its mark. To make matters worse, an Avenger which had just landed was standing on the forward elevator when the Zero crashed right on top of it. Both planes plus the Zero's bomb exploded instantly, killing the pilot and two crewmen of the Avenger and wrecking the elevator. Then, writes Woodward: "Fires spread on the flight-deck until they set fire to seven fighters and two torpedo-planes. The planes started exploding, causing fires that raged for several hours. Flaming gasoline flowed over the side, into the gun buckets and over the men manning the guns."

As dense clouds of smoke rose from the carrier, her crew again set about the task of saving her. Once again Chief Ship's Fitter William Brooks turned on the sprinkler system in the hangar deck thus preventing the planes there from catching fire — this despite having been wounded and temporarily knocked unconscious by an explosion. Several injured officers and men, including Captain Johnson, were trapped on the bridge by fires, but were rescued after the navigator Lieutenant Premo had fought his way through the flames to get help — but Premo who was already wounded, was badly burned in the process; he died a few hours afterwards.

This type of unselfish action became commonplace as the fight to save *Suwanee* continued. One splendid, though tragic instance is told by her executive officer, Commander Van Mater. An enlisted man, unable to bear the thought of a number of wounded trapped on the forecastle without medical supplies, informed Chief Electrician's Mate

Barr that he would carry supplies through the fires to them. "Despite Barr's efforts to stop him, the man climbed to the 20-mm mounts just forward of the flight-deck. A second later a torpedo-bomber directly in his path exploded and the man was seen holding on the starboard side of the flight-deck with one leg blown off. A moment later he fell into the water, and was not seen again. Every effort to ascertain his name has proved unavailing."

Such sacrifices were not in vain. After several hours, the fires were finally extinguished. The ship survived; though she lost 143 killed or missing and 102 wounded some of whom died later, in this and the previous attack. 'Taffy 1' now also retired to Manus for repairs.

This was the last raid by the Kamikazes – indeed the last Japanese attack of any kind – in the Battle of Leyte Gulf. But the Kamikaze strikes were to continue throughout the Leyte campaign, particularly in the later landings at Ormoc Bay. They recommenced during the assaults on Mindoro, Luzon and Iwo Jima, finally reaching a hideous peak at Okinawa with massed attacks called *kikusai* (floating chrysanthemums); the largest of which on 6–7 April 1945 contained 355 aircraft. At Okinawa, a special suicide-plane, the *Oka* (Cherry-Blossom) – *Baka* (Madman) as the Americans called it – also appeared. This was virtually a manned flying-bomb only 20 feet long with a $16\frac{1}{2}$ foot wing-span and 4,700 pounds of explosive in its nose, which was carried to the target area under the belly of a Betty bomber. It was then cast off, after which, propelled on its way by its three rockets, it fell upon its victim at the almost unstoppable speed of 600 m.p.h.

The destruction wrought by the Kamikazes was quite incredible. Although the American sailors fought off attacks with astonishing persistence, very often the Kamikazes simply burst past the most gallant defence – as witness this description by Morison of an attack on 7 December 1944 on destroyer *Mahan* in Ormoc Bay. A raid was intercepted by P-38s (Lockheed Lightning fighters) but nine enemy bombers still came through to attack the destroyer:

> No 1 burst into flames and splashed about 50 yards short of *Mahan*, knocked down by her machine guns. No 2 passed right over the ship. Nos 3 and 4 bombers were shot down at a safe distance. No 5 hit *Mahan* just abaft the bridge. No 6 hit her at the waterline; and almost simultaneously No 2, which had turned back, hit her between waterline and forecastle deck. No 7 contented itself with a thorough strafing, in the course of which it was splashed by the ship's gunfire. No 8, already in flames from

its conflict with the P-38s, tried to crash but splashed instead. No 9 passed over the ship and disappeared. All this within four minutes.

The destroyer was abandoned shortly afterwards.

When the Kamikazes broke through in this way, they often caused appalling casualties. Thus on 11 May 1945, fleet carrier *Bunker Hill* was struck off Okinawa; first by a Zero which crashed through planes on the flight-deck causing huge fires before falling over the side while its bomb went through the flight-deck; then by a Judy which came down in a vertical dive, to plunge clean through the flight-deck at the base of the island structure. Literally in a flash, the great carrier was reduced to a smoking hulk. She was saved eventually but of her crew 392 were dead and 264 wounded.

The total losses caused by the Kamikazes were terrible. At Okinawa, 32 ships were sunk, mostly by Kamikaze attack, 368 were damaged some 50 of them being put out of action for the remainder of the war, over 4,900 sailors were killed and over 4,800 were wounded – the majority hideously burnt by the flames that were the almost inevitable consequences of a crash. The United States Strategic Bombing Survey (Pacific War) concluded that if such attacks had been carried out "in greater power and concentration they might have been able to cause us to withdraw or revise our strategic plans".

This comment suffices to show that Morison's description of the attacks as causing "senseless destruction and suffering" is itself senseless. The attacks were launched with a definite object in view; they came close to achieving their aim. The same is true of the strikes in Philippine waters – particularly those on the landings at Lingayen Gulf, Luzon. During this campaign, the Kamikazes sank 16 ships and damaged 87 others. They were far fewer in number than those at Okinawa – indeed plane for plane the Philippine Kamikazes made the more profitable attacks. It is also worth remarking that the Americans were inspired to 'ride out' these onslaughts by the knowledge of their success at Leyte Gulf which had given them indisputable command of the seas. What one wonders might have happened to their morale if Kurita had slaughtered the escort carriers and the beach-head forces on Leyte, the Japanese Army had then thrown back the disorganized remainder of the land-forces; and then this fearful havoc by the Kamikazes had befallen forces already shaken by these disasters.

Yet the fact is that although the Kamikaze tactics came close to success on more than one occasion, they did not achieve that success. No pilot could make two Kamikaze attacks so that the Kamikazes were inevitably a wasting asset necessitating a lengthy pause after each campaign while new pilots were trained even to the low level of skill required. It might well be argued indeed that their very effectiveness was to have terrible results, for it was partly the fear of further such attacks with their consequent heavy casualties in the course of landings on the Japanese homeland that prompted the Americans to use the atomic bomb.

Therefore it might seem that the raids were merely a vain waste of the young men who were killed during them. In the short view this is no doubt true; but there is another factor worthy of consideration. For whatever one's views on the tactics, there can be nothing but praise for the total unselfishness of the pilots who went knowingly to their deaths. After the war, when Japan lay in ruins, her leading figures arrested, her industrial combines forcibly broken-up, her people near starvation, it was this same determination and absence of selfishness, applied in constructive not destructive forms, which in the short space of 15 years pulled the country out of her despair to bring about a miracle of economic, political and industrial recovery.

When Japan surrendered, the founder of the Kamikaze Corps, Admiral Onishi committed *seppuku*. This did not kill him outright. Refusing both medical aid and a quick death, he lingered in agony all day before finally expiring, as an act of atonement to his fliers for his part in failing to achieve ultimate victory. Just before his death he wrote a *haiku* – a poem of seventeen syllables – which stands not only as a summary of the hopes of the Kamikaze pilots but also as a prophecy of the subsequent revival of Japan. It translates thus:

> Refreshingly
> After the violent storm
> The moon rose radiant.

10

Death of a Navy

The final round of the Battle of Leyte Gulf took the form of American air attacks on the various fleeing Japanese forces – appropriately, for it was American air-power which was the decisive factor in that battle. Kurita's Central Force was, naturally, the chief target. Night-flying 'shadowers' from *Independence* of Bogan's Task Group 38:2 trailed Kurita during the night of 25–26 October as he made his way from the San Bernardino Strait to the Sibuyan Sea. At about 0230 on the twenty-sixth, however, the aircraft in contact with Central Force lost touch in a violent thunderstorm. As a result, a strike of four Avengers with torpedoes and five fighter-bomber Hellcats each carrying a 500-pound bomb, launched from *Independence* at about 0315, was unable to locate any targets, returning with nothing to show for its efforts.

The remainder of the night passed uneventfully, giving Kurita's exhausted gunners a desperately-needed opportunity to gain some uneasy rest. Before dawn on the twenty-sixth, however, all were again at their stations, heads throbbing with weariness, eyes aching, faces drawn. As the light increased to show the island of Panay to port, they prepared for the inevitable revenge of the aroused American air armadas.

They did not have long to wait. McCain's and Bogan's task groups rendezvoused at 0500 north-east of San Bernardino Strait. Search-planes were promptly sent off. The first strikes were launched at 0600 from *Wasp, Hornet, Hancock* and *Cowpens* of McCain's Task Group 38:1 and from *Intrepid* and *Cabot* in Bogan's Group 2. They headed westward awaiting news from the scouts.

At about 0810, Central Force was spotted by two search-planes from *Wasp* in the Tablas Strait steaming south at a good speed some 10 miles north-west of the northern capes of Panay. Kurita had with him his four battleships, *Yamato, Nagato, Kongo* and *Haruna*; heavy cruisers *Tone* and *Haguro*; light cruisers *Noshiro* and *Yahagi*; and seven destroyers. Lagging behind the main body came crippled

Kumano, escorted by destroyer *Hamanami*, and damaged destroyer *Hayashimo* which having run out of fuel in the Sibuyan Sea, had been forced to borrow from her escorting destroyer *Okinami*.

Due to over-eagerness or to various misunderstandings, a large number of planes attacked the stragglers. However, at about 0830, aircraft from *Intrepid* and *Cabot*, followed shortly by others from *Wasp* and *Cowpens*, concentrated on Kurita's main force. These assaults were handicapped by heavy cloud-cover which made co-ordination difficult. Also the enemy gunners still showed admirable spirit, demonstrated in an extremely practical manner by an immense amount of anti-aircraft fire which destroyed eight U.S. aircraft during the day. Four more, damaged, crash-landed short of their parent ships.

Despite natural or hostile hazards, the attackers left their mark on Kurita, though not nearly to the extent that they would have liked. *Yamato* took two more bomb-hits, one on her Number 1 turret – but it would need more than this to stop such a monster. Since no torpedoes reached her, she was able to make good her escape – as in fact did all the ships with Kurita except one. Light cruiser *Noshiro*, hit by two torpedoes from *Wasp*'s airmen at about 0910, was left dead in the water.

While the majority of the American pilots were attacking Kurita, the luckless stragglers were also having attention. *Hornet*'s airmen bombed a destroyer but without result. A force of four bombers, seven torpedo-planes and twelve fighters from *Hancock* went for *Kumano* then steaming west off the southern tip of Mindoro. At about 0850, a 1,000-pound bomb hit her in the boiler-room leaving her dead in the water with huge clouds of smoke belching from her. Yet, as has already been noticed, Japanese ships – especially heavy cruisers of the *Mogami*-class – were capable of withstanding extremely heavy punishment. *Kumano* managed to move on again at 5 knots. Accompanied by faithful *Hamanami*, she proceeded to Coron Bay and thence to Manila.

Subsequent raids from McCain's forces could not inflict further harm on Kurita's main body which now steamed south into the Sulu Sea out of range, but they were able to deal with some of his detached vessels. *Hornet*'s pilots, spotting crippled *Noshiro* off Batbatan Island, finished her off with a bomb-hit. She sank at about 1137.

Aircraft from *Wasp* attacked destroyer *Hayashimo*. A bomb blew her bow off. She had to be run aground at Semirara Island, south of Mindoro, sinking in the shallows with her decks sticking out of the water. Not realizing that she was finished already, American airmen spent the next week making certain by systematically blasting her to pieces. The later strikes on the twenty-sixth incidentally met enemy land-based aircraft trying to provide Kurita with badly-needed protection; they shot down twelve of these.

Nor was Central Force the only target for air attack on the twenty-sixth. Admiral Shima's ships, the Rear of the Southern Forces, now consisting of two heavy cruisers with three escorting destroyers — the fourth destroyer, *Kasumi*, having been detached to assist damaged light cruiser *Abukuma* — was raided at 1500 in the Mindanao Sea, but escaped with only minor damage to destroyer *Shiranuhi*. Another group, however, was less fortunate. This was Vice-Admiral Sakonju's Transport Unit which, it may be recalled, numbered light cruiser *Kinu*, destroyer *Uranami* and four transports. This formation has been overlooked of late in the narrative due to a preoccupation with more important events. It had also been overlooked by the American commanders for the self-same reason.

Taking advantage of their foes' numerous other problems, the ships of Transport Unit landed 2,000 men at Ormoc Bay on the western side of Leyte in the early hours of the twenty-sixth. They then headed westward into the Visayan Sea. Here between Leyte and Cebu Islands, they were sighted by reconnaissance aircraft of Seventh Fleet. Despite the savage encounters of the previous day, to say nothing of the need for air-cover over the Leyte Beaches, Admiral Stump was able to send twenty-three bombers and twenty-nine fighters from his CVEs against these ships.

The resourcefulness of the escort carrier pilots was vividly demonstrated once more in this attack. They had no heavy bombs or torpedoes left after the fighting off Samar, being limited to the use of rockets or small contact bombs or strafing attacks by the fighters. However, starting at about noon, they used all weapons at their command with persistent determination, relentlessly pounding Sakonju as he tried to escape. Early in the afternoon, destroyer *Uranami*, repeatedly bombed and strafed, sank south of Masbate Island. Light cruiser *Kinu*, after suffering similar but even greater punishment, eventually went to the bottom in the same area at about 1730. It was a last well-deserved fanfare of triumphant defiance from the magnificent warriors of Seventh Fleet.

Finally, as if the Japanese had not suffered enough at the hands of the American Navy, the American Army Air Force, somewhat belatedly, also entered the fight. At about 1000 hours on the twenty-sixth, a strong force of forty-four B-24 (Liberator) and B-25 (Mitchell) bombers attacked light cruiser *Abukuma* and destroyer *Kasumi* off the south-west of Negros. The destroyer was not hurt but the luckless light cruiser had been too badly damaged by the earlier hit from *PT137* to make more than 9 knots, neither could she manoeuvre properly. In consequence, the bombers made several hits on her, starting fires which spread until they finally detonated her torpedoes. The resulting explosion doomed *Abukuma*. She sank at 1242.

About an hour after the attack on *Abukuma* began, forty-seven more Liberators in several groups made the final attacks on Central Force's battleships. These were still unpleasantly aggressive. As in the fighting on 24 October, they fired their main batteries at their attackers from several miles' range. They brought down three of the heavy bombers and damaged fourteen others. In return the airmen claimed numerous hits on varying targets all of which, it turned out, were over-optimistic. However, twelve, 1,000-pound bombs exploding very near *Yamato*, sent splinters flying into her superstructure, and, among other casualties, wounded Kurita's Chief of Staff, Rear-Admiral Koyanagi.

It was the last of Central Force's ordeals. On 28 October at 2130, the remaining ships of this once splendid fleet returned dejectedly to Brunei Bay, Borneo, from which they had sailed with such high hopes six days previously.

There is no doubt whatever that for the Americans the Battle of Leyte Gulf was a striking, far-reaching victory; for the Japanese a crushing defeat which must have been made all the more bitter by the fact that their surface vessels which in previous encounters had always performed so admirably had on this occasion been slaughtered in Surigao Strait with nothing to show for their losses, and ignominiously repulsed by a far smaller fleet off Samar. It is true that the defeat was not as overwhelming as it might have been had the Americans deployed their superior strength better. The sinking of the four carriers was not as important as was believed at the time – indeed is still believed to judge from the comment by Captain B.H. Liddell Hart in his *History of the Second World War* that their loss was of "major significance" on the ground that "without any carriers, the six remaining Japanese battleships were helpless". This judgement, however, cannot be correct for it ignores not only the fact that the carriers sunk were already made useless by being virtually empty of planes, but also the fact that even after the engagement, Japan still had several carriers in reserve for use, if only time could be found in which

Death of a Navy

their pilots could be trained. On the other hand, Kurita's four surviving battleships (plus *Hyuga* and *Ise*) did escape to provide a powerful potential threat — a "fleet in being" that would be a source of anxiety, though unfounded as it turned out, to MacArthur and Kinkaid in their plans for further operations in the Philippines.

Yet if the Japanese Navy did not perish in one vast holocaust of destruction as the Russian Navy had done at Tsushima, and as it might well have done if slightly different events had occurred, its defeat was no less irremediable. The numbers of ships sunk alone make clear the extent of the catastrophe — twenty-six vessels, of nearly 306,000 tonnage, went down during the fighting:

    1 18-inch gunned battleship: *Musashi.*
    2 14-inch gunned battleships: *Yamashiro, Fuso.*
    1 Fleet carrier: *Zuikaku.*
    3 Light carriers: *Zuiho, Chiyoda, Chitose.*
    6 Heavy cruisers: *Atago, Maya, Suzuya, Chokai, Chikuma, Mogami.*
    4 Light cruisers: *Noshiro, Abukuma, Tama, Kinu.*
    9 Destroyers: *Nowake, Hayashimo, Yamagumo, Asagumo, Michishio, Akitsuki, Hatsutsuki, Wakaba, Uranami.*

For this devastation the United States paid a cheap price of six ships of almost 37,000 tons:

    1 Light carrier: *Princeton.*
    2 Escort carriers: *Gambier Bay, St Lo.*
    2 Destroyers: *Hoel, Johnston.*
    1 Destroyer-escort: *Samuel B. Roberts.*

The real significance of the Japanese defeat, however, goes beyond the number of sunken ships — their real loss was of the ability to fight another full-scale action. In this respect, the escape of the battleships in practice was to mean less than the destruction of so many of their supporting vessels without which the big ships could not adequately be defended. The battle was the death-sentence for Japan's Navy; hence for the country as a whole.

After the war, Admiral Ozawa stated that as a result of Leyte Gulf, Japanese "surface forces became strictly auxiliary, so that we relied on land forces, special (i.e. Kamikaze) attacks and air power". He added: "There was no further use assigned to surface vessels, with exception of some special ships". A study of the role of the surviving vessels after the battle confirms the truth of these remarks. Those doughty fighters *Hyuga* and *Ise* for example, were used to ferry loads of petrol from Singapore to the Japanese homeland. Most of the remaining vessels skulked in port until finished off by air attacks. Only mighty *Yamato*, on 7 April 1945, again ventured an encounter with the American fleet, when with only enough fuel to take her to Okinawa but none for her return, she went deliberately to a warrior's death. Nor did she reach the amphibious forces which were her target, for Mitscher's airmen, finding her in the East China Sea, in overwhelming numbers battered the giant to her doom.

One other major reason for the hopeless position of the Japanese Navy after the battle was that this had ensured the American conquest of the Philippines. As seen, the *Sho* plan was designed to prevent this situation at all costs. Its failure meant that defeat for Japan was inevitable for she was now certain to be cut off from her resources in the area of her southern conquests. There was no longer enough fuel to send her warships to sea, even had they been capable of forming a sufficiently well-balanced fleet to face the Americans. The disastrous results of the loss of the Philippines which the Japanese had foreseen were soon to befall them; as their Emperor admitted to MacArthur after the war, their subsequent efforts were largely those of desperation.

We may summarize the results of Leyte Gulf by quoting the opinions of two very senior officers, one from each country which fought the action. Admiral Nimitz in his book *The Great Sea War* stated that: "The Battle for Leyte Gulf was the Trafalgar of World War II. Halsey and Kinkaid in 1944, like Nelson in 1805, had finally wiped out the Japanese fleet as an effective fighting force. There would be no more stand-up battles at sea in this war." Admiral Mitsumasa Yonai, the Japanese Navy Minister at the time of the battle, stated when interrogated at the conclusion of hostilities: "Our defeat at Leyte was tantamount to the loss of the Philippines. When you took the Philippines, that was the end of our resources."

In extenuation of their defeat, the Japanese could truthfully point to several initial disadvantages. Their forces were considerably weaker in numbers than those of their opponents. They were especially deficient in the vital element of air-power; though their possession of many airfields on hand while the Americans relied solely on carrier-planes did something to redress the balance. Their various fleets were widely separated, making co-ordination very difficult and their wretched communications made it quite impossible. Also the fleets had suffered from lack of battle experience; several of their techniques showed a great fall in standards from those of former years.

Yet it is clear that the *Sho* plan all but worked; that it did not do so was due not to these disadvantages but to the various actions taken in the course of the battle. "The Japanese sailors fought bravely as usual" remarks Morison — the real compliment lies in the last two words — so it is to the tactical decisions of their commanders that one must look when assessing the reason's for the plan's breakdown.

Of the four principal enemy leaders, Ozawa acted splendidly; this has already been made sufficiently clear to obviate the need for any further elaboration. It is true as Morison points out, that it was one of the greatest of the many ironies in the battle that "this sacrificial Northern Force should have been superbly handled tactically; whilst the commanders of the other two, which might have accomplished something positive, fumbled so miserably" — but this was not the fault of the decoys' great-hearted Admiral.

Regarding the two Southern Forces, it seems only fair to exempt Admiral Shima from blame. Such errors as were attributed to him should really be debited to the High Command. Shima, without proper instructions, without adequate numbers, was supposed to co-operate with another force of whose existence he learnt only by accident, while he remained completely ignorant of its plans. It can scarcely be a matter of wonder if he achieved nothing. He was quite right to make a swift withdrawal from the ridiculous position into which his superiors had placed him.

His colleage Admiral Nishimura stands more open to criticism. It is difficult to find much trace of either strategic or tactical skill in his actions. On the other hand, it seems very probable that whatever brilliance he had displayed he would still have been unable to break through the vast, cleverly-positioned ranks of his enemies. His personal courage was unquestionable. He paid for his errors with his life. Perhaps it would be unkind if he were to be blamed too harshly.

This leaves only Admiral Kurita for consideration. It will already have been apparent that it was his failure to push home his advantage when unexpectedly encountering Sprague's escort carriers off Samar which robbed Japan of a spectacular victory. Instead, he vacillated for some time, finally abandoned his progress towards the vital, vulnerable beaches of Leyte, and, having suffered heavier losses than he inflicted, fled back the way he came. When the extent of his previous ordeal is remembered, there can be ample room for understanding or sympathy. However, it remains true that it was Kurita's hesitation which provided the final, most crucial factor in bringing about the ultimate destruction of the Japanese Navy.

Not all the mistakes made were committed by the Japanese. One fundamental American error was the absence of a Supreme Commander. This resulted in a lack of liaison between the various American fleets involved, which was made worse by deficiencies in communication.

Again, however, it seems difficult to escape the conclusion that it was the tactical errors during the battle which were really responsible for the perilous position in which the American forces found themselves as well as for the escape of sizable portions of the Central and Northern Forces. It is also hard to avoid placing the bulk of the blame squarely on Admiral Halsey. His various actions have been discussed too thoroughly to need further repetition – suffice to record the verdict of Nimitz that "Halsey carried the main American surface strength fruitlessly north and then south through the most crucial hours of the battle, leaving inferior forces to deal with the enemy in two areas".

Halsey, of course, did not share this view. From later accounts which he gave he seems to have felt that blame attached to everyone but himself. He also proclaimed loudly that it is easy to be wise after the event. This indeed is very true – yet, as has been seen, it is surely unarguable that several of Halsey's fellow-commanders were wiser than he was at the time. In any case he was not above using wisdom after the event on his own behalf; he claimed his northward rush, leaving San Bernardino Strait unguarded, was "happily vindicated" by "the Japs' inability to deal with the CVEs and small fry"; a somewhat cavalier way incidentally of describing the fighting off Samar which cost the Americans four ships – or five if one counts *St Lo*, a Kamikaze victim – with over 2,000 casualties.

Yet the commander of the "the CVEs and small fry" Admiral Clifton Sprague attributed his escape from Kurita not to his enemy's inability to destroy him but to "the definite partiality of Almighty God". Can Halsey really claim much justification for his action when disaster was averted by a miracle? Did he really foresee that Kurita would throw away success which was within his grasp? Even the mild-mannered Kinkaid on reading this statement by Halsey could not resist the tart retort: "If so, his crystal ball was certainly in fine working order". It would be grossly unjust not to recall that Halsey was a fine strategist as well as a tremendous morale-raiser. Yet in this action he cuts a sorry figure; he presents a famous warning of the perils inherent in making that potentially most fatal of all mistakes – underestimating the enemy.

The other Third Fleet commanders show to better advantage.

Death of a Navy

Admiral Lee's feelings as his splendid battleships rushed about uselessly can well be imagined — but the error was not his, nor would it have occurred had his advice been followed. Admiral Mitscher with his usual cool decision was responsible for the destruction of the four enemy carriers. All the Task Group Commanders — McCain (when finally he entered the fight), Sherman, Davison, perhaps especially Bogan — did well, while their airmen whether attacking or defending showed such calm, skilful determination that they ensured that maximum use was made of America's aerial might.

Seventh Fleet can claim even greater credit. It was the smaller of the American Fleets yet was responsible for the enemy's repulse in the two most crucial areas of the battle. Its chief, Vice-Admiral Kinkaid, had, says Morison, "an unfortunate position in the chain of command, under MacArthur but unable to control Halsey; within these limitations he acquitted himself very well, and is entitled to no small part of the glory reaped by Oldendorf in Surigao Strait and Clifton Sprague off Samar". MacArthur clearly valued Kinkaid even more highly, summing up the action thus: "Seventh Fleet of my force performed magnificently, as they always had, and always would, and Admiral Kinkaid wrote his name in this engagement among the greatest leaders in our naval annals." Kinkaid was promoted to Admiral in April 1945, retiring with this rank in 1950.

Rear-Admirals Thomas Sprague and Stump also attained the rank of admiral after the war, as they well deserved on their showing in the difficult situations they faced in this action. Their colleague Rear-Admiral Oldendorf was certainly fortunate in having immense strength at his disposal, but, as was demonstrated off Samar, superior might is useless if not properly employed. Oldendorf's tactics in Surigao Strait were splendid in concept, while the courage and ability of the men of his command caused them to be magnificent in realization also.

Most credit of all, however, must belong to Rear-Admiral Clifton Sprague, the officers and men of his 'Taffy 3'. Sprague later commanded Escort Carrier Divisions in the Iwo Jima and Okinawa operations, but, sad to recall, did not live to enjoy a lengthy retirement after the war as did so many of his comrades. He died in April 1955, just over 10 years from the time of his greatest triumph when, in the "ultimate of desperate circumstances" off Samar, he had remained cool, quick-thinking and resolute, and his sailors defiant, valiant and indomitable. As Admiral Nimitz, proclaimed,

Here Admiral Clifton Sprague, backed by Admiral Stump and Admiral Thomas Sprague, squeezed every possible advantage from wind, rain, smoke, interior position, and air and surface attack to confuse and repulse an immensely superior enemy. Overhead, the escort carrier planes, untrained for attacking ships, performed like fast carrier aircraft at their best. On the surface, Clifton Sprague's little screening vessels, steaming boldly into battleships and cruiser fire, dodging through smoke and rain, chasing salvos, opposing 14- and 16-inch shells with 5-inch when they had expended their torpedoes, provided the slender margin that enabled the air-attack to succeed and most of the escort carriers to escape. The history of the United States Navy records no more glorious two hours of resolution, sacrifice, and success.

Finally, it is a pleasure to record that the corroding hatred of the enemy which is one of the inevitable but most degrading consequences of war was largely absent in this action. The majority of the seamen on both sides found they were able to respect, even admire, their opponents. Halsey, of course, was an exception to this rule, but at this distance of time, it would seem kinder to recall Commander Winters, who did not fail to report how the dying enemy carrier flew her battle flag to the end; or the Japanese destroyer captain who saluted as *Johnston* took her final plunge; for they more fittingly represent the spirit of the men who fought in the largest naval battle in history.

Bibliography

The Second World War, Vol. VI Triumph and Tragedy, Winston S. Churchill (Cassell & Co. Ltd)

The Second World War 1939-1945, Major-General J.F.C. Fuller (Eyre & Spottiswoode)

The Navy at War 1939-1945, Captain S.W. Roskill (William Collins Sons & Co. Ltd.)

The three titles listed above are useful for background detail

The Battle for Leyte Gulf, C. Vann Woodward (Macmillan Ltd.)

History of United States Naval Operations in World War II, Vol. XII Leyte June 1944-January 1945, Samuel Eliot Morison (Little, Brown & Co.)

The Two Ocean War, Samuel Eliot Morison, (Little, Brown & Co.) A one-volume edition of Morison's *History* listed above, but up-dated from later information

The Great Sea War, E.B. Potter and Chester W. Nimitz (George G. Harrap & Company Ltd.)

The Thunder of the Guns, Captain Donald Macintyre (Frederick Muller Ltd.)

The Battle for the Pacific, Captain Donald Macintyre (B.T. Batsford Ltd.)

Naval Battles of World War II, Geoffrey Bennett (B.T. Batsford Ltd.)

The War at Sea 1939-1945, Vol. III The Offensive Part II 1st June 1944-14th August 1945 (H.M.S.O.)

Death of a Navy, Andrieu D'albas (Robert Hale Ltd.) The war from the Japanese viewpoint

Reminiscences, Douglas MacArthur (William Heinemann Ltd.)

The Decisive Battles of the Western World, Vol. III, Major-General J.F.C. Fuller (Eyre & Spottiswoode)

The Divine Wind, Captain Rikihei Inoguchi and Commander Tadachi Nakajima with Roger Pineau (Hutchinson). The Kamikazes.

Divine Thunder, Bernard Millot (Macdonald). The Kamikazes.

"Central Pacific: The Great Debate", Robert Coakley and "Battle of Leyte", Stanley L. Falk, from Purnell's *History of the Second World War*, Vol. V

The Battle of Leyte Gulf, Stan Smith, (Belmont Productions Inc., New York). Contains details of battle reports at the time which, while now known to be in many cases inaccurate, are marvellous for giving the atmosphere.

"The Battle for Leyte Gulf", Hanson W. Baldwin, from *Combat Pacific Theater* (Dell Publishing Co.). This article was reprinted from *Sea Fights and Shipwrecks*, Hanson W. Baldwin (Doubleday & Company Inc. and London Museum Press Ltd.)

Deadly Magic, Edward Van Der Rhoer (Robert Hale Ltd) American Intelligence, particularly code breaking.

Index

Abukuma IJN, 50, 102, 116, 120, 207-9
Acuff, Capt. J., 45, 49, 85, 123
Adams, Lt M., 47-9, 61, 76
Akebono IJN, 50, 120-1
Akitsuki IJN, 70-1, 128, 134, 141, 209
Alabama USS, 47, 81, 124, 134
Albert W. Grant USS, 94, 113-15, 118
Aoba IJN, 44
Arima, Rear-Adm. M., 23
Arunta HMAS, 94, 106-9
Asagumo IJN, 50, 98, 100, 106-8, 119-21, 209
Asashimo IJN, 38, 41
Ashigara IJN, 50, 116-17
Atago IJN, 38-40, 184, 209
Australia HMAS, 27
Avenger USN bomber, 47, 56, 61-4, 121, 126-9, 146-7, 150, 153, 164, 170-6, 181-2, 186, 201, 205

Bache USS, 94, 106-7
Badger, Rear-Adm. O., 133-4, 187-8
Barbey, Rear-Adm. D., 25, 32
Bates, Capt. R., 93, 95, 157
Beale USS, 94, 106-7
Belleau Wood USS, 46, 129, 134
Berkey, Rear-Adm. R., 93-4, 106-7, 110, 112
'Betty' IJN bomber, 23, 202
Beyer, Lt-Comdr A., 145, 164
Biloxi USS, 46, 124, 133, 187
Birmingham USS, 46, 57-61, 115
Bogan, Rear-Adm. G., 46, 49, 54, 57, 61, 79-83, 87-8, 132-4, 205, 213
Boise USS, 94, 110
Bream USS, 44
Brunei Bay, 29, 41, 50, 62, 208
Buchanan, Comdr A., 107, 112
Buracker, Capt. W., 57-9

Cabot USS, 46, 65, 132, 205-6
California USS, 94-5, 110-12, 115, 157
Canberra HMAS, 20
Canberra USS, 20
Cape Engano, 31, 71, 122, 126, 144
Cassin Young USS, 46, 57
Catalina USN flying-boat, 92, 148, 188
Cebu Island, 23, 199, 207
Chikuma IJN, 38-9, 147, 156, 164-7, 170-3, 179, 187-8, 209
China, 10-11, 16, 22
Chitose IJN, 30, 69, 122, 128, 134, 209
Chiyoda IJN, 30, 69, 122, 128-9, 134-9, 209
Chokai IJN, 38-9, 147, 156, 162-7, 170, 174, 179, 209
Churchill, W.S., 11, 70, 184
Claggett, Comdr B., 38, 41-4
Clarence K. Bronson USS, 46, 138-9
Claxton USS, 94, 111, 119-20
Columbia USS, 24, 94, 110-11, 119
Coolbaugh USS, 144, 200
Cony USS, 94, 119
Copeland, Lt-Comdr R., 145, 160, 168-9
Cotten USS, 46, 138-9

Coward, Capt. J., 92, 96, 101-5
Cowpens USS, 45, 205-6

Dace USS, 38-44
Daly USS, 94, 106-7, 112
Darter USS, 38-44, 184
Davison, Rear-Adm. R., 46, 49-52, 64, 79-81, 92, 97, 129, 137, 213
Dennis USS, 145, 164, 167-8, 200
Denver USS, 24, 94, 110-13, 119
Deschaineux, Capt. E., 29
Dinagat Island, 24, 29, 94, 105
DuBose, Rear-Adm. L., 21, 138-41

Enterprise USS, 46, 51, 64, 72-3, 90, 125, 136-7
Essex USS, 46, 49, 54-5, 59, 62-4, 125, 128, 135-6, 139
Evans, Comdr E., 145, 154-6, 161, 166, 176-7, 189

Fanshaw Bay USS, 145-7, 150, 158, 165-7, 170, 175, 198
Formosa, 9-16, 19-24, 30, 79, 82, 140, 190
Fowler, Comdr R., 153-4, 174, 185
Franklin USS, 20, 23, 46-50, 64, 125, 129, 135-6
Fukudome, Vice-Adm. S., 19-22, 30, 52, 54, 59, 62-7, 129, 183, 186
Fuso IJN, 50-2, 96, 100, 105, 108, 116, 209

Gambier Bay USS, 145, 153, 165-71, 188-9, 209
Gatling USS, 46, 57, 60-1
Guadalcanal, 23, 32-3, 40, 72, 88, 90, 96, 102-3, 112, 138, 193

Hagen, Lt R., 154*n*, 155, 166, 168, 176-7
Haguro IJN, 38-41, 147, 156, 161-6, 170, 174-8, 205
Halsey, Adm. W.,
    Previous Career, 72-4
    Strategy of, 11-12
    In Formosa operations, 19-25
    Commands Third Fleet and role of, 26-7, 31-5, 74-5
    In preliminary actions, 44-9, 52, 54
    Pursues Japanese 'decoys', 67-72, 78-9
    In action off Cape Engano, 122-5
    Turns back to assist Seventh Fleet, 130-4
    Mentioned, 38, 79, 90, 92-3, 95, 148, 156, 172, 178, 181-2, 187-8
    Summary of achievements, 210-14
Hamakaze IJN, 38, 65
Hamanami IJN, 38, 172, 179, 206
Hancock USS, 45, 185-6, 205-6
Hansen, Lt-Comdr S., 145, 164
Haruna IJN, 38-9, 64, 77, 147, 151, 161-3, 172, 205
Hathaway Comdr A., 145, 160, 163, 166-7, 200
Hatsutsuki IJN, 70-1, 137-41, 209
Hayashimo IJN, 38, 172, 206, 209
Hayler, Rear-Adm. R., 24, 119-20
Heermann USS, 145, 158-67, 173, 199-200
Hellcat USN fighter, 17, 47, 51, 54-5, 59-63, 69, 123, 146, 185, 190, 197, 205
Helldiver USN bomber, 47, 49, 61-4, 67, 126, 129, 185-6
Hibuson Island, 92, 94, 117, 157
Hoel USS, 145, 159-61, 168, 188, 209
Homonhon Island 24, 103
Honolulu USS, 27
Hornet USS, 45, 185-6, 205-6
Houston USS, 20-1
Hubbard, Comdr M., 94-5, 108, 118
Hutchins USS, 94, 106-8, 112
Hyuga IJN, 19, 30, 69-71, 80-1, 122-6, 129, 134-42, 209

I 56 IJN, 197
Independence USS, 46, 86-9, 123-4, 132, 187, 205
Inglis, Capt. T., 57-9
Inoguchi, Rear-Adm. T., 64-5
Intrepid USS, 46, 49, 61, 65, 128, 132, 205-6

Index

Iowa USS, 46-7, 81, 124, 133, 187
Irwin USS, 46, 57-61
Ise IJN, 19, 30, 69-71, 80-1, 122-6, 134-42, 209
Ishii, Comdr H., 30, 50
Isokaze IJN, 38, 147, 175
Isuzu IJN, 69, 129, 134-7, 140, 142
Iwo Jima, 194, 202, 213

'Jake' IJN floatplane, 171
Jallao USS, 140, 142
Japan, 9-12, 15-16, 22, 192-5, 204, 209-11
'Jill' IJN bomber, 57, 70-1
John C. Butler USS, 145, 164, 167-8, 200
Johnston USS, 145, 153-6, 159-68, 176-7, 188-9, 209, 214
'Judy' IJN bomber, 20, 56-9, 70-1, 199, 203

Kadashan Bay USS, 145, 165, 175-6, 200
Kalinin Bay USS, 145, 165, 175-6, 200
Kamikaze Corps, 23, 27, 30, 35, 52-3, 82, 135, 190-204, 209, 212
Kasumi IJN, 50, 120, 207-8
'Kate' IJN bomber, 70
Kenney, Gen. G., 25, 91, 171
Killen USS, 94, 106-7
Kimura, Rear-Adm. S., 175-6
King, Fleet-Adm. E., 84, 132, 148
Kinkaid, Vice-Adm. T.,
  Previous Career, 90-3
  In Leyte Landings, 24-6
  Commands Seventh Fleet and Role of, 26-7, 85-7
  In preliminary actions, 45, 52
  In action in Surigao Strait, 83-4, 92, 99, 121
  In action off Samar Island, 130-32, 148, 156-8
  In final actions, 189, 200
  Mentioned, 32, 75, 80, 82, 125, 146, 182, 184-5, 209
  Summary of achievements, 210, 212-13
Kintberger, Comdr L., 145, 159, 162

Kinu IJN, 44, 49, 207, 209
Kishinami IJN, 38, 41-2
Kitkun Bay USS, 145, 153, 165, 171, 174-5, 181, 185-6, 198-200
Kiyoshimo IJN, 38, 65
Kongo IJN, 38-41, 77, 147, 151-4, 159-63, 168-73, 205
Koyanagi, Rear-Adm. T., 34, 63, 79, 178-80, 208
Krueger, Lt-Gen. W., 24, 26
Kumano IJN, 38-9, 147, 154-5, 159, 179, 185, 206
Kurita, Vice-Adm. T.,
  Previous Career, 39-40
  Commands Central Force and role of, 15-18, 22, 29-36
  In preliminary actions, 38-44, 49-52
  Attacked in Sibuyan Sea, 61-5
  Penetrates San Bernardino Strait, 66, 81-9
  In action off Samar Island, 130-4, 147-59, 163-4, 170-4
  Breaks off attack, 177-88
  In final actions, 205-9
  Mentioned, 50, 70, 71, 77, 79, 95-7, 118, 122, 125, 129, 142, 190, 198, 200, 203
  Summary of achievements, 211-12

Langley USS, 46, 54-9, 129, 135
Lee, Vice-Adm. W., 47, 80-2, 88, 90, 123-5, 130-3, 150, 156, 213
Lewis Hancock USS, 46, 187
Lexington USS, 46, 54, 58-9, 62-4, 67, 78, 123-4, 128-9, 135, 138, 144
Leyte Gulf, 15-18, 21, 24, 29, 33-7, 41, 51, 53, 66-7, 84, 89-90, 93-6, 102-3, 116, 130-1, 141, 145, 156-8, 178-9, 182, 200-4, 208-10
Leyte Island, 10-14, 19-36, 72, 82 87, 91-4, 98, 103, 106, 113, 131, 171, 177, 183, 185, 188, 194, 201, 203, 207, 210-11
Liberator USAAF bomber, 208
Lightning USAAF fighter, 202-3
Louisville USS, 93-4, 106, 110, 114, 117, 119, 157

Luzon, 10-12, 19, 23, 29, 31, 46-7, 54, 63, 71, 122, 140, 183, 186, 190, 194, 198, 202-3

MacArthur, Gen. D.,
  Strategy of, 9-12, 16
  Returns to Philippines, 9, 24-7, 32-5
  During naval battles, 75, 79, 91-3, 125, 131, 157, 171, 209, 213
Maki IJN, 70, 129, 134-7
Manila, 17, 20, 22, 44, 50, 54, 65, 117, 181, 206
Manila Bay USS, 144, 171, 185
Marcus Island USS, 144, 146
Marshall, Gen. G., 10-11
Maryland USS, 94, 110, 115
Massachusetts USS, 46, 81, 124, 134
Matsuda, Rear-Adm. C., 71-2, 76, 80, 122-3, 129, 135, 137
'Mavis' IJN flying-boat, 123
Maya IJN, 38-42, 209
McCain, Vice-Adm. J., 45-6, 49, 85, 123, 125n, 131, 156, 185-6, 205-6, 213
McCampbell, Comdr D., 55-6, 125, 128
McClintock, Comdr D., 38-43
McDermut USS, 92, 103-6
McGowan USS, 92, 103
McKenna, Capt. F., 145, 199
McManes, Capt. K., 94-5, 106-8, 111-13, 119
Melvin USS, 92, 103-5
Miami USS, 46, 124, 133, 187
Michishio IJN, 50, 98, 100, 106-8, 209
Mikawa, Vice-Adm. G., 17, 117
Miller USS, 46, 187
Mindanao, 10, 12, 25, 35, 47, 50, 120
Mindanao Sea, 29, 52, 92, 96, 98, 101, 117, 207
Mindoro Island, 29, 49, 202, 206
Minneapolis USS, 94, 110, 112, 157
Mississippi USS, 94, 110, 115
Mitchell, USAAF bomber, 72, 208
Mitscher, Vice-Adm. M.,
  In Battle of Philippine Sea, 17, 45, 68, 74, 78
  In preliminary actions, 45-6, 49, 78-88
  In action off Cape Engano, 123-6, 131-40
  Mentioned, 172, 185, 210
  Summary of achievements, 213
Mobile USS, 46, 124, 132, 138-9
Mogami IJN, 50, 96, 98, 100-1, 107, 111-21, 206, 209
Monssen USS, 92, 103-6
Monterey USS, 45
Morotai Island, 11-14, 25, 92
Morrison USS, 46, 57-8, 61
Musashi IJN, 38-9, 47-9, 62-5, 76-7, 151, 184, 209
Myoko IJN, 38-41, 62, 77

Nachi IJN, 41-2, 50, 102, 116-17, 120
Naganami IJN, 38, 41
Nagato IJN, 38-9, 64, 147, 161-3, 181, 185, 205
Nakase, Rear-Adm. N., 137
Nashville USS, 12n, 24, 32, 93, 157
Natoma Bay USS, 144, 173
Newcomb USS, 113-15, 118
New Jersey USS, 46-7, 79, 81, 87, 124, 130-3, 187
New Orleans USS, 47, 124, 132, 138
Nimitz, Adm. C., 9-11, 26-7, 34, 49, 72-5, 79, 82-5, 91, 102, 121, 125, 131-2, 156, 188, 210-13
Nisewaner, Comdr T., 113-15
Nishimura, Vice-Adm. S.,
  Commands Van of Southern Force and role of, 29-31
  In preliminary actions, 44, 50-2, 77, 85, 92
  In action in Surigao Strait, 100-12, 115
  Mentioned, 116, 118-21, 125, 180, 184
  Summary of achievements, 211
Nishino, Comdr S., 97, 111, 116, 180
Noshiro IJN, 38, 147, 166, 175, 205-6, 209

Index

Nowake IJN, 38, 147, 175, 179, 187-8, 209

Ofstie, Rear-Adm. R., 145, 153
Ohmae, Capt. T., 70, 122, 137
Oka IJN suicide-plane, 202
Okinami IJN, 38, 179, 185, 206
Okinawa, 14, 16, 19, 115, 191, 194, 202-3, 209, 213
Oldendorf, Rear-Adm. J.,
  In Leyte Landings, 24-6
  Covers beach-head, 53
  In action in Surigao Strait, 93-6, 99-110, 115-21
  In action off Samar Island, 130-1, 157, 182
  Summary of achievements, 213
Ommaney Bay USS, 144, 150, 172
Onishi, Vice Adm. T., 22-3, 30, 52, 65, 135, 191, 204
Ormoc Bay, 30, 202, 207
Owen USS, 46, 187
Oyodo IJN, 69-70, 130, 134-7, 140-2
Ozawa, Vice Adm. J.,
  Previous Career, 68-9
  Commands Northern Force and role of, 16-17, 21-2, 30-1, 34
  In preliminary actions, 58, 65-7, 70-1
  Decoys Third Fleet north, 82-5, 89, 122-4
  In action off Cape Engano, 125-37, 141-3
  Mentioned, 74, 90, 92, 172, 209
  Summary of achievements, 211

Pace, Lt-Comdr J., 145, 167
Palawan Island, 29, 42, 44
Palawan Passage, 38, 42
Panaon Island, 25, 100-2
Panay Island, 25, 100-2
Patterson USS, 47, 138-9
Pearl Harbour, 10, 39, 50, 58, 69, 72, 94, 110, 130n, 132, 136, 145, 182
Peliliu Island, 11-14, 26, 154
Pennsylvania USS, 94, 110, 157
Petrof Bay USS, 144, 190, 197, 200-1

Phoenix USS, 94, 110
Philippines, 9-17, 21-5, 33-7, 45, 53, 66, 74, 81n, 91, 203, 209-10
Philippine Sea, 29-30, 66, 89
Philippine Sea, Battle of, 17, 40, 46, 55, 69, 74, 82, 88, 130n, 145, 190, 194
Phillips, Comdr R., 103-6
Porterfield USS, 46, 138-9
Portland USS, 94, 110-12, 117-19, 138, 157
Princeton USS, 40, 46, 54-62, 81, 83, 123, 190, 209
PT boats, 96, 98-103, 106, 119-21, 208

Raymond USS, 145, 164, 167-8, 200
Remey USS, 92, 103
Reno USS, 46, 57-61
Richard M. Rowell USS, 144, 200
Richard P. Leary USS, 94, 113-15
Roosevelt, President F., 9
Ryukyu Islands, 10, 16, 19, 23, 29

Sakonji, Vice-Adm. N., 30, 44, 49, 207
Samar Island, 26, 29, 46, 49, 66, 79, 144, 147-8, 177, 180-5, 188-9, 207-8, 211-14
Samuel B. Roberts USS, 145, 160-4, 167-9, 188, 209
San Bernardino Strait, 29, 46, 49, 52, 66, 79-89, 122, 123n, 131, 133, 142, 147-8, 156, 180, 183-4, 187, 205, 212
Sangamon USS, 29, 144-6, 171, 190, 197
San Jacinto USS, 46, 128-9, 136
Santa Fe USS, 46, 124, 132, 138-9
Santee USS, 144-5, 190, 196-8
Savo Island USS, 144, 171, 181
Sherman, Rear-Adm. F., 46, 49, 54, 57-61, 67, 70-1, 76-8, 81-4, 87, 123, 213
Shigure IJN, 50, 52, 97-100, 105-7, 111-21, 180
Shima, Vice-Adm. K.,
  Commands Rear of Southern

Force and role of, 16-17, 21, 29-31
In preliminary actions, 44, 50-2
In action in Surigao Strait, 96-7, 101-2, 108, 116-20
In final actions, 207
Mentioned, 157, 158, 180, 184
Summary of achievements, 211
Shimotsuke IJN, 70-1, 129, 134-7
Shiraishi, Vice-Adm. K., 154-5, 185
Shiranuhi IJN, 50, 120, 207
Sho Plan, 16-18, 22, 29-30, 34-6, 54, 62, 72, 125, 191, 210
Shropshire HMAS, 94, 110-12, 157
Sibuyan Sea, 29, 44, 47, 62, 79, 96, 147, 172, 174, 205-6
Smoot, Capt, R., 94-5, 108, 111-15, 118
South Dakota USS, 46, 81, 124, 134
Sprague, Rear-Adm. C.A.F.,
In action off Samar Island, 145-60, 164-7, 170-80
Attacked by Kamikazes, 198, 200
Mentioned, 86, 125, 131, 133
Summary of achievements, 211-14
Sprague, Rear-Adm. T.,
In Leyte Landings, 24-7
Covers Beach-head, 53
Attacks Southern Forces, 121
In action off Samar Island, 144, 148, 158
Attacked by Kamikazes, 190, 198
Mentioned, 92, 93
Summary of achievements, 213-14
Spruance, Adm. R., 17, 45, 69, 74-5, 83
St Lo USS, 145, 153, 165, 171, 176, 198-200, 209, 212
Struble, Rear-Adm. A., 24-5
Stump, Rear-Adm. F., 144-50, 158, 171-4, 179-86, 207, 213-14
Sullivan, Capt. D., 145, 156
Suluan Island, 24, 29, 144
Sulu Sea, 29, 44, 47, 50, 52, 97
Surigao Strait, 29, 34, 52, 84, 92-3, 96-100, 118, 122, 144, 151, 156, 208, 213
Suwanee USS, 144-6, 190, 197-8, 201
Suzuki, Lt-Gen. S., 25-6, 30, 33
Suzuya IJN, 38-9, 147, 154-5, 170-2, 179, 182, 185, 188, 209

Tablas Strait, 29, 49, 61, 205
Tacloban, 26, 32, 34, 51, 53, 158, 171, 174, 181-2, 185-6
'Taffy 1' 144-6, 158, 171, 181, 189-90, 196-201
'Taffy 2' 144-6, 150, 155, 158-60, 170-7, 182, 185-6
'Taffy 3' 144-53, 156-7, 160-2, 165, 170-4, 177, 180-4, 188-90, 198, 200, 213
Takao IJN, 38-42
Tama IJN, 69, 71, 128-9, 134-7, 142, 209
Task Force 34, 80-6, 89, 123-4, 129-33
Task Force 34:5, 133, 187-8
Task Force 38, 11, 45-7, 61, 85, 89, 125
Task Group 38:1, 45, 49, 85, 123, 131, 185-6, 205
Task Group 38:2, 46, 49, 61-2, 79, 84, 87-8, 123, 132, 205
Task Group 38:3, 46, 54, 62-3, 67, 76-8, 81, 123, 129, 135-6
Task Group 38:4, 46, 64, 77, 84, 92, 123, 129, 135-7
Tennessee USS, 94-5, 110, 112, 115, 157
Terutsuki-class destroyers IJN, 67, 70, 76, 128, 139
Thomas, Comdr W., 145, 159-62
Thorn USS, 94, 119
Tominaga, Lt-Gen. K., 22, 30, 52
Tone IJN, 38-9, 53, 64-5, 77, 147, 156, 164-8, 174-8, 185-6, 205
Toyoda, Adm. S., 15-22, 29-31, 51, 65-6, 69n, 72, 97, 180-4, 187
Trathen USS, 144, 197

Ugaki, Rear-Adm. M., 42, 65
Ulithi Island, 11, 14, 21, 45-6, 61
Urakaze IJN, 38, 147, 175

Index

Uranami IJN, 44, 207, 209
Ushio IJN, 50, 120

'Val' IJN bomber, 191
Vieweg, Capt. W., 145, 165, 167
Vincennes USS, 46, 124, 133, 187

Wakaba IJN, 49-50, 209
Wakatsuki IJN, 70-1, 137
Washington USS, 47, 81, 124, 134
Wasp USS, 45, 145, 135, 205-6
West Virginia USS, 94-5, 110-11, 115
Weyler, Rear-Adm. G., 93, 115
Whitehead, Capt. R., 32, 158, 171, 182
White Plains USS, 145, 152-3, 156, 164-5, 170-1, 175, 181, 198-9
Wichita USS, 47, 124, 132, 138
Wildcat USN fighter, 146-7, 170-4, 182, 185-6
Wilkinson, Vice-Adm. T., 25, 32, 45, 96
Williamson, Capt. T., 145

Winters, Comdr H., 135-8, 214

Yahagi IJN, 38, 147, 175-6, 205
Yamagumo IJN, 50, 98, 100, 106, 209
Yamamoto, Adm. I., 15, 26n, 73, 143
Yamashiro IJN, 50, 96, 100, 105-7, 110-16, 209
Yamashita, Gen. T., 25, 26n
Yamato IJN, 38-9, 42, 49, 63-6, 76-9, 87, 134, 147, 152, 159, 163, 171, 178-81, 199, 205-9
Yap Island, 11, 13, 25, 46, 95
Yonai, Adm. M., 210
Yukikaze IJN, 38, 147, 175, 184

Zero IJN fighter, 17, 33, 53, 55, 58, 68-71, 74, 126, 186, 190, 193-4, 197-203
Zuiho IJN, 30, 69, 122, 126-30, 135-6, 139, 209
Zuikaku IJN, 30, 69, 76, 122, 128-30, 135-6, 139, 209